Belonging in Oceania

**Pacific Perspectives**
Studies of the European Society for Oceanists

Series Editors: Christina Toren, University of St Andrews, and Edvard Hviding, University of Bergen

Oceania is of enduring contemporary significance in global trajectories of history, politics, economy and ecology, and has remained influential for diverse approaches to studying and understanding human life worlds. The books published in this series explore Oceanic values and imaginations, documenting the unique position of the Pacific region – its cultural and linguistic diversity, its ecological and geographical distinctness, and always fascinating experiments with social formations. This series thus conveys the political, economic and moral alternatives that Oceania offers the contemporary world.

**Volume 1**
*The Ethnographic Experiment*
*A.M. Hocart and W.H.R. Rivers in Island Melanesia, 1908*
Edited by Edvard Hviding and Cato Berg

**Volume 2**
*Pacific Futures*
*Projects, Politics and Interests*
Edited by Will Rollason

**Volume 3**
*Belonging in Oceania*
*Movement, Place-Making and Multiple Identifications*
Edited by Elfriede Hermann, Wolfgang Kempf and Toon van Meijl

**Upcoming titles**
*Visible Value*
*Problems with Request, Reciprocity, and Community in Manus, Papua New Guinea*
Anders Rasmussen

*Living Kinship in the Pacific*
Edited by Christina Toren and Simonne Pauwels

# Belonging in Oceania

Movement, Place-Making and Multiple Identifications

♦●♦

Edited by Elfriede Hermann, Wolfgang Kempf and Toon van Meijl

First edition published in 2014 by
Berghahn Books
www.berghahnbooks.com

©2014 Elfriede Hermann, Wolfgang Kempf and Toon van Meijl

All rights reserved. Except for the quotation of short passages for the purposes of criticism and review, no part of this book may be reproduced in any form or by any means, electronic or mechanical, including photocopying, recording, or any information storage and retrieval system now known or to be invented, without written permission of the publisher.

**Library of Congress Cataloging-in-Publication Data**
Belonging in Oceania: movement, place-making and multiple identifications / edited by Elfriede Hermann, Wolfgang Kempf and Toon van Meijl. -- First edition.
    pages cm. -- (Pacific perspectives; volume 3)
Includes bibliographical references.
ISBN 978-1-78238-415-1 (hardback: alk. paper) -- ISBN 978-1-78238-416-8 (ebook)
    1. Ethnology--Oceania--Case studies. 2. Group identity--Oceania.--Case studies. 3. Intergroup relations--Oceania--Case studies. 4. Belonging (Social psychology)--Oceania--Case studies. 5. Place (Philosophy)--Case studies. I. Hermann, Elfriede, editor of compilation. II. Kempf, Wolfgang (Anthropologist) editor of compilation. III. Meijl, Toon van, editor of compilation.
  GN662.B45 2014
  302.3--dc23
                                                                                    2014009647

**British Library Cataloguing in Publication Data**
A catalogue record for this book is available from the British Library

ISBN 978-1-78238-415-1 (hardback)
ISBN 978-1-78238-416-8 (ebook)

# Contents

| | | |
|---|---|---|
| **Acknowledgements** | | vii |
| **Introduction** | | 1 |
| **Movement, Place-making and Cultural Identification** | | |
| Multiplicities of Belonging | | |
| *Wolfgang Kempf, Toon van Meijl and Elfriede Hermann* | | |
| 1 **Culture as Experience** | | 25 |
| Constructing Identities through Transpacific Encounters | | |
| *Eveline Dürr* | | |
| 2 **'Forty-plus Different Tribes'** | | 49 |
| Displacement, Place-making and Aboriginal Tribal Names on Palm Island, Australia | | |
| *Lise Garond* | | |
| 3 **Coconuts and the Landscape of Underdevelopment on Panapompom, Papua New Guinea** | | 71 |
| *Will Rollason* | | |
| 4 **Invisible Villages in the City** | | 94 |
| Niuean Constructions of Place and Identity in Auckland | | |
| *Hilke Thode-Arora* | | |
| 5 **Migration and Identity** | | 117 |
| Cook Islanders' Relation to Land | | |
| *Arno Pascht* | | |
| 6 **Protestantism among Pacific Peoples in New Zealand** | | 142 |
| Mobility, Cultural Identifications and Generational Shifts | | |
| *Yannick Fer and Gwendoline Malogne-Fer* | | |
| 7 **Identity and Belonging in Cross-cultural Friendship** | | 164 |
| Māori and Pākehā Experiences | | |
| *Agnes Brandt* | | |

**Epilogue**     189
   **Uncertain Futures of Belonging**
   Consequences of Climate Change and Sea-level Rise in Oceania
   *Wolfgang Kempf and Elfriede Hermann*

**Notes on Contributors**     214

**Index**     217

# Acknowledgements

Our greatest debt is to our interlocutors in the Pacific, with whom we were, and remain, in constant personal and imaginative dialogue. We are endlessly grateful to them, not least for insights shared into their cultural discourses and practices relating to movement, place-making, multiple identifications and diverse modes of belonging. The idea for this volume came when the authors were exchanging research results under the auspices of the European Society for Oceanists (ESfO), and it was realized in close cooperation. Our warmest thanks go to Anna Paini and Elisabetta Gnecchi-Ruscone, chairperson und deputy chairperson of ESfO at the time, for helping with the organization. In this connection we are also indebted to the Wenner-Gren Foundation for Anthropological Research for financial assistance. In addition, we are greatly indebted to the editorial board of the ESfO book series, especially to Christina Toren and Tony Crook, for investing time and energy in supporting the publication process. We expressly thank the three anonymous reviewers who read and commented on the manuscript in its entirety. Their critiques, recommendations and comments stimulated us to further ponder the thematic complex treated in this book. In preparing the manuscript for publication, we owe much to the professional skills of René van der Haar, with Steffen Herrmann also contributing valuable expertise. Both were always there when needed. At Berghahn Books, it was chiefly Marion Berghahn (editor and publisher), Ann Przyzycki DeVita (senior editor), Lauren Weiss and Molly Mosher (both editorial assistants) who steered this book through to publication. We are grateful for their efforts on our behalf.

# Introduction

# Movement, Place-making and Cultural Identification

## Multiplicities of Belonging

### Wolfgang Kempf, Toon van Meijl and Elfriede Hermann

Oceania is characterized by a high and increasing level of movement – travel as well as migration. What implications do movement and mobility have for place-making, for cultural identifications and for multiple ways of belonging in the Pacific region? It is our conviction that anthropological studies of Oceania are well suited to analyse ongoing dialogues between formations of place, community, identity and self within a framework of mobility and global connectivity. The present volume therefore aims at studying movement and the cultural constructions of place and identity as an intersecting ensemble.

This collection of chapters specifically seeks to show that movement invests place-making and cultural identifications with a new dimension of multiplicity. Those who set forth in the Pacific do not simply leave behind land and socio-cultural communities, they also acquire a web of multiple spatial and social relationships. Installed in a new environment, they create new places and communities, while often maintaining ties with their homeland as well as with other diasporas. They come to identify – depending on context – with a multiplicity of places and communities. These identifications often attest to divergent ascriptions by self and others at local, national, regional and global levels. Thus, they point to exclusions and multiplicities of belonging entangled with relations of power. To explore and enhance the understanding of these complexities of belonging, we adopt an analytical approach aimed at pursuing the intricate links between the dimensions of movement, place-making and multiple identifications through a series of ethnographic case studies. This approach will, we believe, allow an improved understanding of the current praxis of Pacific Islanders. The point of focusing on these three dimensions is to examine what they tell us about belonging, not to claim that such a tripartite scheme is in any way final or binding. But if this scheme can serve as a springboard (necessarily provisional) for developing anthropological perspectives conducive to exploring how these – and other – dimensions interact, it will have served its purpose. Hence our scheme is to be seen as open-ended, one able to accommodate additional dimensions, such as the dimension of things (see Latour 1993). So we would wish our conceptual framework to be received as but one possible way of binding together several dimensions for analytic purposes, the better to understand how multiplicities are constituted.

The chapters collected here illuminate processes in which Māori, Niueans and members of other cultural communities in New Zealand, but also Cook Islanders, Aboriginal people in Australia, island societies in Papua New Guinea and in Kiribati, come to be embedded, if we may use that expression, as they make contact and interact with diverse social actors (both real and imagined) inside and outside their own society. In publishing these studies, we make no claim to have given equal weighting to all so-called culture areas of Oceania. Rather, our sustaining hope has been to assemble insights into multiplicities of belonging, such as have resulted from intersections of movement, place-making and cultural identifications. It is our hope that the insights gathered within these pages prove fruitful in stimulating study of other similar processes within the region of Oceania and beyond.

## Movement

One element of our integrated conceptual frame is movement. The concept is used here as an overarching category that includes mobility, travel, tourism, migration, flight, displacement, border zones, diaspora and transnationalism. These aspects feature whenever the dynamics of societies, cultures, identities and spatial networks are considered in the context of global currents and power relationships. By focusing on the aspect of movement, we are endorsing a theoretical development that has arisen from a critique of static models and representations in anthropology.[1]

Doubts have been raised about an earlier tendency to accord centrality to such aspects as the stability and coherence of social systems and cultural orders, the rootedness and the immobility of indigenous peoples, and the primordial nexus of places, persons and cultures, whereas mobility and migration were rather left out of the picture or construed as disruptions of localized, bounded communities. This retreat from old certainties was accompanied by a theoretical realignment, the aim being to mobilize the metaphorical potential of movement, of flux and flow generally, for purposes of revising key concepts in the social sciences and humanities (Pile and Thrift 1995: 19; see also Inda and Rosaldo 2008: 10–15). In a more recent publication, Kirby (2009: 15) even promised to redeem anthropology from the evils of Cartesian space, dismissed as a 'static', 'empty' and 'soulless' continuum; this goal would be achieved by attending more to the living and dynamic aspects of the movements of social actors in their immediate environment. Our own analytic approach pursues a rather more profane goal, building primarily on a theoretical perspective that allows movement and displacement to be seen as constituting forces of place, culture and identity (see Clifford 1997: 276–77).

Oceania has at all times been home to movements and expansions, contacts and articulations. Epeli Hau'ofa, in his seminal text 'Our Sea of Islands' (Hau'ofa 1994), broke new ground in giving us a graphic account of this circumstance. Hau'ofa objected to what he saw as a one-sided focus on 'islands in a far sea', a focus on smallness and fragmentation that he deemed in no way adequate to the historical praxis of Pacific Islanders. He pointed out that the inhabitants of Oceania, in the course of their long history of exploration, trade, interlinking and networking – including the transnational migrant flows of recent decades – had moved to expand their oceanic world, and that they are still doing so. Hau'ofa's concern was to sketch a new and positive perspective, very much the reverse of the old one; instead of focusing on scattered Pacific islands, he argued for the need to treat Oceania as a constellation of relationships. In his own words, instead of 'islands in a far sea' the reality was 'a sea of islands'. Thus the key parameters were not isolation, limitation and smallness, but movement, connectivity and enlargement.

Hau'ofa's alternative vision of an enlarged Oceania was criticized by some commentators for its romanticizing and idealizing tendencies. Two principal points were made: first, that the poverty, marginalization and exploitation that was the lot of many Pacific Islanders in a globalizing context had been neglected; and second, that a maritime way of life – applicable, at best, to Polynesia and Micronesia – had been generalized to cover the entire Pacific region (see e.g., Chandra 1993; Griffen 1993; Naidu 1993). However, Hau'ofa's narrative matters still, from our perspective, for two reasons. The first is that it marks the transition from an insular to a relational perspective on Oceania (Nero 1997). Second, Hauʻofa's argument constitutes an important link between earlier studies of mobility, diffusion, voyaging and migration in Oceania, and more recent studies of translocal and transnational networks between Oceanian societies and their diasporas.[2]

Against this background of theoretical developments and regional refocusing, the challenge, for us, consists in systematically including in our analysis historically and culturally specific forms and directions of movement on the part of men and women, with due consideration given to power relationships, and doing this based on concrete ethnography. Writing about movement and mobility, we primarily have in mind physical movement involving, in one sense or another, a change of place (cf. McKay 2006). In the case of Oceania, what this specifically means is internal migration (such as movements from hinterland to coast, from island to island, from rural regions to town and city, from town to peri-urban or rural locations) as well as international migration.

The issue of how international migration plays out involves not just the migrants themselves and the people they interact with in their country of residence, but also those they leave behind; nor is this simply a matter of the remittances that migrants send home. In our treatment of movement we want to go further and incorporate the dimension of imagination as well (see Dawson and Johnson 2001: 321; cf. Appadurai 1996: 53–56). Imagination enters into play when the stay-at-homes view themselves in relation to their migrant kinfolk; it is in this context that they organize and define how they think, feel and act in terms of transnational relationships and contacts (e.g. Young Leslie 2004; Gershon 2007; Besnier 2011). Of course, this also holds, conversely, for the migrants and the networks they maintain with their lands of origin (e.g. Hermann 2004) and with other diasporic communities. A further example of imagined movement might be future scenarios of forced migration, such as in view of scientific projections of the likely consequences of climate change and sea-level rise. Such scenarios are now firmly lodged in the imaginations of the youth of the region, especially in low-lying atoll states like Tuvalu, Kiribati and the Marshall Islands (Kempf and Hermann, this volume). In our view, an integrated perspective of physical and imagined movement can be usefully combined with a need to incorporate indigenous conceptualizations of movement and social space into the analysis of mobility and migration (see Lilomaiava-Doktor 2009).

The contributions to this volume relate to a broad spectrum of movements. Eveline Dürr looks at Māori pupils who travelled from New Zealand to Mexico. This excursion forms the framework for her analysis of the construction and representation of identity in the context of intercultural encounters. Lise Garond and Will Rollason address the forms and consequences of displacement and migration in Australia and Papua New Guinea, respectively. Thus Garond's study of the multiple belongings and contemporary mobility of reservation dwellers on Palm Island is based on the historical fact of the forced relocation of Aboriginal people by the Australian state. Rollason analyses the nexus between local discourses of place, economic decline and marginalization on Panapompom in southeast Papua New Guinea. He turns his attention to a heterogeneous community, whose pioneers came from different corners of the immediate region and who settled, in the second half of the twentieth century, on what was then an uninhabited island. In each of these case studies, movement designates a mode of internal migration.

International migration flows are, on the other hand, central to how Hilke Thode-Arora, Arno Pascht, and Yannick Fer and Gwendoline Malogne-Fer analyse the multiple belongings of Polynesians living in New Zealand. Thode-Arora looks at the case of Niueans in Auckland and their efforts to reconstitute place and identity in the diaspora. The reality of absentee landowners in the Cook Islands lets Pascht unpack the symbolism, and the associated issues, of land which émigré Cook Islanders continue to regard as their property. Fer and Malogne-Fer, for their part, target international migration too, shedding much light on the important role now being played by Polynesia's Protestant churches as places of orientation and social reorganization for Pacific Islanders who have migrated to New Zealand.

Migration processes from an earlier era form the background against which Agnes Brandt studies the boundaries as well as intercultural ties between Māori and non-Māori, or Pākehā, in New Zealand. She is primarily concerned to analyse constructions of self, identity and belonging at the points of encounter between cultural others. But she also hints at the fact that international migration movements in the past supplied the structural prerequisites for New Zealand's present-day practices and politics of biculturalism. Here it is important to stress generally the historical dimension of movement. Movement is never a singular event or moment, not even in conjunction with place-making and identification. It is invariably pervaded by a multiplicity of preceding movements. A glance at the history of Asian-Pacific migration flows conveys a sense of the complexity of these plural events in space and time (Goss and Lindquist 2000).

## Place-making

In emphasizing the movements of people in Oceania, our intention is at one and the same time to draw attention to the dynamics of place, which are invariably implied in processes of mobility. Hence the importance of 'place-making', the second element of the conceptual frame advanced here. By 'place' is meant the spatial dimension *per se*, considered as an object of investigation. But the hyphenated nature of the concept used here – 'place-making' – cautions us that places are not to be thought of as static, self-enclosed entities, but rather as changing products of historical praxis. In our view, place-making allows us to think of place – each and every place – as a dynamic configuration crafted by history in a unique melding of practices, linkages and power relationships (cf. Kabachnik 2012).

In introducing their volume on senses of place, Feld and Basso (1996: 7, 11) call for a phenomenologically oriented and explicit ethnography of indigenous constructions of place via language, knowledge and praxis, the better to achieve an adequate understanding of the manner in which places are perceived, experienced, lived out, negotiated and associated with different identities. At the same time, they refer to a theoretical development within anthropology that would have us construe 'place largely from the standpoint of its contestation and its linkage to local and global power relations' (ibid.: 4). Astonishingly, however, they base their own essays about the Western Apache in the USA (Basso 1996) and the Kaluli in Papua New Guinea (Feld 1996) on the same idealized and seemingly static world of locally anchored people, songs and stories, far removed from government offices, church precincts, migration processes (or other forms of new presences and absences) – a closed off world whose validity had been questioned by this very theoretical development. True, it is important to carefully document how people relate to places proactively, in the sense of developing embodied relationships with localities and endowing them with cultural meanings (see Casey 1996). However, such an ethnographic undertaking must actually deliver in terms of offering a systematic account of the broader interconnections, movements, transformations and power constellations that make up the lived texture of a specific place.

Gupta and Ferguson (1997a, 1997b), in particular, have stressed the importance of mobility, migration and displacement when studying constructions of place and identity. Such an expanded notion of the mutability and multi-dimensionality of places necessitates, in their view, a concrete analysis of 'processes and practices of place-making' (Gupta und Ferguson 1997a: 6). We prefer to talk of place-making rather than invoke the related concepts of deterritorialization and reterritorialization, or of de/territorialization.[3] Although the conceptual pair of deterritorialization and reterritorialization was used within the anthropological context of globalization and migration theory to highlight the causal sequence of a process of movement, migration or displacement followed by a process of reconstituting place, culture and identity, its semantic field is rather more complicated than is generally thought. The reason for this lies in the conceptual position within the theoretical edifice of Deleuze and Guattari from which it derives (see esp. Deleuze and Guattari 1987). Deleuze and Guattari construe deterritorialization as integral to a 'nomadic' theory of counter-movements and displacements, with which they seek to destabilize Western models, mindsets, orders and routines. Caren Kaplan has objected that Deleuze and Guattari conceptualize deterritorialization primarily as another form of (colonial) expansion: 'Deterritorialization is always reterritorialization, an increase of territory, an imperialization' (Kaplan 1996: 89).

The idea of the rhizome – a key analytic concept in Deleuze and Guattari's work – represents, according to Kaplan (ibid.: 87), a variant of this neo-colonial discourse. It is a botanical metaphor for multi-directionality, extension and displacement. As such, it has gained entry into the anthropological literature on globalization, migration and interstitiality (e.g. Appadurai 1996: 29; Bottomley 1995: 31–32; Malkki 1995: 174–75; 1997: 67–68). Deleuze and Guattari first introduced the idea of the rhizome to contrapose the arborescent model of unity, order and hierarchy with an alternative embracing of multiplicity, disorder, and reticulation. The fact that these authors assigned Oceania to the rhizomatic type – the West, by contrast, they deemed arborescent – caused Rumsey (2001) to deconstruct this dichotomy from the perspective of an Oceania specialist. Trees and arborescent structures generally – Rumsey objected – are also encountered in connection with the placing of traditional cosmologies and local identities in Oceania. Constituting the 'other' as an oppositional category and fundamental counterforce to Western modernity is symptomatic of the deficits contained in Deleuze and Guattari's theoretical project of the subversion and displacement of dominant orders and paradigms (see Kaplan 1996: 86–91; cf. Lattas 1991; Miller 1993). One contradiction is especially noticeable. Deleuze and Guattari strive, on the one hand, to table a notion of multiplicity that cannot be reduced to an origin, an essence or a totality (cf. Deleuze and Parnet 2007: 34–35). On the other hand, they perpetuate with their theoretical concepts of nomadology, rhizomes, deterritorialization and reterritorialization, a colonial discourse turning on essences and absolute difference, a discourse which happens to be diametrically opposed to the decentred way in which they first conceived multiplicity.

We propose to skirt these troubled waters of theoretical counter-models and contentious metaphors by deploying our own preferred concept of place-making. The theoretical agenda is to study those historical processes, political projects and social practices that contribute to the ongoing constitution of place, locality, homeland and community in the context of local, regional and global entwinements (Low and Lawrence-Zuniga

2003). From the perspective of viewing places as open-ended processes, embedded in – and articulating with – a larger system, it is possible to see localities as interfaces, as points where relationships and interactions meet (Massey 1994: 154–56). For Biersack, places 'are constructed historically in processes that spatially exceed the local and in which the extralocal is as constitutive as the local' (Biersack 2006: 16). Wherever external influences and forces make deep inroads into a particular locality, the resultant transformation processes will be considerable. The loss of land, landscape and villages through mining, say, can result in resettlement projects; these, in turn, occasion the articulation of different places in different states, laying the basis for multiple relationships of a long-term kind.[4] A method of analytically scrutinizing the historical transformation of the landscape as a consequence of pollution caused by mine tailings was proposed by Kirsch (2004), combining a phenomenological approach with political-economy. Here ecological degradation and destruction give rise to an altered self-understanding among landowners, which, in Kirsch's opinion, is behind an indigenous discourse opposing the capitalist logic of resource extraction. Missing from his account, however, are the discourses and practices of refugees living in the area under study who have fled from nearby West Papua (see King 1998: 79–80); yet such discourses and practices might be seen as a useful adjunct to the debate over the historical process of local transformations, since these refugees have their own ways of conceptualizing place and identity, loss and change. At this point a number of questions suggest themselves: What sort of sense of place have these refugees forged? How do their voices contribute to the multiplicity of experiences, perceptions and transformations found on the ground?

The multiplicity of place poses a challenge for the analytical repertoire of anthropologists, a challenge Margaret Rodman (1992) has tried to resolve using the twin concepts of multilocality and multivocality. Basically, multilocality designates the heterogeneity of place. Multiple relationships and networks as well as diverse actors, power positionings and polysemes fall under this concept as constitutive elements. From Rodman's praxis-oriented approach can likewise be derived conceptual overlaps between multilocality and multivocality. How different voices are represented is based on structuring factors such as age, status, gender and (ethnic) identity. So, multivocality means exploring diverging perspectives for spatial configurations that yield key insights into the multi-dimensionality of places (ibid.: 646–47, 649; cf. Kahn 1996).

In order to accentuate the multiple nature of places, we construe the latter not only as heterogeneous ensembles, but also as contested entities and variable configurations in the making. By placing the multiplicity of spatial formations and events centre stage, we acquire a conceptual lens indispensable to any adequate understanding of Oceania today, including its transnational extensions and diasporas. The chapters in this volume treat the multi-dimensionality of place in all its many guises, whether resulting from mobility, travel or internal and international migration. Movements of this kind make a difference. They are constitutive of the multiplicities of places and identifications in Oceania and beyond. They extend the multilocal referentiality of place. They transform multivocality by involving new rhythms and intensities of local absence and presence. They bring their historically and culturally specific influence to bear on localities, working through social actors who – dependent on their positioning – set up and consolidate or even contest and refashion diverse relationships. In this way, places are imbued with new meanings, which often give rise, in turn, to unexpected connotations, or even to new contradictions and ambiguities. This spectrum of meanings – multifaceted as well as lacking in uniformity – ultimately feeds back into the praxis of those persons and groups who are embedded within such multiple spatial relationships.

Reservations and plantations are exemplary landscapes of displacement, marginalization and ambivalence within postcolonial nation-states. It is upon this terrain that the consequences of colonial dominance and discipline still resonate, even now, in the manner in which these places are constituted. Garond stresses just how central tribal names are for the multiple bonds which displaced Palm Island Aboriginal people maintain with places both on and off their island home. She also elucidates how antagonisms and conflicts over land rights particularly nurture a sense of alienation among these Aboriginal people, who have found a new home in such a multilocal setting. Rollason views local interpretations of the rundown coconut plantations on Panapompom as spatial manifestations of a general state of disorder, stagnation and underdevelopment. For him, discourses of decline, oriented as they are to a transformed image of these plantations, are the product of a mnemonic praxis associating such places with the erection of new socio-political and economic structures during the colonial era. Yet the historical fact of immigration, in combination with disputed aspects of land ownership on Panapompom, gives rise to ambivalences within the contemporary population over their rightful place on the island.

Pascht focuses on the multiple meanings attached to land on Rarotonga, land which is claimed by Cook Island migrants to New Zealand, as a material symbol of their origins, kinship ties and cultural belonging. Pascht's perspective reveals a new dimension of place-making: land matters as much for Cook Islanders living abroad as it does for those living at home. The undeniable multivocality stemming from the reality of the multiple ownership of land on the Cook Islands is further compounded, within a context of transnational ties, by the different standpoints of those living abroad and those at home.

Thode-Arora as well as Fer and Malogne-Fer show, by studying Polynesian migrants within the urban contexts of New Zealand, that reversion to village and/or Christian structures from people's islands of origin is an important benchmark for reconstituting place and identity abroad. Hence, migrants from Niue, who can be found scattered throughout Auckland, have turned certain churches and meeting halls into social and cultural nodes of diasporic existence. The multilocal character of these urban meeting points is further underscored by the fact that Niueans share these buildings, where they perform religious rituals and cultural activities based on village affiliations, with ethnic groups other than their own. Reviewing the heterogeneous landscape of the Protestant Polynesian churches in New Zealand, Fer and Malogne-Fer confirm the central role these play (as institutions as well as places) in spatially anchoring the multiple relationships immigrants maintain with their countries of residence and of origin. Additionally, Thode-Arora and Fer and Malogne-Fer point out that the second generation of migrants, who were born and bred in New Zealand, already invoke new places, orientations and identifications, thus clearly setting themselves apart from the pioneer generation.

Places figure also in the chapters by Dürr and Brandt, who both stress the centrality of cross-cultural encounters and relationships of various forms. Thus, Dürr analyses the dialogical process by which perceptions and representations of places and/or landscapes back home are shaped by exchange with culturally different others. She shows how Māori pupils created an idealized place called New Zealand in interaction with their Mexican hosts, and under the spell of a new landscape. On the Mexican side, the same cross-cultural encounter led pupils to perceive and evaluate culturally significant places within Mexico itself in a novel way. At the same time, it also created imaginative references to a largely unknown New Zealand they had never visited. The study by Brandt of the texture of cross-cultural friendships between Māori and Pākehā let us conclude that differences between these two groups have been consolidated and reproduced across time – not least through the daily process of constituting discrete places and belonging.

## Cultural Identifications

Recent processes of movement and place-making have also had tremendous implications for the central, anthropological concepts of culture and identity, which in turn have raised new questions that require new theoretical approaches. Indeed, culture can no longer be considered as bounded, as relatively static and as a comparatively coherent set of ideas or meanings that are shared by a whole population of homogeneous individuals. Following large-scale processes of transnational migration across the globe, the meaning of the concept of culture has instead shifted to include the diversity and derivations of individual constructions, representations and interpretations. The dynamics of contemporary migration meanwhile make it necessary not only to look critically at the essentializing construction of culture, but since fluidity, non-fixity, contingency, contextuality and multiplicity are the order of the day, new imaginative sets of epistemologies and methodologies are required to address the multifarious dimension of contemporary culture (Eagleton 2000). Or should we perhaps say 'cultures'? After all, a 'culture' can no longer be considered to speak with one voice, so to speak, but it has become apparent that we need to take account of internal differentiation, and therefore culture has gradually come to be regarded as multivocal and polyphonous. For that reason, too, a distinction must be made between, on the one hand, a traditional discourse of culture in which culture was equated with a group of people that can be delineated with a boundary and, on the other hand, a new discourse of culture which is not represented as a reified essence, but instead as a political process of contestation among individual members or groupings over the power to define social situations (e.g. Wright 1998). The dynamic relationship between individual and community has in other words become characteristic of the anthropological concept of culture in recent history (Van Meijl 2008).

Obviously, the shifting meaning of culture also has far-reaching implications for our understanding and interpretation of identity. A clarification of the new meaning of culture not only sheds light on the contemporary context in which identities are being reconstituted, but it also clarifies the need to situate the analysis of identity in different dimensions of social and cultural situations. Any contextual analysis of contemporary representations of identity will necessarily have to pay attention to the cultural complexity and inherent ambiguity of identity (Hannerz 1992). In the global era, identity implies not only sameness and uniqueness, as it used to in the past; indeed, it has become abundantly clear that the features of identity cannot be defined in isolation of other – cultural – identities. In increasingly multicultural and transnational contexts, identity obtains its meaning primarily from the identity of the other with whom self is contrasted. Indeed, any construction of identity is preceded by a recognition of difference and an awareness of what self is not, but this psychological process is particularly prominent in inter-cultural situations (e.g. Woodward 1997). Not until difference between individuals with a different cultural background has become apparent will the sameness and uniqueness of the cultural identity of self come to the surface. Thus, the new conception of identity refers simultaneously to the difference and sameness of self and other, both with psychological and sociological connotations (Van Meijl 2010).

As the aspect of sameness has been eclipsed by difference, so has the aspect of uniqueness been substituted by plurality in contemporary perspectives on identity. Identity is no longer seen as exclusive, as individual or indivisible, but as multiply constructed across different, often intersecting and antagonistic, discourses, practices and positions. As a result, attention has shifted from a singular identity to multiple identities, although this emphasis is literally contradictory to the original, etymological meaning of the sameness of self (Sökefeld 1999: 417; 2001). Nevertheless, the focus is now on fractured identities as well as on their flexibility and changeability. In this context it is also relevant to refer to Stuart Hall's definition of identity as 'the point of *suture* between on the one hand the discourses and practices which attempt to "interpellate", speak to us or hail us into place as the social subjects of particular discourses, and on the other hand, the processes which produce subjectivities, which construct us as subjects which can be "spoken"' (Hall 1996: 5–6, original emphasis). Identity, in other words, is a kind of nexus at which different constructions of self coincide, and sometimes also collide.

Since the processes of contemporary constructions of identity, or rather identities, are never-ending and always incomplete, unfinished and open-ended, Hall (ibid.: 6) also proposes the term 'identification' above the essentialist concept of identity, an idea later developed by the influential sociologist and philosopher Zygmunt Bauman (2001: 129). Rather than being characterized by a singular and stable identity, in the contemporary global world the subject is constantly 'suturing' itself to different articulations between discourse and practice, a process which leads in turn to multiple identifications (see also Cohen 2000; Van Meijl and Driessen 2003; see also Hermann 2003).

These developments have now raised new questions for anthropology: To what extent is the differentiation of contemporary cultures reflected in the construction of identities and the emergence of multiple identifications? How do multiple identifications come about in individual lives? And how do multiple identifications of an individual relate to the identifications of other people in a dynamic socio-cultural context? In this volume, these questions are addressed in particular by Dürr and Thode-Arora. The latter examines the relationship between place and identity among the Niuean community in Auckland, New Zealand, which is characterized by multiplicity in two ways: both place and identity are multi-layered, in New Zealand as well as on the island of origin, Niue, with which Niuean immigrants in New Zealand continue to maintain strong connections. The cultural position of Niuean immigrants in New Zealand may have become displaced, but the link to their homeland remains a crucial component of their conception of self, reflected even in the organization of expatriate social groups on the basis of original village identities. Dürr, on the other hand, focuses on the reification of culture in encounters between Māori and Mexican students. She demonstrates that travel and movement shape not only cultural representations of other and self, but also that they lead to a variety of cultural identifications. In Mexico, Māori pupils, for example, represent themselves through performances of traditional songs and dances, but in New Zealand there is usually no need to express their cultural identity in a theatrical fashion.

In addition to the questions mentioned above regarding the sociological implications of changing cultures and changing identities, it is important to examine the psychological implications of contemporary cultural developments. The main question in this respect concerns the relationship between multiple identifications within individual constructions of personhood rather than between or among individuals (Van Meijl 2010). How are multiple identifications mediated within individual consciousness? And how do individuals relate different representations of their identifications within their experiences of themselves? Agnes Brandt addresses these questions in her study of cross-cultural friendships and relationships between Māori and non-Māori in New Zealand. In her approach she follows the cutting edge of research into multiple identifications in anthropology and psychology by showing that the self of individuals entwined in cross-cultural relationships is engaged in a continuous dialogue between the various cultural dimensions that impact directly upon their existence.

Questions regarding the balance between multiple identifications of a person's self are currently being addressed from a variety of different angles and orientations, the most promising one of which is situated in cognitive anthropology and social psychology, in which the idea of plural, competing identifications is linked up with the notion of a person as a composite of many, often contradictory self-understandings.[5] This strand of analysis has been inspired mainly by the Russian literary critic Mikhail Bakhtin, and has resulted in a view of the person as a multiplicity of I-positions among which dialogical relationships are established. The most important implication of the dialogical perspective on the person is that it is not an intra-psychological but a relational phenomenon that transcends the boundaries between inside and outside, self and other. In our view, this perspective on the relationship between multiple identifications also constitutes a promising point of departure for the final dimension of our conceptual frame: belonging.

## Multiplicities of Belonging

In the context of movement, place-making and multiple identifications always raise issues of belonging: belonging to certain places as well as to specific (and imagined) communities at local, national and transnational levels. The contributors to Lovell (1998b) reveal important ways in which loyalties are tied to localities and give rise to collective identities. Taking up where their discussions left off, we will attempt to delve more deeply into various aspects of belonging, making use of the theoretical approaches mentioned above.

Theories of movement and constituting place prompt us, via an analysis of relationships, to focus on cultural conceptions of spatial belonging. Such relationships include, above all, culturally constituted attachments to localities, that is, practices that anchor ideas of belonging in certain places and in the communities living there (Lovell 1998a; hooks 2009). Thus, we are interested in relationships that generate multiple belonging. Theoretical leads developed to elucidate multiple identifications can also yield insights into the shaping of such pluralities of belonging. Using the dialogical theory of Bakhtin, it is possible to construe belonging as a function of dialogue. Utterances by persons do not (in Bakhtin's eyes) simply represent 'the talk of individuals, but also the voices of their surrounding groups and institutions' (Van Meijl 2006: 930) with whom they are involved in a process of dialogue. These groups and institutions do not necessarily have to be physically present; they can be, indeed usually are, co-present in the speaker's imagination (ibid.: 930; Merlan 2005: 169). For Bakhtin, it is the anticipated response of others that shapes each utterance, as Francesca Merlan (2005: 178) has noted. This theoretical perspective implies that social actors constitute plural nodes of spatial and social belonging and that they do so in both their place of origin and their place of residence, in dialogue with the many voices and actions of others. Often, after migrating, they maintain a dialogue with persons and groups from their place of origin, while also engaging in dialogical relationships with those from their place of residence.

To see how multiple belonging results from such dialogical processes, we only need to turn to those contributions that treat international migration from Polynesia to New Zealand (see the chapters by Pascht, Thode-Arora, and Fer and Malogne-Fer, this volume). Land, village and church are constituted in discourses with real and imagined – but also with near and far – persons, communities and institutions. Whether it be the estates of absentee owners on Rarotonga, Niuean village structures or Polynesian churches in the urban areas of New Zealand, these function as signs and symbols of belonging in a transnational landscape of relationships and contacts maintained on a basis of dialogical activity and reflection. Thus, the changes, displacements and reorientations experienced by the second generation of Polynesians living in New Zealand can be explained (see Thode-Arora, Fer and Malogne-Fer, this volume), bearing in mind that their lives are constituted in a different, more diverse socio-cultural setting. A comparable praxis of negotiating origin and homeland can be found in the context of travel (Dürr, this volume) when belonging is represented and transformed in dialogue with others.

The manner in which loyalties are articulated concretely in such dialogical interactions depends always on historical and political developments, as well as on power relationships. Accordingly, it is important to pick up not just on processes of 'identifying with a place', but also on 'identifying against a place' and even on 'not identifying', as Gillian Rose (1995: 89–98) has suggested. In this context it is also crucial, by incorporating an analysis of power relationships, to study whether parts of a particular society deny to certain persons and groups the right of belonging to places, territories and communities (of whatever size). The instilling and preserving of loyalties, but also contesting the rights of others to the same attachments, can be additionally studied in light of further aspects of these processes.

The continuing structural effects of the colonial era on present-day constructions of place and identity leave no doubt that multiple belonging holds its share of ambiguities. The dialogical constitutions of belonging and not-belonging by, respectively, Aboriginal people relocated to Palm Island (Garond, this volume) and the inhabitants of Panapompom (Rollason, this volume) supply insights into such a political praxis of association and exclusion. Here, we find continuities, but also discontinuities and contradictions, pervading fields of multiple belonging. The contours of these fields are, in an ongoing process of negotiating distance and proximity, determined, called into question, altered and reshaped.

The factor of land (or land ownership) frequently appears as *movens* behind this ambiguity of belonging. On Palm Island and Panapompom, it is dialogues concerning past and present relations to land – both between newcomers themselves and between newcomers and (traditional) landowners – that drive such ambiguities. With the Māori of New Zealand (Brandt, this volume), where belonging is negotiated via spiritual ties to land, we find urban life itself operating as a source of alienation and ambiguity. Moreover, links to land constitute a dimension differentiating Māori from Pākehā and cut across various forms of cross-cultural relations. On Niue (Thode-Arora, this volume) and Rarotonga (Pascht, this volume) the ongoing dialogue between migrants and those who have stayed behind concerning land is the driving force behind the ambiguities of multiple belonging. The intention of Niue's prime minister to block access to the land-claim court for émigrés who had turned their backs on the island for decades shows that belonging requires a modicum of continuity. In Oceania we find continuity, thus construed, resting primarily on presence and proximity, on obligation and interaction. Movement and distance do not only multiply belonging but also exert a decisive influence on its structure and intensity. Such malleability reflects the fact that multiplicities of belonging are the product of dialogical processes operating within the frame of specific power relationships.

## Ethnographic Case Studies from Oceania

The chapter by Eveline Dürr investigates the construction of 'culture' in encounters between Māori and Mexican secondary-school students during a prolonged cultural exchange. It analyses how face-to-face relationships and lived experiences not only shape the perception of the 'other', but also how differences are played out and how alterity is created and understood in cross-cultural encounters. Drawing on translocal fieldwork in Mexico and New Zealand, Dürr places emphasis on the impact of cultural encounters on the formation of cultural identifications, imaginations and representations of one's own 'culture' in contrast to the 'other'. These experiences are embedded in movement and travelling to new places in both physical and imaginative ways.

Dürr conceives of travel as both a mode of place-making and interaction, impacting on travellers as well as on the people with whom they engage. Following a transcultural approach, Dürr reveals complex ways of creating both culture and places interactively and shows which cultural aspects are challenged, evoked and prioritized. By doing so, she draws attention to the ambivalent consequences of cross-cultural experiences. Although travel and movement may enhance people's tolerance for cultural otherness, they may simultaneously reinforce and partially essentialize one's own cultural patterns, identities and viewpoints. Thus, it becomes evident that travel, movement and border crossing shape cultural representation and identification in a multi-layered process.

Lise Garond focuses on the way Aboriginal inhabitants of Palm Island reservation articulate their sense of attachment to their island home, as well as to multiple places on mainland Australia, from which they or their forebears were forcibly removed. She stresses that they often express these attachments by reverting to multiple tribal names. She views such praxis as part of an emerging interest among the people of Palm Island in reappropriating identities recognized by the contemporary state, but also in reconstituting, to the fullest extent possible, their own disrupted histories. Another aspect is that the manner in which such names are used today harks back to a particular history of social relations and place-making within the reservation that is now home to the present community. According to Garond, reverting to tribal names reveals a way of identifying self and 'community' that differs greatly from the objectified and unifying Aboriginal identities represented in contemporary state discourses.

Will Rollason's chapter is about the way in which Panapompom people in south-east Papua New Guinea see their underdevelopment figured in the decaying landscape of a defunct copra plantation. His essay demonstrates how contemporary Panapompom people are constituted by their placement in shifting assemblages of material, people and relationships which, in turn, locate and contextualize them while also defining the movements, flows and connections that locate them in the wider world. Rollason argues that the plantation is entwined in competing dynamics and histories of place-making. On the one hand, it exists in an uneasy relationship with genealogical claims to land along customary lines, thus attaching it to narratives and memories of kinship. On the other, the plantation was a site of work and production in the colonial and postcolonial periods. It constituted a space-time that still contextualizes Panapompom within an orderly world of law, development and potential riches. The derelict state of the plantation symbolizes both the collapse of this order and what Panapompom people see as their exclusion from the expansive space-time of development.

Based on fieldwork among the Niuean community in Auckland, Hilke Thode-Arora explores Niuean constructions of place and identity. Taking her inspiration from Henri Lefebvre, she postulates a three dimensional grid: place as spatial praxis, place as perception and space as imagination. In her view, Niuean 'space-making' and ethnic marking can be shown to follow a similar pattern: while being unobtrusive and often rather pan-Polynesian in many of the city's polyethnic settings, Niueanness, overlaid as it is with village identity, sends out strong intra-ethnic signals. Village-based social groupings are constantly recreated and spatially expressed in Niuean gatherings. Power relations and social practices are linked with space-making and ideas of belonging, as 'true' Niueanness is highly contested and strategically negotiated between old and young, but also between Niueans living on the island and those living in New Zealand.

In the Cook Islands, absentee landowners are often seen as posing a most serious problem for contemporary land tenure. Arno Pascht shows that interpretations of this phenomenon often concentrate on economic or moral factors, but this is to neglect another important factor, namely the centrality of identity and belonging for Cook Islanders who, while not living permanently on their land, still wish to retain rights in it. Pascht explains that 'land rights' not only have to do with the right to use, or to take decisions about, a certain piece of land, but also involve ideas about belonging to a specific place and a specific family connected with it. In certain circumstances, land rights even mean full ownership. The relation to land and family – which is tantamount to identification with both – is by no means a given but must be actively maintained. In the case of family members living in New Zealand or Australia, this is typically done through visits, communication, gifts and, not least, remittances. Maintaining a relation can also be part of the process of resolving disputes over land rights. Pascht shows how identification is thus connected with notions of family and kinship, which is to say that it is also to do with history and the basic political and spatial organization of the island.

Yannick Fer and Gwendoline Malogne-Fer present a case-study of Polynesian communities formed as a result of Polynesian migration to New Zealand. Stressing the importance of Christian faith and religious praxis, they argue that churches have been nodes around which the distinctive identity of such communities has coalesced, given their central location between inclusion in New Zealand on the one side, and maintenance of enduring transnational links with the home islands on the other. Thus, in urban areas where most of these migrants now live, Protestant churches can be said to have contributed historically to the perpetuation of a collective memory, at once religious and cultural, while adapting the patterns of parish life to the urban context. But Fer and Malogne-Fer also stress that, in recent years, traditional Protestant churches have faced competition from evangelical Protestantism, inducing internal tensions. In this context, they refer to the Island Breeze movement, a branch of an international network known as Youth with a Mission. This missionizing body encourages young New Zealand-born Pacific people to define personal and multiple identities within the framework of local, regional and global circles of belonging, this by disentangling Christian faith, culture and traditional structures of authority. What this trend shows, according to Fer and Malogne-Fer, is how complex relationships forged between a common religious memory derived from Polynesian Protestantism and the multicultural context of contemporary New Zealand can give rise to a plethora of self-identifications.

In postcolonial New Zealand, the construction of identity is invariably influenced by popular and political debates about recent immigration from the Pacific islands and Asia, but even more so around the political process that aims at settling colonial grievances of the country's indigenous population, the Māori, especially about violations of the treaty signed between Māori and the colonial government at Waitangi in 1840. The official espousal of biculturalism since the 1980s has meant the acknowledgement of Māori indigeneity and their cultural differences, which, in turn, has led to an ongoing debate about the place of Māori and non-Māori people in New Zealand society. Increasing socio-cultural diversity through immigration has added further complexity.

In her contribution, Agnes Brandt addresses the question of how these processes impact upon New Zealanders' everyday social relations. She takes up this question by investigating the dynamics of cross-cultural friendships between Māori and Pākehā individuals. Special attention is given to the dynamics of actors' identities and senses of belonging in friendship, and the question how these relate to the wider socio-political context in which they occur. As the empirical analysis reveals, wider identity-making processes are not only reproduced, but at the same time they are often creatively deconstructed and re-imagined in cross-cultural friendships. A sense of belonging constitutes an important factor for the ways in which individuals establish and maintain close relations across socio-cultural and economic boundaries. A dialogical perspective is explored as a promising analytical avenue, which accounts for the complexities of this dynamic field of discourse, friendship and belonging.

## Notes

1. See e.g. Appadurai (1988, 1996), Malkki (1995), Lavie and Swedenburg (1996), Clifford (1997), Gupta and Ferguson (1997b) and Hastrup and Olwig (1997).
2. For earlier studies, see e.g. Lieber (1977), Finney (1979), Bonnemaison (1985) and Chapman (1985). For more recent studies of translocal and transnational networks, see e.g. Shankman (1993), Macpherson (1997), Lee (2003), Marshall (2004) and Gershon (2007). See also the contributions to the volumes edited by Spickard, Rondilla and Wright (2002), Lockwood (2004), Lee and Francis (2009) and Rensel and Howard (2012).
3. On deterritorialization and reterritorialization, see Appadurai (1996: 188), Gupta and Ferguson (1997b: 33, 37), Hastrup and Olwig (1997: 7), Malkki (1997: 52) and Olwig (1997: 18–23). On de/territorialization, see Inda and Rosaldo (2008: 12–15).
4. See e.g. the case of the Banabans (Kempf and Hermann 2005, this volume).
5. For examples from cognitive anthropology, see e.g. Holland et al. (1998) and Holland and Lave (2001). For work in social psychology, see e.g. Hermans and Kempen (1993) and Hermans (2002).

## References

Appadurai, A. 1988. 'Putting Hierarchy in its Place', *Cultural Anthropology* 3(1): 36–49.

_____ 1996. *Modernity at Large: Cultural Dimensions of Globalization.* Minneapolis: University of Minnesota Press.

Basso, K.H. 1996. 'Wisdom Sits in Places: Notes on a Western Apache Landscape', in S. Feld and K.H. Basso (eds), *Senses of Place.* Santa Fe, NM: School of American Research Press, pp.53–90.

Bauman, Z. 2001. 'Identity in the Globalising World', *Social Anthropology* 9(2): 121–29.

Besnier, N. 2011. *On the Edge of the Global: Modern Anxieties in a Pacific Island Nation.* Stanford: Stanford University Press.

Biersack, A. 2006. 'Reimagining Political Ecology: Culture/Power/History/Nature' in A. Biersack and J.B. Greenberg (eds), *Reimagining Political Ecology.* Durham, NC: Duke University Press, pp.3–40.

Bonnemaison, J. 1985. 'The Tree and the Canoe: Roots and Mobility in Vanuatu Societies', *Pacific Viewpoint* (special issue) 26(1): 30–62.

Bottomley, G. 1998. 'Anthropologists and the Rhizomatic Study of Migration', *Australian Journal of Anthropology* 9(1): 31–44.

Casey, E.S. 1996. 'How to Get from Space to Place in a Fairly Short Stretch of Time: Phenomenological Prolegomena', in S. Feld and K.H. Basso (eds), *Senses of Place.* Santa Fe, NM: School of American Research Press, pp.13–52.

Chandra, R. 1993. 'Where Do We Go From Here?' in E. Waddell, V. Naidu and E. Hau'ofa (eds), *A New Oceania: Rediscovering Our Sea of Islands.* Suva: School of Social and Economic Development, University of the South Pacific, pp.76–81.

Chapman, M. (ed.). 1985. 'Mobility and Identity in the Island Pacific', *Pacific Viewpoint* (special issue) 26(1).

Clifford, J. 1997. *Routes: Travel and Translation in the Late Twentieth Century.* Cambridge: Harvard University Press.

Cohen, A.P. (ed.). 2000. *Signifying Identities: Anthropological Perspectives on Boundaries and Contested Values.* London: Routledge.

Dawson, A., and M. Johnson. 2001. 'Migration, Exile and Landscapes of the Imagination', in B. Bender and M. Winer (eds), *Contested Landscapes: Movement, Exile and Place.* Oxford: Berg, pp.319–32.

Deleuze, G., and F. Guattari. 1987. *A Thousand Plateaus: Capitalism and Schizophrenia.* Minneapolis: University of Minnesota Press.

Deleuze, G., and C. Parnet. 2007. *Dialogues*, Vol. 2. New York: Columbia University Press.

Eagleton, T. 2000. *The Idea of Culture.* Oxford: Blackwell.

Feld, S. 1996. 'Waterfalls of Song: An Acoustemology of Place Resounding in Bosavi, Papua New Guinea', in S. Feld and K.H. Basso (eds), *Senses of Place.* Santa Fe, NM: School of American Research Press, pp.91–135.

Feld, S., and K.H. Basso. 1996. 'Introduction', in S. Feld and K.H. Basso (eds), *Senses of Place.* Santa Fe, NM: School of American Research Press, pp.3–11.

Finney, B. 1979. *Hokulea: The Way to Tahiti.* New York: Dodd, Mead.

Gershon, I. 2007. 'Viewing Diasporas from the Pacific: What Pacific Ethnographies Offer Pacific Diaspora Studies', *Contemporary Pacific* 19(2): 474–502.

Goss, J., and B. Lindquist. 2000. 'Placing Movers: An Overview of the Asian-Pacific Migration System', *Contemporary Pacific* 12(4): 385–414.

Griffen, V. 1993. 'Putting Our Minds to Alternatives', in E. Waddell, V. Naidu and E. Hauʻofa (eds), *A New Oceania: Rediscovering Our Sea of Islands*. Suva: School of Social and Economic Development, University of the South Pacific, pp.56–65.

Gupta, A., and J. Ferguson. 1997a. 'Culture, Power, Place: Ethnography at the End of an Era', in A. Gupta and J. Ferguson (eds), *Culture, Power, Place: Explorations in Critical Anthropology*. Durham, NC: Duke University Press, pp.1–29.

―――― 1997b. 'Beyond "Culture": Space, Identity, and the Politics of Difference', in A. Gupta and J. Ferguson (eds), *Culture, Power, Place: Explorations in Critical Anthropology*. Durham, NC: Duke University Press, pp.33–51.

Hall, S. 1996. 'Who Needs Identity?' in S. Hall and P.Du Gay (eds), *Questions of Cultural Identity*. London: Sage, pp.1–17.

Hannerz, U. 1992. *Cultural Complexity: Studies in the Social Organization of Meaning*. New York: Columbia University Press.

Hastrup, K., and K.F. Olwig. 1997. 'Introduction', in K.F. Olwig and K. Hastrup (eds), *Siting Culture: The Shifting Anthropological Object*. London: Routledge, pp.1–14.

Hauʻofa, E. 1994. 'Our Sea of Islands', *Contemporary Pacific* 6(1): 148–61.

Hermann, E. 2003. 'Manifold Identifications within Differentiations: Shapings of Self among the Relocated Banabans of Fiji', *Focaal* (special section) 42: 77–88.

―――― 2004. 'Emotions, Agency and the Dis/placed Self of the Banabans in Fiji', in T. van Meijl and J. Miedema (eds), *Shifting Images of Identity in the Pacific*. Leiden: KITLV Press, pp.191–217.

Hermans, H.J.M. 2002. 'The Dialogical Self as a Society of Mind', *Theory and Psychology* 12(2): 147–60.

Hermans, H.J.M., and H.J.G. Kempen. 1993. *The Dialogical Self: Meaning as Movement*. San Diego: Academic Press.

Holland, D., W. Lachicotte, D. Skinner and C. Caine. 1998. *Identity and Agency in Cultural Worlds*. Cambridge, MA: Harvard University Press.

Holland, D., and J. Lave (eds). 2001. *History in Person: Enduring Struggles, Contentious Practice, Intimate Identities*. Santa Fe, NM: School of American Research Press.

hooks, b. 2009. *Belonging: A Culture of Place*. New York: Routledge.

Inda, J.X., and R. Rosaldo. 2008. 'Tracking Global Flows', in J.X. Inda and R. Rosaldo (eds), *The Anthropology of Globalization: A Reader*, 2nd edn. Malden, MA: Blackwell, pp.3–46.

Kabachnik, P. 2012. 'Nomads and Mobile Places: Disentangling Place, Space and Mobility', *Identities: Global Studies in Culture and Power* 19(2): 210–28.

Kahn, M. 1996. 'Your Place and Mine: Sharing Emotional Landscapes in Wamira, Papua New Guinea', in S. Feld and K.H. Basso (eds), *Senses of Place*. Santa Fe, NM: School of American Research Press, pp.167–96.

Kaplan, C. 1996. *Questions of Travel: Postmodern Discourses of Displacement*. Durham, NC: Duke University Press.

Kempf, W., and E. Hermann. 2005. 'Reconfigurations of Place and Ethnicity: Positionings, Performances, and Politics of Relocated Banabans in Fiji', *Oceania* (special issue) 75(4): 368–86.

King, D. 1998. 'Refugees and Border Crossers on the Papua New Guinea–Indonesia Border', in L. Zimmer-Tamakoshi (ed.), *Modern Papua New Guinea*. Kirksville, MO: Thomas Jefferson University Press, pp.67–84.

Kirby, P.W. 2009. 'Lost in "Space": An Anthropological Approach to Movement', in P.W. Kirby (ed.), *Boundless Worlds: An Anthropological Approach to Movement*. New York: Berghahn, pp.1–27.

Kirsch, S. 2004. 'Changing Views of Place and Time along the Ok Tedi', in A. Rumsey and J. Weiner (eds), *Mining and Indigenous Lifeworlds in Australia and Papua New Guinea*. Wantage: Sean Kingston, pp.182–207.

Latour, B. 1993. *We Have Never Been Modern*. New York: Harvester.

Lattas, A. 1991. 'Primitivism in Deleuze and Guattari's "A Thousand Plateaus"', *Social Analysis* 30: 98–115.

Lavie, S., and T. Swedenburg. 1996. 'Introduction: Displacement, Diaspora, and Geographies of Identity', in S. Lavie and T. Swedenburg (eds), *Displacement, Diaspora, and Geographies of Identity*. Durham, NC: Duke University Press, pp.1–25.

Lee, H.M. 2003. *Tongans Overseas: Between Two Shores*. Honolulu: University of Hawai'i Press.

Lee, H., and S.T. Francis (eds). 2009. *Migration and Transnationalism: Pacific Perspectives*. Canberra: ANU ePress.

Lieber, M.D. (ed.). 1977. *Exiles and Migrants in Oceania*. Honolulu: University of Hawai'i Press.

Lilomaiava-Doktor, S. 2009. 'Beyond "Migration": Samoan Population Movement (*Malaga*) and the Geography of Social Space (*Va*)', *Contemporary Pacific* 21(1): 1–32.

Lockwood, V.S. (ed.). 2004. *Globalization and Culture Change in the Pacific Islands*. Upper Saddle River, NJ: Pearson and Prentice Hall.

Lovell, N. 1998a. 'Introduction: Belonging in Need of Emplacement?' in N. Lovell (ed.), *Locality and Belonging*. London: Routledge, pp.1–24.

―――― (ed.). 1998b. *Locality and Belonging*. London: Routledge.

Low, S.M., and D. Lawrence-Zuniga. 2003. 'Locating Culture', in S.M. Low and D. Lawrence-Zuniga, (eds), *The Anthropology of Space and Place*. Malden, MA: Blackwell, pp.1–47.

Macpherson, C. 1997. 'The Polynesian Diaspora: New Communities and New Questions' in K. Sudo and S. Yoshida (eds), *Population Movement in the Modern World*, Vol. I: *Contemporary Migration in Oceania: Diaspora and Network*. Osaka: Japan Center for Area Studies, National Museum of Ethnology, pp.77–100.

Malkki, L.H. 1995. *Purity and Exile: Violence, Memory, and National Cosmology among Hutu Refugees in Tanzania*. Chicago: University of Chicago Press.

―――― 1997. 'National Geographic: The Rooting of Peoples and the Territorialization of National Identity among Scholars and Refugees', in A. Gupta and J. Ferguson (eds), *Culture, Power, Place: Explorations in Critical Anthropology*. Durham, NC: Duke University Press, pp.52–74.

Marshall, M. 2004. *Namoluk beyond the Reef: The Transformation of a Micronesian Community*. Boulder, CO: Westview Press.

Massey, D. 1994. *Space, Place and Gender*. Cambridge: Polity Press.

McKay, D. (ed.). 2006. 'Place in Motion: New Ethnographies of Locality in the Asia-Pacific', *Asia Pacific Journal of Anthropology* 7(3).

Merlan, F. 2005. 'Explorations towards Intercultural Accounts of Socio-cultural Reproduction and Change', *Oceania* 75(3): 167–82.

Miller, C.L. 1993. 'The Postidentitarian Predicament in the Footnotes of A Thousand Plateaus: Nomadology, Anthropology and Authority', *Diacritics* 23(3): 6–35.

Naidu, V. 1993. 'Whose Sea of Islands?' in E. Waddell, V. Naidun and E. Hau'ofa (eds), *A New Oceania: Rediscovering Our Sea of Islands*. Suva: School of Social and Economic Development, University of the South Pacific, pp.49–55.

Nero, K.L. 1997. 'The End of Insularity', in D. Denoon (ed.), *The Cambridge History of Pacific Islanders*. Cambridge: Cambridge University Press, pp.439–67.

Olwig, K.F. 1997. 'Cultural Sites: Sustaining a Home in a Deterritorialized World', in K.F Olwig and K. Hastrup (eds), *Siting Culture: The Shifting Anthropological Object*. London: Routledge, pp.17–38.

Pile, S., and N. Thrift. 1995. 'Mapping the Subject', in S. Pile and N. Thrift (eds), *Mapping the Subject: Geographies of Cultural Transformation*. London: Routledge, pp.13–51.

Rensel, J., and A. Howard (eds). 2012. 'Pacific Islands Diaspora, Identity, and Incorporation', *Pacific Studies* (special issue) 35(1/2).

Rodman, M.C. 1992. 'Empowering Place: Multilocality and Multivocality', *American Anthropologist* 94(3): 640–56.

Rose, G. 1995. 'Place and Identity: A Sense of Place', in D. Massey and P. Jess (eds), *A Place in the World? Places, Cultures and Globalization*. Oxford: Oxford University Press, pp.87–132.

Rumsey, A. 2001. 'Tracks, Traces, and Links to Land in Aboriginal Australia, New Guinea, and Beyond', in A. Rumsey and J.F. Weiner (eds), *Emplaced Myth: Space, Narrative, and Knowledge in Aboriginal Australia and Papua New Guinea*. Honolulu: University of Hawai'i Press, pp.19–42.

Shankman, P. 1993. 'The Samoan Exodus', in V.S. Lockwood, T.G. Harding and B.J. Wallace (eds), *Contemporary Pacific Societies: Studies in Development and Change*. Englewood Cliffs, NJ: Prentice Hall, pp.156–70.

Sökefeld, M. 1999. 'Debating Self, Identity and Culture in Anthropology', *Current Anthropology* 40(4): 417–47.

―――― 2001. 'Reconsidering Identity', *Anthropos* 96(2): 527–44.

Spickard, R., R.J. Rondilla and D.H. Wright (eds). 2002. *Pacific Diaspora: Island Peoples in the United States and Across the Pacific*. Honolulu: University of Hawai'i Press.

Van Meijl, T. 2006. 'Multiple Identifications and the Dialogical Self: Urban Maori Youngsters and the Cultural Renaissance', *Journal of the Royal Anthropological Institute* 12(4): 917–33.

―――― 2008. 'Culture and Identity in Anthropology: Reflections on "Unity" and "Uncertainty" in the Dialogical Self', *International Journal for Dialogical Science* 3(1): 165–90.

―――― 2010. 'Anthropological Perspectives on Identity: From Sameness to Difference', in M. Wetherell and C.T. Mohanty (eds), *The Sage Handbook of Identities*. London: Sage, pp.63–81.

Van Meijl, T., and H. Driessen. 2003. 'Introduction: Multiple Identifications and the Self', *Focaal* (special section) 42: 17–29.

Woodward, K. (ed.). 1997. *Identity and Difference*. London: Sage.

Wright, S. 1998. 'The Politicization of "Culture"', *Anthropology Today* 14(1): 7–15.

Young Leslie, H. 2004. 'Pushing Children Up: Maternal Obligation, Modernity and Medicine in the Tongan Ethnoscape', in V.S. Lockwood (ed.), *Globalization and Culture Change in the Pacific Islands*. Upper Saddle River, NJ: Pearson and Prentice Hall, pp.390–413.

# 1

# Culture as Experience

## Constructing Identities through Transpacific Encounters

### Eveline Dürr

In this chapter,[1] I investigate an encounter of Māori and Mexican secondary-school students, which was initiated and organized by a Māori immersion school located on Aotearoa New Zealand's North Island. In 2006, thirty-one Māori school students, aged roughly between twelve and seventeen, and five teachers and parents visited a private school in a state capital in southern Mexico.[2] The aims of their visit were to improve the students' Spanish language skills, as Spanish is part of the school's curriculum, and to provide a window onto the world for the students, trying to enhance their knowledge about other cultures and foster cultural understanding. This encounter took place on a home-stay basis, and the Māori students lived for approximately three months in Mexican middle-class households.[3] The Māori students were expected to try and become part of the Mexican families they stayed with by participating in their daily routine and practices, adapting to their food habits, timetable and language.

This transpacific, cross-cultural encounter, in which the participants met each other for the first time, left a deep impression on both the Māori and Mexican students. In the course of this face-to face-encounter, the students reformulated their own cultural identities and those of the people they met through interaction and experience. I wish to explore this process and analyse the impact of this encounter on the formation of cultural identities, imaginations and representations of one's own 'culture' in contrast to the 'other'. How do cultural identities alter when they travel, and what impact does this have on the individuals they encounter and interact with? How does physical movement to new places and engagement with foreign cultures invoke the unfamiliar and construct alterity? Following Clifford (1999: 7), I conceptualize this travel experience and encounter as a particular contact zone, where culture, identity and indigeneity are displayed and negotiated. While moving through particular sites and engaging with foreignness, both similarities and dissimilarities become apparent in individuals' encounters (ibid.: 3). Thus, I seek to analyse how concepts of self and alterity evolve and are modified in the course of lived experiences. Increasingly, cultures are shaped in cross-cultural contacts, mutually appropriating facets of the 'other' and thus creating trans-cultural dialogues and new cultural formations (Welsch 1999). In this vein, I will also show which cultural aspects are evoked, rejected, challenged or appropriated, and what is prioritized in the process of cultural representation. As the example of travel I am concerned with here entails a tourist experience, I refer also to perceptions of foreign places and to concepts of place-making and mobility. As the students travelled together, they saw, at least partially, their countries through the eyes of the other. Places were mediated through the students' narratives and constructed intersubjectively, thus acquiring new emotionality and meaning. Further, places became mobile and interconnected as they were included in this network of cross-cultural relationships. They were made close through personal contacts and subsequently reproduced in practices and performances.

In conclusion, I highlight the complexity of cross-cultural representations, and point to the ambivalent outcomes of cross-cultural experiences. While tolerance for cultural otherness may increase, one's own cultural patterns, identities and viewpoints may also be strengthened and partially essentialized. Simultaneously, the blurring of boundaries, openness towards the 'other', as well as trans-cultural tendencies may become apparent. This shows once more that self and other are interrelated and shifting categories, and may be sometimes even contradictory constructs (Hallam and Street 2000: 5). It also reveals that cultural practices are not meaningful in themselves but rather are a product of interaction and experience, and that travel and movement constitute forces of cultural identification. Mobility is of paramount importance as a crucial component of social life (Kirby 2009: 4).

Encounters between different cultures have long been a key subject in anthropology. At the heart of the anthropological inquiry lies the very nature of these encounters and the question how individuals perceive, represent and make sense of each other. Cross-cultural encounters evolve in extremely diverse ways and can result in ambivalent experiences, entailing facets of both attraction and repulsion. These issues have been expatiated in myriad contexts and constellations, such as first contacts during European expansion and under colonialism, when cultural contacts were mainly framed by subordination and asymmetrical relationships between the colonizer and the colonized (Schieffelin et al. 1991; Schwartz 1994). Other studies conceive of cross-cultural encounters as multilayered acts of translation between virtually incommensurate worlds, with some actors searching for comparability and common denominators (Fuchs 2002, 2004; Maranhão and Streck 2003). These inquiries have gained new momentum due to research into globalization and mobility, with increased transnational activities and faster communication networks intensifying the exposure of different cultures to each other. Studies now emphasize interconnection, the importance of movement across borders and between cultures, and cultures in motion (Inda and Rosaldo 2008). Interest centres on various forms of mobility (Sheller and Urry 2006), travel, border crossing and self-location (Clifford 1999), and the cultures, ideas, discourses and performances encountered through tourism (Rojek and Urry 1997b; Bruner 2005; Jaworski and Pritchard 2005b). As Clifford (1999: 3) has pointed out in his work on culture, travel and movement, travel is part of the human condition and entails a complex set of experiences. Travel requires multiple forms of identification, attachment and belonging, and travellers develop diverse strategies of translation. As a way of stepping beyond the horizon and leaving 'home', travel has become a metaphor for the postmodern condition.[4]

In this vein, anthropologists have long deconstructed the concept of culture, arguing that it is a process rather than a set of fixed and bounded entities. Anthropological theory highlights that 'culture' is a constantly changing formation, shaped by specific contexts, power relations and representations. This implies that 'culture', or what is perceived as the 'other', is not set in terms of a pre-existing unit but is rather constructed through interaction. Therefore, the dichotomy between self and other which shaped binary discourses on relationships and interaction patterns in terms of East/West, traditional/modern, civilized/primitive and so on has been revised. It has become obvious that these categories are interrelated and constitute each other (Hallam and Street 2000: 3, 5–6). The research focus has shifted to reflexivity, overlap and mixture, emphasizing the constant renegotiation of cultural meanings and identities as a response to changing contexts and interests. This revised view of the meaning of culture also points to considerable variation within one cultural group, and stresses diversity and polyphony rather than unity and homogeneity.

As societies become culturally more diverse, various forms of crossover, meetings and mixings of world-views and practices have come under close scrutiny. Emphasis has been given to transgression and the dissolution of firm boundaries between cultural groups which were formerly perceived as separate, and to the interplay of cultural appropriation, assemblages and agency (Hall 1996; Werbner and Modood 1997). However, empirical research reveals additional results from cross-cultural encounters. A long time ago, Frederik Barth (1969) pointed out that boundaries may be reinforced and reinvigorated through cultural contact. Besides processes of mixing, creolization, bricolage and hybridity as results of increasing mobility, travel and interconnectedness, intensified exchange and encounters also revive cultural boundaries or even create new ones as individuals search for orientations and fixed points in their life-worlds. Rather than embracing fusion and mixing, some cultural identities seem to resist amalgamation, and emphasize 'purity' and uniqueness (Werbner 1997: 3). More often than not, culture contact makes individuals become aware and proud of difference, and reinforces distinctiveness (Meyer and Geschiere 2003; Harrison 2006: 8, 97). This occurs for a variety of reasons. Groups and individuals may perceive and represent themselves as bounded, rooted, fixed and static in a territory, and thus with an unchanged cultural repertoire. In these ways they define themselves and exclude others. This may be because they feel threatened or endangered, and this kind of representation becomes vital for their survival (Hastrup 1995; Harrison 2006: 120). These processes are evident in the political usage of cultural symbols which can be observed throughout the Pacific and elsewhere. The reasons for this mode of representation and self-perception are myriad and need to be understood in the light of a group's historical experience and contemporary condition. They are also key to the understanding of the emergence of both more or less clearly contoured 'cultures' and cultural identifications, that is, the range of ways individuals relate to, emphasize or reject specific aspects of what they perceive as core features of their respective cultural repertoire.

This article is guided by these lines of inquiry. It aims to advance our understanding of the complex interactive constructions of culture as they emerge from concrete experiences and their impact on identity formation in pluricultural contexts. It also calls for a more thorough consideration of the wider embeddedness of these processes in terms of social structure, class and other structural conditions. Drawing on ethnographic fieldwork conducted in Mexico and New Zealand in 2007, and on interviews with all the parties involved (students, teachers and parents), I examine individuals' retrospective appraisal of their subjective experiences of immersion in a culture different to their own. The trans-local and cross-cultural nature of this research added to its complexity and sometimes caused confusion. During the preparation phase of this project, I discussed my research aims and methods with the principals of the schools in Mexico and New Zealand respectively, and informed them that I sought to talk to all individuals involved in both countries. In Mexico, some of the participants wondered about my interest in this encounter and, given the fact that I came from New Zealand but am a German national, some assumed that this project was carried out on behalf of the school in New Zealand. Others were keen to know what I was told by the other 'side' and hesitated to deliver their personal views at the beginning of the research process. It took some time to create a trustful relationship and to convince the participants of the independent, academic nature of this research. My own national background as a German rather than a New Zealander or Mexican might have been an advantage in this context, and helped to stress the fact that I had no personal preference or interest in either 'side'. As a German, I was perceived as an outsider by both cultures, but simultaneously as somebody who was familiar with both cultural contexts, as all participants knew that I had lived in both New Zealand and Mexico for some time. In this research, some knowledge of both cultures was crucial as they differ considerably, a fact that adds to the complexity of cross-cultural hermeneutics.

## Interacting in Cultural Context: Indigenous Māori Meet the Mexican Middle Class

The peculiarities of this encounter merit special attention as not only the cultural contexts and historical experiences of the individuals involved, but also the societies that they came from, are diverse. Even though all students were adolescent and in a formative phase in their life-cycles, their backgrounds regarding class, culture and social positioning in their respective societies differed considerably. It is also important to note that the Māori and Mexican students were mostly unaware of each other and had only vague, if any, ideas about what to expect before the actual encounter took place. For the majority of the students, it was the first time to experience such an intense border crossing in terms of cultural, geographic, economic and social boundaries. This is also tied into the divergent public perception and political impact of indigenous peoples in New Zealand and Mexico.

While the pre-European cultures of Mexico, often glorified and romanticized, are crucial to Mexico's representation and national identity, the contemporary indigenous population is marginalized in economic, social and political terms. In everyday life and interactions, indigenous peoples are widely perceived as backward, and a hindrance to progress and modernity. However, there has been a tendency to revise this perception and to revalue indigeneity in Mexico, as has been observed in other Latin American countries (Reina 2002; Sieder 2002). This development became politically manifest in the revision of Mexico's constitution in 1992, when the country officially acknowledged cultural diversity and indigenous customs. In New Zealand, however, this tendency is far more accentuated than in Mexico, as the country is officially a bicultural nation, based on an ideal of equal partnership between indigenous Māori and Pākehā (European New Zealanders) as it is articulated in the Treaty of Waitangi of 1840.[5] However, the Treaty has long been ignored, and biculturalism as a fairly recent political agenda has its roots in the Māori renaissance movement in the 1960s (Sharp 1997; Durie 1998). To this day, doubts persist about the realities of New Zealand's bicultural framework, as relative disparities between Māori and Pākehā remain in place (Walker 2004; Maaka and Fleras 2005: 69).

In the postwar period, decolonization processes gave rise to the revival of ethnic identities and the emergence of indigenous movements in many parts of the world. Political independence came to the Pacific in the 1970s and 1980s (Clifford 2001: 473). It was in this time frame that Māori culture gained new momentum in New Zealand. Māori demands for recognition placed emphasis on a revaluation of Māori culture, as it is the Crown's obligation to protect Māori *taonga*, that is tangible and intangible cultural 'treasures'.[6] These treasures include artefacts and material objects, as well as specific cultural knowledge and practices such as *te reo Māori* (Māori language), ceremonial speech-making, songs, dances and craft skills, like carving and weaving. *Taonga* are seen as exclusive Māori possessions which are in need of protection against hegemonic forces. Loss or replacement of *taonga*, which only Māori own and have the power to define (Bishop and Glynn 1999: 170), is equated with a loss of identity and dignity. In public discourses and representations, Māori culture is defined by these features, and culture itself became synonymous with language, symbolic practices, skills and crafts. Regaining control over these cultural characteristics is seen as a sign of success and counter-hegemonic agency, and has therefore become of paramount importance (Van Meijl 2006). Thus, culture is conceived of as a reified essence and identity marker which helps to dissociate Māori from European New Zealanders and other groups in New Zealand society. As such, it is mobilized as symbolic capital and used to achieve political aims in Māori struggles over power and self-determination in New Zealand society. Furthermore, 'culture' in terms of symbolic practices and skills is also refashioned and commercialized for the tourist gaze, and put on display in theme-park-like environments as tourist attractions, staging an imagined pre-colonial past. However, not all Māori see symbolic practices and traditional performances as key features of their identity. Critical voices posit that culturalist orientations and representations of Māori identity may not include all categories of Māori individuals, but may even cause pressure and tension for those who do not belong to the privileged indigenous middle class (Rata 1996, 2006; Van Meijl 2006).[7] Nevertheless, the dominant discourse in New Zealand is shaped by an exceptional pride of Māori in their specific culture and consequently in a particular concept of indigeneity as *tangata whenua* (people of the land).

These conditions differ considerably from the social and political context concerning the Mexican families in this study, and which consequently impact on their understanding of 'culture' and perceptions of indigeneity. While most of the Māori students came from mixed social backgrounds, most of the Mexican students belong to the non-indigenous urban middle class, and some families even form part of the town's elite and practise an extravagant lifestyle. While embracing and performing 'traditional culture' is crucial for the constitution of a Māori identity, this is not the case for affluent Mexican families. In most Mexican middle-class households, the notion of 'culture' refers more to an individual's habitus and class, whereas traditional knowledge and practices are more associated with indigenous peoples and referred to as *cultura indígena*, 'indigenous culture', which does not have the same powerful connotation as it does in New Zealand. The Mexican families rather tend to express their class identity and middle-class affiliation through status symbols such as cars, housing, clothing, modern technology and so on. This is also indicated by the fact that many such Mexican households have domestic workers, like servants, chauffeurs and gardeners, to assist them in everyday tasks – this is in marked contrast to most Māori households in New Zealand. Also, Mexican middle-class families place emphasis on 'cultural experiences', which usually means a journey abroad, preferably to the USA or Europe, but does not include involvement in Mexico's indigenous communities and their symbolic practices.

These diverse conceptualizations and social significations of 'culture' in both countries find apparent expression in the school systems. In New Zealand, the school system has been fiercely criticized for its Eurocentric teaching style and lack of cultural sensitivity. Māori have felt discriminated against in Pākehā-dominated schools and have sought to provide a culturally adequate alternative space to mainstream education. As a result, Māori-language pre-schools, so called 'Māori language nests' (*te kōhanga reo*), came into existence in 1982 (Fleras and Elliot 1992: 212; King 2001). They aimed at promoting Māori cultural aspirations and resistance to Pākehā hegemony in the education system (Bishop 2008: 439). As culturally sensitive and community-based Māori language immersion schools, they used Māori language as a means of instruction to fight the gradual erosion of language and, subsequently, cultural identity. Thus, these institutions encouraged Māori to identify with Māori language and cultural values in order to enhance self-esteem and to promote Māori social and cultural values (Fleras and Elliot 1992: 213).

The success of Māori-language pre-schools gave rise to further immersion schools, at all levels of the education system, known as *kura kaupapa Māori* (Bishop 2008: 439). They are based on Māori pedagogy and philosophy, although national curriculum guidelines are considered to ensure credibility and support. These schools have assisted in installing Māori language in everyday conversation, politicized Māori concerns and provided a forum for a politically engaged discussion on social equity, discrimination and justice, with particular reference to commitment to the Treaty of Waitangi (Fleras and Elliot 1992: 211; Bishop 2008: 439). The immersion school approach also reaches into students' homes. Participation of students' parents in school activities, and their support for their children's education, are seen as crucial to the success of this pedagogy (Bishop and Glynn 2003: 81; Bishop 2008: 443).

The New Zealand school involved in the visit to Mexico is influenced by this educational context, and therefore committed to Māori pedagogy. This had a strong impact on the students' mode of self-representation in Mexico. Given their specific educational background, they are trained to excel in Māori culture, comprising language, song and dance. Doing and performing culture play a significant role in the school, entailing a range of activities, skills and attitudes which reflect the survival of specific Māori values and practices, such as *kapa haka*, a performance including specific dances and choreography, ceremonial speech-making, *waiata* (Māori songs and chants), oratory, oral history and modes of hospitality. Excelling in culture adds to the *mana* of the students and the school alike.[8] The school also has a *marae*, a meeting house in combination with a courtyard to carry out ceremonies and assemblies, a space which requires a specific *marae* protocol that the students are trained in and familiar with. Thus, the role of the school reaches far beyond education, and provides a vital source for the constitution of a specific Māori cultural identity and self-definition. Also, many students feel a deep emotional attachment to their school and keep contact with it after they have left. Airini, a teacher at the school involved in this research, pertinently expresses the activities of the school and their impact on the students. As a source of pride, the students are encouraged to display their culture outside the school and New Zealand contexts: 'A lot of *kura*[9] schools like ours are focused on language and retention of traditions and things like that. That is important here, but what we want our children to do that for is so that they can go out into the world on their own terms, and when they go somewhere they've got something to show'.

In contrast to the philosophy of Māori immersion schools, 'culture' is not of paramount importance in the Mexican school's curriculum, nor is it considered to be a key source of the students' identity and education, even though cultural activities, in terms of Mexican heritage and performances, are taught. Furthermore, the two schools have different approaches to education and conduct, teaching style, philosophy and constituency. While the Māori immersion school in New Zealand places emphasis on respect toward seniors as part of Māori protocol, the Mexican school privileges a more relaxed teaching atmosphere. This may result in less disciplined behaviour in the classroom, which is not favoured in Māori pedagogy.

In order to place these differences in perspective, it is important to bear in mind that the roles of these schools in the wider society differ considerably in New Zealand and in Mexico. While the immersion schools in New Zealand are a response to colonial forces and assimilationist tendencies, the expensive private schools in Mexico provide a space for the upbringing of the city's future elite, which has hardly any affiliation with indigenous cultures. More often than not, Mexican private schools are associated with the politics of the local elite and power struggles within the local political scene. In this vein, the Mexican private schools facilitate and perpetuate social networks and political alliances of a specific segment of society. Thus, both schools contribute to the production and reproduction of a politically engaged value system and constituency, be it Māori or Mexican middle class.

Prior to their visit to Mexico, the New Zealand school prepared its students and provided information on Mexico's social and cultural history and current situation. Other than this, hardly any pre-formed images, cultural experiences or spatial imaginaries existed, and neither the Mexican nor the Māori students knew much of each others' existence before their actual encounter took place. The majority of the Māori students were quite New Zealand-focused, and only a few had travelled beyond their homeland's shores.[10] For most of the students, this trip marked their first experience outside New Zealand's North Island, on an aeroplane, and away from their families for a lengthy period of time. However, family linkages and kinship bonds were not totally broken up during the trip, as some of the students were related to each other and to some of the teachers. They were 'alone' only when staying with their Mexican host families; otherwise they created a sense of community amongst themselves.

In a similar way, their Mexican counterparts had been mostly unaware of New Zealand before they encountered the Māori students. Some had heard of the country in the context of the famous movie trilogy *The Lord of the Rings*, and located it at the 'end of the world'. One family took New Zealand for a US state or city, in line with names for such places as New Jersey, New Orleans and New Mexico. Others searched for New Zealand on the globe, and scrutinized the internet for information prior to the arrival of their guests. Patricia, a host-mother described their preparations as follows:

> Yes, we had heard of New Zealand, but when we finally looked it up on the globe – well – we saw how far away it really is. But this made us even more curious to get to know a person from down there. We did not know what colour they are or what language they speak, we were really ignorant in this regard. But then we realized that they speak English and their indigenous language as well.

Because of the information these families gathered before the actual encounter took place, they had a vague idea about New Zealand, but they were still utterly surprised to host New Zealand's indigenous population.

Their surprise might be related to the fact that travel has long been perceived as a privilege of the white, mostly male, middle class (Rojek and Urry 1997a: 16). To this day, it is still considered unusual that indigenous peoples are mobile, leave 'their place' in order to explore and learn from the 'other'. Instead, they are constructed as static and bound to a particular place or territory to which they belong and where they can be visited. Mobility in order to explore other cultures and places is still seen as a privilege of non-indigenous actors. Rights to travel are unequal and tied into status and power. This is tentatively expressed by Pedro, a host-family father, who was surprised to receive a Māori girl as his guest-daughter:

> I did not know that they represent a native group – travelling all this way! I had only a vague idea of New Zealand. We expected tall whites with green eyes! But then we enjoyed getting to know the Māori and we checked their history in books and pictures. Our guest-daughter told us about her culture and the life in New Zealand. But we did not know anything about them before their actual visit.

In many ways, this travel experience involved an intense engagement with both the familiar and unfamiliar for all the individuals involved. The dynamics of identification became apparent as they were both constituted and changed in relation to each other. This open and unfinished process entails an awareness of difference and sameness, stressing the uniqueness of cultural identities as they emerge from these contexts. This is particularly evident with regard to different and even competing conceptions of culture. The divergent life-worlds and social contexts of Māori and the Mexican students, teachers and parents did not help understanding.

Miscomprehension and misinterpretation of each other's cultural aspirations stemmed from diverse expectations that were grounded in their own views and their respective ways of making sense of differences. The perceived differences were explained with regard to 'culture' or 'lack of culture', rather than with class, history or social conditions.

## Culture as Gift, Distinction, Performance and Experience

From the very beginning of this encounter, performative representations played a crucial role in interactions between the two groups. In line with the Māori immersion school's philosophy and focus on cultural practices, the Māori students proudly performed songs and dances in traditional costumes, such as the *haka*, an intimidating dance with aggressive gestures including foot-stamping, fiercely poking the tongue out, eye rolling and chanting, or the *poi*, a dance with light balls swung on the end of a string, or *waiata*, songs covering a range of topics from love and sincerity to lament, and generally celebrating ancient and pre-colonial life. While performances are common practices to establish contact and introduce one another in the Pacific context (Balme 2007: 6), they are not used as a means of interpersonal introduction in Mexican middle-class first-contact situations. Furthermore, these performances should not just display Māori culture, but also honour and pay respect to the Mexican hosts by 'offering' those symbolic acts and 'sharing' the *taonga*, Māori cultural treasures, with them. From a Māori perspective, this was a way to invite the hosts 'into their culture', in terms of facilitating dialogue and participation. Thus, the Māori in Mexico proudly talked about their cultural heritage, performed dances and songs, and referred to a range of their *taonga* – in their understanding, the core of Māori culture and essence of their representation as non-European. Putting these extraordinary practices on display added to the exoticism and mystification of Māori, and stressed their foreignness and distinctiveness. At the same time, they demonstrated a distinctive concept of indigeneity.

The Māori performances caused surprise and irritation amongst the Mexican students. They were rather puzzled by these acts as they were familiar with neither their meaning nor their history, nor could they situate these practices in New Zealand's cultural and political context. Simultaneously, they became aware of the cultural pride, devotion and seriousness when the Māori were performing – an attitude they could make little sense of at the beginning of their encounter. This unexpected mode of conduct made them curious and keen to know more. The Māori in turn noticed their interest with pleasure, as is pertinently described by Emere, a fifteen-year-old Māori student:

Yeah, well, that's the thing. Not only did we go over to Mexico to learn Spanish and learn about them, we also went over there to offer them *our culture* and show them how we are, because some of them don't even know where New Zealand is … at the bottom of the earth [...] Well, they were really scared when we did the *haka* and stuff, and that's something that they tried to learn. They loved the *haka*, the boy's did. And we taught them that, and they absolutely loved it, they couldn't stop doing it, and we taught them some of our old Māori games and yeah they loved it. It was a new experience for them, so we were happy to offer it to them. But yeah, they loved it.

The Māori students had hoped that the Mexican students would act in a similar way, and thus introduce them to their cultural treasures. But the Mexican students did not respond to this invitation to 'exchange' culture and to celebrate each others' culture instantly – or at least not in the way the Māori students had expected. Instead, the Mexicans reacted both with irritation and admiration to the Māori's expressive performances and skills. The Mexican students' perplexity in turn had an interesting effect on the Māori, which points to the interactive construction of cultural identities. In the light of the Mexican students' response, the Māori students experienced their culture as even 'stronger', as they felt that the Mexicans are lacking similar practices which are defined as 'culture' from a Māori perspective. Hanaha explained that the Mexicans might have 'lost' their culture due to colonization, globalization and Americanization, whereas the Māori were able to resist these hegemonic forces. His interpretation is based on the political connotation of Māori culture in New Zealand, which challenges Pākehā dominance and efforts to assimilate Māori (Van Meijl 2006: 918). Hanaha expressed how proud he was to perform his culture in Mexico:

Because seeing how lucky we are compared to another culture, I'm proud that we still maintain traditions and the language, and it was different putting out the Māori tradition in another country. Yeah – that was awesome seeing their reactions – and seeing how they reacted to us doing our cultural performances. [...] I feel lucky that we still have a strong cultural background. Because I noticed that they were impressed by our cultural performances … Māori is still maintained and it is strong in between us … we maintained a high level of culture.

This aspect is strongly remembered by most of the Māori students, and considered a key experience of their stay in Mexico. In the retrospective interviews, many students felt that their encounter with the Mexican students strengthened their identification as Māori because of the Mexicans' response to their performative acts. The Mexican students turned into the Māori's admiring audience. This reinforced and solidified ideas about the power and significance of performance, or 'culture', in their understanding. It made them more self-confident, 'stronger' and prouder of their cultural heritage, as articulated by sixteen-year-old Hanaha: 'Yeah, yeah, I'm more eager to kind of promote or to kind of put the Māori identity out there. I'm not shy to share that, I'm not shy to tell people that I'm Māori, and because showing, because seeing the reaction of another culture to our culture, it's made me feel better about the Māori culture'.

This reaction had an immense impact on the Mexican students as well. The Māori's cultural pride challenged the Mexican hosts to balance this attitude, and to respond accordingly. They started to promote their own culture and to put 'Mexicanness' on display. At the beginning, however, this was not an easy task. Elena remembered this vividly: 'First, we did not really know what to do, because our dances are very different, not so popular and less expressive. So we thought, 'hmmm, what could we do?' [...] I also thought that we will lose these [dances, songs] unless we conserve our [indigenous] groups in Latin America – and I thought this would be wonderful'.

The Mexican hosts' counter-strategy consisted in exploring the rich history and famous tourist attractions of both their immediate surroundings and wider Mexico. They organized excursions, family members volunteered to deliver explanations regarding pre-Columbian architecture and cultures, the traditional crafts in indigenous villages and the colonial art on display in churches and museums. Thus, the students turned into travellers, tourists and tourist guides alike. Many Mexican families became gradually skilled in their own culture during the Māori visit as they gained a deeper knowledge of Mexico's cultural history. Simultaneously, they took pride in displaying the various facets of 'their Mexican culture' to their guests. By doing so, they applied a similar mode of cultural representation as the Māori, that is, is constructing a historical trajectory from pre-colonial times to the present, with an emphasis on the past. This in turn strengthened the Māori's impression that Mexican culture is synonymous with ancient monuments and traditions that do not or hardly exist anymore. This view was also supported by the fact that some of the Mexican students were named after famous pre-Columbian Zapotec rulers because their parents took great pride in Mexico's past. This, however, does not necessarily mean that the current indigenous population is equally valued and respected.

As a result of their interaction, the Mexican hosts reshaped their identification with and definition of 'Mexican culture'. For some Mexican families, this was the first time that they reflected intensively on what 'Mexican culture' precisely entails and they tried to define Mexicanness in contrast to other national cultures. They also altered their perception of places as they acquired new meanings for them in the course of their travel experiences. The Mexican hosts turned into tourists themselves, and revived their cultural heritage through excursions, putting it on display to their guests. In this process, places were constructed intersubjectively (Jaworski and Pritchard 2005a: 9), and they gained a new significance and sense. They were reloaded with meaning and provided a stage for identification. Distinctions between people and places blurred as both became rather interconnected and related to each other.

This experience added to the students' novel interest in and respect towards their own Mexican heritage. Some students reflected on their changing identification with 'Mexicanness', and on the processes of place-making that evolved in the course of their encounter with an 'other', through which they learned a stronger appreciation of their own cultural background. Intriguingly, they also included aspects that they defined as 'indigenous' in their reflections. Elena stated that while she was rather bored by, or even ridiculed, traditional music or dances before the Māori visit, she would now perceive these performances in a different light. She summarized this as follows:

> I think that I learned a lot about my own culture when the Māori came to visit. We were visiting all those historic sites and explored the villages, and we went through our whole history. We kind of had forgotten to go there, because it is just around the corner. And for us this is not so important. But they [the Māori], they knew a lot of their culture, and when they asked us something we answered: 'Well, I don't know', or we would know some basic things, but I felt we did not know as much as they did. [...] They [the Māori] could explain all details and various forms of their dances. Their culture is very important to them, also on a personal level. But here, when people talk to us about the Zapotec, one would say: 'Well, this is very far away from me', or some would even ridicule this. But the Māori take it very serious. [...] Their visit made me understand that I have to respect my culture – not just to respect, to be proud of my culture. They were very proud to be Māori. What impressed me most were their dances, because they kind of transform when performing. And here, we watch the dances and that's it, but they transform themselves. It is like they live in their dances.

The Mexican students' parents regarded their children's novel awareness of 'culture' favourably, and appreciated their curiosity toward Mexico's history and the pre-Columbian past.[11] They helped organize excursions to pre-colonial sites and indigenous villages. But there were also critical voices regarding the influence of the Māori on their children. Some parents struggled with the fact that Māori were dark-skinned and indigenous, because these attributes do not fit with their ideas about socially appropriate identities for inclusion in the town's future elite. While there was never any blunt racism, this is still an ambivalent issue in the context of wider Mexican society. Others, for instance, expressed concern that their children might be impressed by and try to emulate Māori tattoos. Even though they understood that tattooing is a widespread and highly symbolic practice in the Pacific, they rejected this idea as tattoos are not seen as appropriate for Mexican middle-class offspring. For them, tattooing is seen as a social stigma and a marker of being outside mainstream society, practised by criminals, prisoners or individuals involved in gang-related activities. In some host families, there were also divergent views regarding the question of which language should be favoured, as they wanted their children to practise English while the Māori's interest was in improving their Spanish. In their daily interactions, however, most students applied a mix of languages and alternated between Spanish and English.

Other differences became apparent in the daily routine. Some of the Mexican middle-class households placed an emphasis on an appropriate dress code, such as ironed shirts, long trousers and clean shoes. Dress code and a spotless appearance are signs of respect and point to class and 'culture', in particular when visiting family members or attending formal events. In New Zealand, however, casual dress, including sandals, is common and accepted. In the school, the students took off their shoes before entering the classroom, which is in accord with Māori protocol, but rather strange in Mexico, where bare feet are a sign of poverty. In addition to dress code, personal hygiene is also an important feature, and many Mexicans shower at least once a day. Both personal hygiene and class affiliation are displayed in a trim appearance and by use of make-up. This attitude was noticed by the Māori students, but sometimes perceived as vain or even arrogant behaviour. Kaewa, a fourteen-year-old Māori girl, observed:

> The way they [the Mexican girls] dress, and especially their image, their image is such a big thing over there, the students were walking around with mirrors on their necks and, you know, they'd always, always wear make-up. [...] They're really, really pretty, aye? They like to keep themselves looking good all the time. Like we'll be in class and there will be all the girls in the back row, and they'll pull out their make-up and their mirrors and stuff.

In considering each others' appearance and conduct, each party applied their own understanding of 'culture' to the other, which stemmed from their own society and experiences. As a consequence, they tentatively concluded, therefore, that the other 'has no culture' or lacked a specific set of cultural practices which were perceived as crucial cultural expressions. The perception of cultural differences reinforced the respective understanding and righteousness of the groups' own cultural concepts, and they assessed the other accordingly. Thus, cultural differences were constructed by applying one's own concepts to a distinct cultural context, with the result that each side concluded, tentatively, that the other had a 'loss' or 'lack of culture'. This corresponds with dominant discourses and categories in their respective societies: stereotyped perceptions of indigenous cultures in Mexico, and Māori views of Pākehā in New Zealand.

It is important to note, however, that besides these perceived differences both groups also identified commonalities, in particular with regard to family life and reciprocity between relatives. The discoveries of similar features helped to bridge differences between the two groups, and were seen as something particularly valuable and meaningful. Kauri expressed this as follows:

> Yeah, I found that they were quite similar because, just how they all live in big families, and they're real generous to one another and help each other out. It sort of reminds me of how we are in New Zealand, with our big families, look[ing] after one another, stuff like that. It just made me realize again how important that is.

Furthermore, this encounter impacted not just on individual identity constructions, but also on a sense of community and group identity amongst Māori and Mexicans. The fact that all Mexican students had a Māori visitor staying with them created a sense of commonality and fostered common activities. The Mexican families met more frequently, shared their respective experiences regarding their foreign guests and organized trips together. These activities crossed ideological divisions which were otherwise more accentuated, in particular amongst the adults. The Mexican students reported a similar experience. They felt like 'Mexicans' and a Mexican community on display to their Māori guests, which created a bond between them. A similar tendency developed amongst the Māori students. This cross-cultural encounter also brought about an integrative effect regarding the latter community. Kaewa expressed this as follows:

> The other amazing thing was that we learnt a lot about each other, it wasn't just about them and teaching them our culture, it was also ... – well, a lot of us were quite amazed at how close we became with the younger students who came with us. Because, you know, at school you might say 'hello', and we were always sort of like family, but over there [Mexico] we became a real family because it was just amazing, you know, to get to know one another. I mean, they became my best friends over there and they were third formers, and we still keep in touch now. And, yeah, it was just amazing to learn about one another over in another country, and we developed a real bond between us.

It is interesting to note that all students became more sensitive to place in the course of this encounter. Just as most of the Māori students explored Mexico through the lens of their host family and their peers, New Zealand was represented via the Māori students. The perception of place was mediated through the narratives of the Māori students so that New Zealand was personalized – that is, the imaginary of the country became inextricably associated with the personal experience with the particular Māori who lived in the Mexican's household. Thus, New Zealand turned from an unknown country into an emotionally loaded place, full of memories and imaginaries, which were also reinforced when the Māori students gave souvenirs. This created a sense of familiarity with an unknown and foreign place, as is expressed in this quote from Patricia, a Mexican host-mother:

> When I think of New Zealand, I always think of the Māori student who stayed with us. I feel like New Zealand came to my house, and that we had the opportunity to get to know something of New Zealand through the Māori student. […] It was like New Zealand was a hidden place, nobody knew about it, and now suddenly it is so familiar, even [though] I have not been there yet.

While the Mexicans' perception of New Zealand was mainly shaped by representation, the Māori students' perception of Mexico was based on concrete experience and direct comparisons of the two countries. They noticed the dryness of the land, and in turn the greenness of New Zealand, as something special. They were also surprised by the level of poverty in Mexico, which is apparent in public spaces. By comparing New Zealand and Mexico, they re-evaluated the richness of their country and developed a new appreciation for New Zealand. Kaewa stated:

> Yeah, and that's another great thing that I've learnt is, you never know, what is it, you know, like, how lucky you are until you leave home. You know the small things, like water over there is scarce, whereas over here we take it for granted. Just little things, power and stuff like that, whereas some people over there, they have nothing at all and … It's funny that you have to leave home to find that out.

Besides gaining a new perception of New Zealand, the students also took pride in the accomplishments of their voyage, which was in many ways a challenge for them as most of them were relatively inexperienced at travelling. They all considered their trip a successful endeavour and, when coming back to New Zealand, this experience became an asset that most of their peers did not have. This had an impact on their self-confidence and made them curious to explore more. Kauri expressed this pertinently:

> Yeah, I did, I did change a lot. The way I see life, it was sort of closed before I went. But when, after I got back, I knew I had a whole life to make the most out of. Yeah, like I could go around the world if I wanted to. [...] The world had opened to me now because I've been to LA, to Disneyland, to Mexico, wherever else, and I've seen a lot of things, different things which I've learnt from, and if I made a mistake I think I won't make those mistakes again.

The end of their stay was marked by a particular experience which all participants recalled vividly, described as the most striking and unforgettable event in their encounter. The Mexican school organized a 'cultural evening', and the students put their cultures on display to each other. The school provided music and dances, a large buffet with Mexican delicacies, and the Māori performed in their traditional costumes. This cross-cultural theatricality blurred differences which they had experienced in their daily routine, and transcended clear demarcations. It created a sense of community and commonality between them. By staging culture, they indulged in the vice-versa celebration of each other's ancient glories, referring to an imagined pre-contact, pre-European 'authentic' and aestheticized culture. By performing for each other, the two groups not only shared their dominant modes of representation in terms of performance and appearance, but they also emulated each other, and even to some extent converged in the cultural evening's theatricality, which was strongly emotionally charged. By staging themselves for the other, they mirrored themselves in the other in however distorted a manner. This emotionally loaded experience of 'sharing' culture, and in some ways merging with the other, was commented on by Mahuta, one of the Māori teachers, with pride: 'our kids have not been exposed to that until the final night when we had the final concert, which was when they actually got a chance to see it in action, their culture'.

## Conclusion

In pluricultural contexts, identity is formed primarily by comparing and contrasting oneself with the 'other'. This process is particularly prominent in cross-cultural face-to-face situations. An awareness of difference and sameness is crucial in these encounters, and it contributes to a nuanced perception of one's own uniqueness and originality (Woodward 1997; Cohen 2000). However, this is not a unilinear and predictable process but rather ambiguous, as it intersects with a range of different and constantly changing positions, practices, discourses and interests. These dynamics are shaped by negotiations of understandings and evaluations on both sides of the encounter. Thus, as members of diverse groups interact, their identities are remodelled and transformed through interaction, exchange and dialogue.

This research shows that cultures get remade as a result of movement, travel and border crossing as they cannot be closed off from each other but exist rather in relation to each other. Borders and edges gain centrality, and lines of cultural demarcation evolve and are redrawn in this kind of encounter. However, all cultural articulations are relational and incomplete; that is, they are situated in and entangled with a wider context and evolve constantly. Culture and identity are formed in a never-ending process of encounters and translations, thus constantly changing contours and margins.

Travel and contact are crucial for cross-cultural engagement. Travel as a mode of cultural deterritorialization and spatial practice does not only affect those who are on the move, but has an impact upon the culture of the hosts alike. These changing processes of identification became apparent in the course of the trip. The journey to Mexico entailed a reflection on the value of Māori culture for the identity of the Māori students, and it had implications for Māori cultural conceptions. It encompassed recognition of differences, similarities and uniqueness in terms of cultural identity. This encounter also had a strong impact on the Mexican students, who re-evaluated their cultural heritage. They developed new representational strategies and created a specific notion of Mexicanness in the course of this encounter. By travelling and changing places with their guests, they saw, at least partially, their country through the eyes of the other. In this process, these places were turned into important localities for identification, and constituted interfaces of relationships and interactions (Massey 1994: 154–56). However, travel does not only affect those who physically move around but may also encompass those who are living in their places of origin. In this vein, the Mexican hosts travelled to New Zealand in an imaginary way, and New Zealand was brought to them by their guests. Through the narratives of their Māori guests, they felt a sort of familiarity with a place and developed a meaningful relationship with a locality they had never been to in person. This shows once more that places and persons cannot be separated but rather depend on each other. It also shows the proliferation and interconnectedness of places, encompassing multilayered processes of identification, emotionality and meaning.

This cross-cultural encounter is intriguing in other ways, and it reveals the simultaneity of seemingly contradictory results. While this experience built tolerance and openness toward otherness, individuals' own perspectives were reinforced and strengthened. Thus, concrete experiences with a culture different from one's own do not necessarily decentre one's own perspective, but may rather strengthen particular aspects of self and of the perceived other. At the same time, such experiences also entail learning opportunities on both sides, in terms of accepting otherness and accumulating cultural knowledge. This cross-cultural encounter stimulated a process in which a self-reflexive cultural awareness developed, a process which transformed and reproduced cultural identification.

## Acknowledgements

The author gratefully acknowledges financial support for this research from the Auckland University of Technology, New Zealand. I also wish to thank all the participants for sharing their experiences with me, and I am particularly grateful to the principals of the schools involved for their engagement and support. Their hospitality and friendliness shaped the relationships in this research process and facilitated this project. I also wish to thank my Māori colleagues at the Auckland University of Technology for their advice, in particular regarding Māori research protocol. Their support was crucial to this research. I conducted the interviews in New Zealand in English, and in Mexico in Spanish. All quotes from Mexican participants have been translated into English by the author, and all the names used have been altered to ensure confidentiality.

## Notes

1. This chapter is based upon an earlier work published in German entitled 'Kulturbegegnung und Identitätsbildung. Ethnologische Perspektiven auf transkulturelle Prozesse', in A. Moosmüller (ed.), *Konzepte kultureller Differenz. Interkulturelle Perspektiven.* München: Waxmann, pp.179–94.
2. In this chapter I focus on secondary-school students even though some younger students took part in this encounter. Only a few of the students were younger than twelve years, and these were the children of the accompanying teachers.
3. On their way to Mexico, the group spent some days in California and visited Los Angeles and Disneyland. Intriguingly, in the USA some of the Māori were thought to be Mexicans because of their skin colour.
4. Clifford (1999: 52–91) outlines these practices with regard to ethnographic fieldwork, and draws intriguing parallels between travel and ethnography.
5. In 1840, representatives of the British government and around 520 Māori *rangatira* (chiefs) signed a treaty at Waitangi, which addressed important issues concerning such matters as Māori sovereignty, access to land and legal rights. This treaty is seen as the founding document of New Zealand (see Durie 1998; Brookfield 2006).
6. *Nga mahi a nga tipuna/taonga tuku iho* is literally translated by Bishop and Glynn as the 'works of the ancestors, or those treasures handed down from the ancestors' (Bishop and Glynn 1999: 171–72).

7. It is also interesting to note that anthropological research on and representation of Māori today shape understandings of Māoridom. For a detailed discussion on these processes and emerging class conflicts among Māori themselves, see Webster (1998) and Openshaw (2006).
8. *Mana* is a complex cultural concept, which is often translated as status, prestige, authority or influence. The concrete meaning of the term needs to be explored in the context of its use. For a discussion regarding the various types of *mana*, see Metge (1995) and Mutu and McCully (2003).
9. *Kura* refers to education and teaching and in this case is meant to signal a Māori immersion programme.
10. However, some exceptions need to be mentioned. Some of the Māori students had already been to Mexico when they were travelling with their parents – but these were few in number.
11. It is interesting to contrast the Mexican parents' evaluation of this encounter with that of Māori parents. Unlike the Mexican families, they did not personally participate in their children's experience, but kept in touch by telephone and e-mail. Overall, they were rather positive about this event, and showed pride in the fact that their children had travelled so far and improved their language skills. Some, however, were critical, and felt that their children had changed during the stay and developed a more distant and independent relationship with them.

## References

Balme, C.B. 2007. *Pacific Performances: Theatricality and Cross-cultural Encounter in the South Seas*. Basingstoke: Palgrave Macmillan.

Barth, F. (ed.). 1969. *Ethnic Groups and Boundaries: The Social Organization of Culture Difference*. Bergen: Universitetsforlaget.

Bishop, R. 2008. 'Te Kotahitanga: Kaupapa Māori in Mainstream Classrooms', in N.K. Denzin, Y.S. Lincoln and L.T. Smith (eds), *Handbook of Critical and Indigenous Methodologies*. Los Angeles: Sage, pp.439–58.

Bishop, R., and T. Glynn. 1999. 'Researching in Māori Contexts: An Interpretation of Participatory Consciousness', *Journal of Intercultural Studies* 20(2): 167–82.

Bishop, R., and T. Glynn. 2003 [1999]. *Culture Counts: Changing Power Relations in Education*. Palmerston North: Dunmore Press.

Brookfield, F.M. 2006. *Waitangi and Indigenous Rights: Revolution, Law and Legitimation*. Auckland: Auckland University Press.

Bruner, E.M. (ed.). 2005. *Culture on Tour: Ethnographies of Travel*. Chicago: University of Chicago Press.

Clifford, J. 1999 [1997]. *Routes: Travel and Translation in the Twentieth Century*. Cambridge, MA: Harvard University Press.

——— 2001. 'Indigenous Articulations', *Contemporary Pacific* 13(2): 468–90.

Cohen, A.P. (ed.). 2000. *Signifying Identities: Anthropological Perspectives on Boundaries and Contested Values*. New York: Routledge.

Durie, M.H. 1998. *Te mana, te kawanatanga: The Politics of Māori Self-determination*. Auckland: Oxford University Press.

Fleras, A., and J.L. Elliot (eds). 1992. *The 'Nations Within': Aboriginal-State Relations in Canada, the United States, and New Zealand*. Toronto: Oxford University Press.

Fuchs, M. 2002. 'The Praxis of Cognition and the Representation of Difference', in H. Friese (ed.), *Identities: Time, Difference, and Boundaries*. New York: Berghahn, pp.109–32.

———— 2004. 'Das Ende der Modelle: Interkulturalität statt (Kultur-)Vergleich', in S. Randeria, M. Fuchs and A. Linkenbach (eds), *Konfigurationen der Moderne: Diskurse zu Indien*. Baden-Baden: Nomos, pp.439–70.

Hall, S. (ed.). 1996. *Questions of Cultural Identity*. London: Sage.

Hallam, E., and B.V. Street. 2000. 'Cultural Encounters: Representing "Otherness"', in E. Hallam and B.V. Street (eds), *Cultural Encounters: Representing 'Otherness'*. London: Routledge, pp.1–10.

Harrison, S. 2006. *Fracturing Resemblances: Identity and Mimetic Conflict in Melanesia and the West*. New York: Berghahn.

Hastrup, K. 1995. *A Passage to Anthropology: Between Experience and Theory*. London: Routledge.

Inda, J.X., and R. Rosaldo. 2008 [2002]. 'Tracking Global Flows: The Anthropology of Globalization', in J.X. Inda and R. Rosaldo (eds), *The Anthropology of Globalization: A Reader*. Oxford: Blackwell, pp.3–46.

Jaworski, A., and A. Pritchard. 2005a. 'Discourse, Communication and Tourism Dialogues', in A. Jaworski and A. Pritchard (eds), *Discourse, Communication and Tourism*. Clevedon: Channel View Publications, pp.1–16.

———— (eds). 2005b. *Discourse, Communication and Tourism*. Clevedon: Channel View Publications.

King, J. 2001. 'Te Kohanga Reo: Maori Language Revitalization', in L. Hinton and K. Hale (eds), *The Green Book of Language Revitalization in Practice*. San Diego: Academic Press, pp.119–128.

Kirby, P.W. 2009. 'Lost in "Space": An Anthropological Approach to Movement', in P.W. Kirby (ed.), *Boundless Worlds: An Anthropological Approach to Movement*. Oxford: Berghahn, pp.1–27.

Maaka, R., and A. Fleras (eds). 2005. *The Politics of Indigeneity: Challenging the State in Canada and Aotearoa New Zealand*. Otago: University of Otago Press.

Maranhão, T., and B. Streck. 2003. *Translation and Ethnography. The Anthropological Challenge of Intercultural Understanding*. Tucson: University of Arizona Press.

Massey, D. (ed.). 1994. *Space, Place and Gender*. Cambridge: Polity Press.

Metge, J. 1995. *New Growth from Old: The Whanau in the Modern World*. Wellington: Victoria University Press.

Meyer, B., and P. Geschiere (eds). 2003 [1999]. *Globalization and Identity: Dialectics of Flow and Closure*. Oxford: Blackwell.

Mutu, M., and M. McCully. 2003. *Te Whānau Moana – Ngā kaupapa me ngā tikanga – Customs and Protocols*. Auckland: Reed Publishing.

Openshaw, R. 2006. 'Putting Ethnicity into Policy: A New Zealand Case Study', in E. Rata and R. Openshaw (eds), *Public Policy and Ethnicity: The Politics of Ethnic Boundary Making*. Houndsmill: Palgrave Macmillan, pp.113–27.

Rata, E. 1996. 'Goodness and Power: The Sociology of Liberal Guilt', *New Zealand Sociology* 11(2): 223–74.

―――― 2006. 'The Political Strategies of Ethnic and Indigenous Elites: Public Policy and Ethnicity', in E. Rata and R. Openshaw (eds), *The Politics of Ethnic Boundary Making*. Houndmills: Palgrave Macmillan, pp.40–53.

Reina, L. 2002. 'Reindianizacion: Paradoja del Liberalismo', *Mexico Indígena* 1(2): 49–57.

Rojek, C., and J. Urry. 1997a. 'Transformations of Travel and Theory', in C. Rojek and J. Urry (eds), *Touring Cultures: Transformations of Travel and Theory*. London: Routledge, pp.1–19.

―――― (eds). 1997b. *Touring Cultures: Transformations of Travel and Theory*. London: Routledge.

Schieffelin, E.L., et al. 1991. *Like People You See in a Dream: First Contact in Six Papuan Societies*. Stanford: Stanford University Press.

Schwartz, S.B. 1994. *Implicit Understandings: Observing, Reporting, and Reflecting on the Encounters between Europeans and Other Peoples in the Early Modern Era*. Cambridge: Cambridge University Press.

Sharp, A. 1997 [1990]. *Justice and the Māori: The Philosophy and Practice of Māori Claims in New Zealand since the 1970s*, 2nd edn. Auckland: Oxford University Press.

Sheller, M., and J. Urry. 2006. 'The New Mobilities Paradigm', *Environment and Planning A* 28(2): 207–26.

Sieder, R. (ed.). 2002. *Multiculturalism in Latin America: Indigenous Rights, Diversity and Democracy*. London: Palgrave Macmillan.

Van Meijl, T. 2006. 'Multiple Identifications and the Dialogical Self: Urban Māori Youngsters and the Cultural Renaissance', *Journal of the Royal Anthropological Institute* 12(4): 917–33.

Walker, R. 2004 [1990]. *Ka whawhai tonu matou: Struggle without End*. Auckland: Penguin.

Webster, S. 1998. *Patrons of Maori Culture: Power, Theory and Ideology in the Māori Renaissance*. Dunedin: University of Otago Press.

Welsch, W. 1999. 'Transculturality: The Puzzling Form of Cultures Today', in M. Featherstone and S. Lash (eds), *Spaces of Culture: City, Nation, World*. London: Sage, pp.194–213.

Werbner, P. 1997. 'The Dialectics of Cultural Hybridity', in P. Werbner and T. Modood (eds), *Debating Cultural Hybridity: Multi-cultural Identities and the Politics of Anti-racism*. London: Zed Books, pp.1–26.

Werbner, P., and T. Modood (eds). 1997. *Debating Cultural Hybridity: Multi-cultural Identites and the Politics of Anti-racism*. London: Zed Books.

Woodward, K. (ed.). 1997. *Identity and Difference*. London: Sage.

## 2

# 'Forty-plus Different Tribes'

Displacement, Place-making and Aboriginal Tribal
Names on Palm Island, Australia

◆●◆

### Lise Garond

Palm Island residents commonly define themselves as Aboriginal and/ or sometimes Torres Strait Islanders, Murris,[1] or 'Blackfellows', as well as 'Palm Islanders'. Many of the islanders also present themselves as belonging to one or several tribes and regions, from which they, or from which their forebears, were removed during the colonial period, when Palm Island was a government reserve. Today, with over three thousand residents, Palm Island, a small island in north-east Queensland, is also one of the largest 'Aboriginal communities' in Australia.[2] Until the late 1970s and early 1980s, most of these localities were known as 'Aboriginal reserves', or 'missions': places where Aboriginal people lived under the supervision of the state and/or various churches.

In 1918 the Queensland government established a new Aboriginal reserve on Palm Island. The new reserve was meant to receive Aboriginal people from various regions in Queensland, a growing number of which were being removed to government reserves and Christian missions, under the authority of the state's 'protective' legislation (namely, the Queensland Aborigines Protection and Restriction of the Sale of Opium Act 1897). From the passing of this legislation at the end of the nineteenth century until the early 1970s, when the removal policies were repealed, several thousand Aboriginal people (and to a lesser extent Torres Strait Islanders) were removed to the Queensland reserves and missions, Palm Island being the reserve which received the most arrivals from the largest number of locations.[3] In the 1970s, changes in government policies allowed people to leave the reserves and freely circulate throughout the state. Some families left Palm Island, but the majority of people remained on the island, which had become, for several generations, 'home'.

While often very vividly expressing their sense of attachment to the island, places of origin – actually known or imagined – seem to remain important to many of the islanders. They often mention several such places or regions of origin as significant to them individually or as members of particular families. As we shall see, the resulting multiple identifications often involved not only relate to histories of origin and displacement to the island,[4] but also to a particular history of place-making on the island itself. One of the ways in which this is made apparent is when islanders describe Palm Island – the place and the community – past and present, as 'made of' the many 'tribes' which were sent to the island (forty, or 'forty plus', is the number often mentioned). Palm Islanders' notion of what is 'tribal', the importance they seem to place on being able to claim one's belonging to a tribe, and indeed on knowing where one or where one's ancestors 'come from', also reveal some of the struggles which the islanders face as Aboriginal subjects. They have been and are subjected to particular discourses which categorize/recognize them as Aboriginal, in diverse ways. By being sent to the Palm Island reserve, for instance, one was also recategorized as a 'problematic' or 'troublesome' Aboriginal subject. Today, Palm Island and Palm Islanders are most often represented in the mainstream media as epitomizing all sorts of 'problems', stereotypically presented as endemic in 'Aboriginal communities', and Palm Island is often portrayed as a place where Aboriginal people have 'lost their culture'. By claiming their belonging to particular tribes, Palm Islanders perhaps 'respond' to such negative stereotypes, while also manifesting a desire to 'belong' to popularly recognized models of Aboriginality, construed as bearing signs of 'traditional culture', models which have come to be fashioned, importantly, in relation to the policies of recognition by the state of indigeneity and indigenous land ownership. But what appears to be a late emphasis by Palm Islanders on affirming their belonging to particular tribes is not reducible to a simple form of a 'mimetic' process of identification. A more complex process is at stake here, one which needs to be considered in relation to Palm Islanders' history of displacement and to place-making on the island. In this chapter, I thus want to pay attention to what Palm Islanders' identifications in terms of tribes and tribal names may tell us about their particular, and often ambivalent, senses of place and belonging (and not belonging) as Aboriginal subjects.

## Place-making in the Palm Island Reserve

Palm Islanders' histories and experiences of displacement, and of place-making on the island, in the former reserve and the present community, are not unique among indigenous Queenslanders, or more broadly among Aboriginal Australians, although the anthropological literature has tended to focus on 'traditional' ways of relating to place in remote areas,[5] and/or in contexts where Aboriginal people had historically rarely experienced large-scale displacements or confinement to a single place.[6] This relative lack of interest has perhaps tended to obscure the fact that there are particular and often ambivalent senses of place and belonging that these historical circumstances have contributed to shape, rather than simply change or erase, among Aboriginal people.

By removing Aboriginal people from their places of belonging, the colonial administrators in charge of the protection policies had several ambitions in mind, including that of 'erasing' the memory of familiar places of belonging and being in order to instil into them new forms of, and reformed, 'habituses' (see Henry 2012).[7] However, permanent displacement from familiar places, and from the familiar senses of self in relation to others that this familiarity with place nurtures, does not only result in the loss of one's day-to-day 'relational' sense of place (Ingold 2000). Displacement, as an experience, can be considered as a particular sense of place; that is, for instance, the sense of missing familiar places, remembering and imagining them, as well as the sense of finding oneself in unfamiliar places, can be viewed as particular 'senses of place' (Feld and Basso 1996). Indeed, as Barbara Bender notes, 'dislocation is also relocation. People are always in some relationship with the landscape they move through' (Bender 2001: 8; see also Bender and Winer 2001). In this sense, displacement not only disrupts but also engenders senses of place, leading to new forms of place-making.

In the first section of this chapter, I will attempt to describe some of the conditions of place-making in the reserve for those who were removed there and had to make their 'place' in this peculiar location. The notion of 'place' can be differentiated from that of 'space' by the process through which a mere spatial location becomes a place as it is invested with lived experiences of being in place, memories and meaning (see Casey 1993; Henry 2012). Place-making is also a process through which social identifications and differentiations are produced, reproduced and contested, that is, a process through which the meaning of place as, for instance, one's site of belonging or exclusion, at the same time as the corresponding social identities and boundaries, are made (Henry 2012; see also Keith and Pile 1993; Massey 1994). Judith Butler (1997) uses the expression 'place-holder' and 'site' (the site of a discourse) to designate the 'subject', somehow figuratively: in some cases, however, discourses literally conflate with 'placing' individuals in spatial locations. The case of prisons, studied by Michel Foucault (1977), is an example, as are the 'Aboriginal reserves'. Indeed, to be removed to the Palm Island reserve meant that one had been and continued to be designated as an 'Aboriginal subject', in need of 'protection' and/or punishment.[8]

Similar to other mission and government reserves, the Palm Island reserve was designed on segregated patterns. The white administration's quarters were located in an enclosed area, adjacent to which stood three enclosed dormitories: these were to receive women and children, a large number of whom were removed to the reserve on the basis that they were of mixed descent.[9] This central area was 'out of bounds' to most Aboriginal residents, and placed under police surveillance. A bell which stood near the police station, as older islanders recall, 'governed' the lives of Aboriginal inmates, signalling times to go to work and to bed. Police patrols, composed of Aboriginal and Torres Strait Islander inmates, also patrolled the rest of the reserve and areas further away from the central area, where the Aboriginal 'camps' (as older Palm Islanders describe them), made of iron-sheds and grass huts, were scattered. Further away from the camps, the surrounding forests, hills and beaches remained uninhabited, and Aboriginal residents were not supposed to venture there without permission. There are many stories of escapes from the dormitories and breakaways from the reserve to these 'wild' areas, as islanders describe them. When sent to the island, Aboriginal people were not allowed to leave the reserve, except when they were able to obtain from the administration, on demonstration of 'good behaviour', a permit which allowed them to spend a night or a couple of days on the mainland, under police escort. By contrast, many tourists visited the reserve. They were received in the central area, and were entertained with Aboriginal and Torres Strait Islander dances. As one older resident put it, hence describing one of the most significant features of life in the former reserve: 'tourists came, but we never go out'. Despite the intense restrictions placed on the movements of Aboriginal people to and from, as well as within, the reserve, the inmates were regularly sent to the mainland to fulfil work arrangements between the administration and various employers in need of cheap labour, especially in the agricultural and cattle industries. Some Palm Island elders remember the time they spent on the mainland as periods of freedom away from the reserve, while others insist, on the contrary, on their bad experiences and their longing for 'home', away from their families. Although they often express much resentment about the past, older Palm Islanders also frequently share fond memories of some aspects of their life in the former reserve; their feelings about the old reserve, and indeed, their sense of attachment to the island, seem to be weaved through with much ambivalence (see Garond 2012a). A place of displacement and exile, the island is also described as a place from which one could be separated and which one longed for; this is one of the ways in which displacement, as a prominent theme in Palm Islanders' accounts of themselves and their family histories, becomes constitutive of place itself.[10]

Within the reserve, the space allocated to the Aboriginal camps was also divided, as some of the older Palm Islanders recall, into several different 'tribal camps', areas within which people from the same 'tribes' grouped together. Most older islanders remember that there were six or seven different tribal camps in the reserve. 'What happened when we came', an elder explained to me, while pointing in different directions:

> all the people in my tribe, and the Clumpoint all stayed in the Clumpoint down Dee Street, that area. And on the other side was the people from further up from Cooktown and that, you know... And here, were most people from Ingham area. And over that side, that was the Sundowners, so they were mostly in that area. But here and right up there were the Lama Lama.

While Lama Lama is the name of an Aboriginal language and a language-named tribe, Cooktown, Clumpoint or Ingham are the names of localities or small towns from which people were sent to the reserve, and at which or near which they had until then lived (when they hadn't been removed there from somewhere else). While the latter are not 'classical' Aboriginal tribal names, Palm Islanders refer to them as such. Up on one small hill was the 'Sundowners' camp': it grouped together those who had been sent from 'out West', or from different places in far-western Queensland. The 'old people' from that camp, I was told, were known to be 'crying for their country' while looking at 'the sun going down', towards the direction of their former homeland.[11]

'Everything was strange. All these strange people. When my mother found somebody that could talk her lingo it wasn't so bad' (Rosser 1985: 160). Iris Clay, in this short account, was telling her friend and Aboriginal author Bill Rosser how it felt like when she first arrived on Palm Island as a child with her parents and some of her siblings in the early 1930s. Other siblings were left behind and never seen again when the family was sent to the island from Mapoon, a Christian mission for Aboriginal people at the north-western tip of Cape York. Iris's father had been convicted of practising 'witchcraft', and so punished by the administration. As more and more people from different regions were sent to the island and had to accommodate to this 'strange place', with 'all its strange people', as Iris Clay puts it, different 'groupings' seemed to have so reformed or formed more or less anew within the reserve. Making one's own place in the reserve was, among other things, a process of boundary-making, in a Barthian sense (Barth 1969), as well as more literally in a 'spatial' sense: a process of creating and recreating identities and differences, in and through place. This process operated on an everyday basis in relation to the white people occupying distinctive areas and distinctive houses (as opposed to 'the camps'). It also operated amongst Aboriginal people, associating with and differentiating from (more or less similar/different) others in place. Islanders in fact often talk literally of 'boundaries', delimiting each camp and separating one camp from another, boundaries which are said to have been the cause of constant tensions among members of different tribes: 'if you crossed that boundary', one middle-age resident thus explained, 'they'd spear you in the leg!' Fighting, sometimes involving spears or boomerangs, is also mentioned as a distinctive 'tribal' way. Maintaining distinct 'boundaries' between the various tribes was necessary to avoid disputes, I was often told, while also allowing for the existence of a sense of 'community' within each camp. However, I was also told that the delimitation of different camps, separating different tribes from each other, had been part of an administrative strategy to 'divide and conquer' those who were under its surveillance, preventing them from organizing a collective uprising, for instance, or 'a riot', as one resident put it.

The notion of tribes as distinct social entities was indeed part of the administration's 'knowledge' of Aboriginal people, in a Foucauldian sense. Some of the bureaucrats who had specialized in 'Aboriginal affairs' in the late nineteenth century, such as Walter E. Roth, who was also one of the earliest ethnographers in Australia, had developed an extensive 'knowledge' of Aboriginal people, ranging from linguistic knowledge to that of ceremonies, kinship, marriage and racial categories (with Aboriginal people commonly classed as 'full-blood' or 'half-caste'). 'Tribes' or 'clans' were conceived as small and bounded social entities.[12] The notion of what was 'tribal' was also somehow synonymous for administrators and experts with what they saw as 'primitive' or 'savage', often with a mixture of both disdain and admiration.[13] Less detailed forms of such knowledge were commonly held by the local administrators of the reserves: in many colonial official letters and reports, it is frequent to find references to 'tribal fights' occurring (or at risk of occurring) within a reserve. The word 'tribal' was in general meant to designate practices (such as 'sorcery') that the administration, in its reformative view, aimed at progressively suppressing within the reserves, but which could be accommodated in some of their features. For instance, while the practice of ceremonies or the use of Aboriginal languages was officially forbidden, the making of 'artefacts' and the performance of 'corroborees', especially for visiting tourists, was encouraged.

It is difficult to know precisely when or how the spatial layout changed, and when the tribal camps started to disappear, but it seems that throughout the 1950s if not earlier the old grass and iron-shed houses were more systematically replaced with sturdier dwellings, this being part of the increased accent in state policies towards 'assimilation', the transformation of Aboriginal habituses into 'European' ones. The ensuing change in the spatial layout, although sometimes understood as a natural outgrowth of inter-marriage between different tribal groups, is also regularly interpreted as a direct result of the administration's will to 'split up the tribes', as an elder described it, to dismantle the scattered camps in order to create a more homogeneous – and less distinctively 'Aboriginal' – space. However, people's 'tribal origins' seem to have continued to play a significant role within the changed residential areas: it is sometimes said to have induced new tensions among residents, and sometimes, on the contrary, people insist on the solidarity existing within new spaces of sociability – all the more remarkable, and in some regards all the more enjoyable, that people 'came from' different places. As one resident, recalling her childhood on Palm Island in the 1960s, put it:

> In our area, the Lama Lama area, everyone sort of knew one another. We all sort of grew up together, and everyone had an open house for people. We used to go to this house, and they would give you a feed, to that house, and they would give you a feed. [...] Some people from Aurukun was there, Kowanyama I should say, and some people from the Torres Strait, so it was ... everyone knew each other, you know?

Somehow, stories about the 'tribal camps' are foundation stories about Palm Island and about the present Aboriginal community. They are histories about place-making, and more precisely about Aboriginal place-making, within and in spite of the reserve. In this narrative, the role of the state appears somehow uncertain. There are different and contradictory hypotheses about the involvement of the administrators in the setting up and demise of the tribal camps. This is perhaps illustrative of a more fundamental questioning among Palm Islanders about of what Trouillot calls 'state effects' (Trouillot 2001). There is a questioning about the degree to which the state, or the experience of living in a reserve and being subjected to the authority of a white administration, has weighed not only on their lives but on the manner in which they experience and represent themselves as Aboriginal people. Nevertheless, Palm Islanders seem to conceive of the notion of tribe as a social, specifically 'Aboriginal', category, one not invested with its colonial connotations, and relatively autonomous from the state. It could be argued that Palm Islanders' conceptualizations of tribal camps as bounded by place, of tribal identities and of what 'tribal' means generally in fact demonstrate how state effects operate. In this case, for instance, it could be argued that it is the very colonial differentiation between what is 'tribal' and what is 'civilized', including in the spatial layout of the reserve and the differentiation of Aboriginal from 'white' spaces of living and types of habitation, which was partly productive of Palm Islanders' conceptions of what is (or is no longer) 'tribal'. But rather than the mere imposition of colonial categories, I would suggest that it is the overall experience of place-making in the reserve which is partly productive of Palm Islanders' perceptions of what is tribal. In addition, Palm Islanders' insistence on this notion today, and the value they attach to it, also stems from their experience of the late recognition, notably by the state, of indigenous identities.

## Tribal Identifications and Desires of Belonging in the Era of Recognition

Palm Islanders of various ages often express a sense of loss, a sense of having been alienated from their 'traditional' Aboriginal culture. This is sometimes expressed with more or less resentment or sadness, as in 'we have been assimilated', 'we have lost our culture' or 'we're not really tribal anymore'.[14] This sense of alienation is not only a consequence of historical experiences of displacement and of living in a government reserve, but also exists in relation to ongoing discourses about the recognition of indigenous identities in terms of recognizable signs of 'authentic difference' (Povinelli 2002: 45). To Palm Islanders, identifying in terms of tribal names, and in reference to a corresponding 'territory', is a sign of 'traditional' Aboriginal culture. This practice has, however, been described by anthropologists as a rather recent phenomenon, notably an effect of the 'native title era' (Fingleton and Finlayson 1995), an era during which new possibilities emerged for indigenous people to claim land ownership on the basis of (and proof of) enduring relationships with the land claimed. These new and regulated possibilities seem to have played a part in a growing tendency amongst many Aboriginal people to rearticulate land-based identifications using broader collective identities or 'tribes' (see Glowczewski 1998; Merlan 1998; Smith 2000, 2006; Bauman 2006).

In the case of those who have been, or whose forebears have been, displaced under colonial legislation, identification with a tribal name and genealogy often becomes the principal means by which claims to land can be effectively made. This may differ greatly from the manner in which those who have not experienced displacement (or at least not to such an extent) formulate their attachment to the land. And while the latter are able to do so on the basis of enduring practice and precise knowledge of the places at stake, they may also contest the validity of the claims made by formerly displaced or 'diaspora' people,[15] which tend to be formulated in a more reified way or on the sole basis of genealogy (Smith 2000, 2006). As Smith mentions, this questioning or rejection by 'local' Aboriginal people of the validity of 'diaspora' people's participation in land claims can be resented by the latter as a form of 'double denial' (Smith 2006: 230): while they were first displaced by the state from their land, their claims can also now be questioned or rejected by other Aboriginal people, if not by the state. Nevertheless, since the early 1990s, the possibilities of recognition have triggered, and persistently trigger, a desire to be part of Aboriginal land claims among many Palm Islanders.

I take as an example that of Lorna, a woman in her eighties who was born and grew up south of Cairns, in the Tablelands, before being sent as a young teenager along with members of her family to Palm Island.[16] She vividly remembered the Tablelands, and despite her removal she had managed to remain in contact with some of her relatives still living there over the years. She had also been able to return to this place while she was still an inmate of the reserve during work placements. In the 1970s, she started to return to the Tablelands more frequently, and during the 1990s she had been included in a native title claim for the area, and had been able to participate regularly in native title meetings, which had given her more occasions to travel there over the years. In her words: 'Whenever I can get a trip back up on the Tablelands, I'll take it, because it's all up there [...] All I think about is going home, I really want to take my grandchildren, take them to show the country, show them this is where I was born, where your grandfathers, where your uncles were born'. The possible recognition of her belonging to this area had triggered an increased desire to 'go back' to this place, one which had remained always significant to her but which now constituted a more tangible reality. However, she did not wish to return there permanently: most of her closest relatives lived on Palm Island and in the nearby coastal city of Townsville, even if, as she put it, 'There's also a big family up there, you know'. She liked her current residence in Townsville because it is relatively close to both Palm Island and the Tablelands, and thus allowed easier access to both 'homes'. As she stated, 'It's home there [the Tablelands], but I sort of like this home too, you know, I grew up here too'. However, she also mentioned the embarrassment she felt once whilst sitting at a native title meeting, finding herself surrounded by people – many of whom were younger than her – who had spent most of their lives at, or close to, the place to which the claim related. Many around her could speak 'in language', as she put it – that is, in the Aboriginal language traditionally spoken in that area – either partly or fluently, whereas she, unable to do so despite her advanced age, felt 'like a child' among them, she added. But this did not appear to undermine her sense of the Tablelands as her 'home', and her sense of pride in being able to identify as 'coming from' this second home.

In many other cases, places of 'origin' are not known or are not known with any precision. This is particularly the case for those, and the descendants of those, who were sent to the island as young children without relatives, or without an administrative record or precise information about the rest of their family and the places where they were born or had lived before being sent to Palm Island. Fairly often, people were sent to other places, missions or reserves, and on work placements, before reaching the island, rendering their descendants' own 'histories of origin' all the more uncertain. The lack of knowledge about one's or one's forebears' places of origin is often experienced as a sense of uncertainty about oneself. As a result, many Palm Islanders undertake research into their 'family tree' in order to 'trace back', as they often put it, their genealogy. Family histories are often searched in the archives kept by different institutions, especially Queensland's state archives, sometimes in order to constitute the genealogies relevant to native title claims. However, this kind of work is more often undertaken as a more general means of reconstituting disrupted histories and genealogies, with the hope of discovering or confirming places of 'origin' or the existence of relatives whose 'trace' was 'lost' as a result of separation and displacement. However, while the archives produced by the churches, the state or the police contain a massive amount of information, including some of a very personal nature, they often lack the very kind of information that people are looking for, and that when they are not inaccurate or have been destroyed.

On a few occasions I was asked if I could help research in the archives, although the Palm Island friends who asked me had usually already contacted the archival institutions at stake, and had been disappointed not to have found what they sought. In one instance, in learning that I was on my way to undertake research in the state archives in Brisbane, Mandy asked me if I could try to find information about her mother, and especially about where her mother was born. 'We don't know who she is', she stated. Yet, to my great surprise, she went on to explain that her mother was alive and living with her. As it goes, her mother had been sent alone to Palm Island in the late 1930s as a young child. She came from south Cape York, 'somewhere in the bush', Mandy explained. Although some relatives on one side of her family were known, uncertainty about the other 'side' meant that places of 'origin' remained only partially known. Her previous research attempts had left her dissatisfied: 'We couldn't trace her', as she put it. Not knowing precisely where her mother 'came from' was causing Mandy (and probably her mother as well) a painful sense of uncertain identity, all the more so because research in the archives had been unsuccessful. Although she was 'from Palm Island', she did not cease to feel that she was also 'from' somewhere else, no matter how uncertain this other location was.

Alongside research attempts, and although they have an exceptional character, stories of reconnection with long-lost family members are also told. Patrick, for instance, a man in his forties, told me of a trip he undertook to Mount Isa, about 1,000 kilometres from Palm Island in western Queensland. This was the approximate area where his mother was born and from which she was sent to Palm Island in her youth. She had not been able to keep in touch with most of the family she left behind, but she had told her own children about them. When Patrick travelled to Mount Isa, he did so in the hope that some of them still lived nearby. At a pub, he happened to sit next to an old man, who suddenly turned to him and asked him where he was from. As Patrick replied that he was 'from Palm Island', the old man 'started crying'. He had recognized Patrick as being his nephew, his 'lost' sister's child. Straight away, recalled Patrick, he met 'all the cousins, nieces and nephews'. He also had family in south Queensland, and found he had 'family all across', as he put it. These relatives, some of whom had only recently been discovered, were closely linked to his parents' and grand-parents' histories of origin and their displacement to the island. By virtue of these relationships and histories, he explained how he identified with several tribal names (some of which related to far-away regions). But Palm Island, he strongly asserted, was his 'home'. He also mentioned that he had 'connection' to the island's 'traditional owners', and thus that he was also Manbarra as well as Bwgcolman, two tribal names which are associated in different ways with Palm Island, and have started to be more commonly used by Palm Islanders (although some of them say that these names were never used before) in the wake of the 'native title era', when a native title claim was lodged regarding the island.

At the beginning of the 1990s, an Aboriginal land title recognition process was engaged on Palm Island. An anthropologist assisted this process by collecting information about those who could be identified as the 'traditional owners' of the island; that is, those whose ancestors were already living on the island before the reserve was established. The identified people were designated as belonging to the Manbarra people, the name of the 'tribe' which originally lived on the island. Since this time they have become more frequently acknowledged, especially on special and public occasions, as the 'traditional owners' of the island and of the other islands surrounding it. In accordance with the process of identification, and the language used in native title claims, the remaining population of the island (that is, nearly all of the island's residents) were identified as 'historical people': those whose belonging was acknowledged as resulting from their 'historical' (rather than 'traditional') relationship to the island, or, in other words, from their displacement to the island.[17] In fact, no native title *per se* has been formally recognized since the early 1990s, and the present land status of the island corresponds to a recent and less formal 'land use agreement' between the local Aboriginal council – representing the 'historical people' – the 'traditional owners' and the state.

Over the last few years there have been periods during which the island's Aboriginal ownership has been more intensely discussed among the islanders, producing tensions between the 'historical people' and the 'traditional owners'. On several occasions, for instance, I was told by different 'historical' people that the Manbarra were 'not really' the traditional owners, either because those who doubted them suspected them of having been brought, like others, to the island, or because they appeared to them to be lacking enough 'traditional' knowledge about the island. The 'historical people' sometimes also express resentment at their belonging to the island being questioned by their differentiation from the 'traditional owners'. Interestingly, however, Palm Islanders very commonly use the term 'historical people' to designate themselves (as well as the term 'history'). One older resident, doubting that the Manbarra were 'really' the 'traditional owners' of the island, thus claimed that 'this place started off as a penal settlement!' Being 'historical', for Palm Islanders, does not necessarily mean that one does not belong to the island. In fact, histories of displacement to the island, and of living in the former reserve 'under the Act' (as the former policies are commonly referred to) are also histories of belonging to the island.

As well as Manbarra, another Aboriginal name, Bwgcolman, which in the local Aboriginal language designated the island, also started to be more commonly used on the island in the 1990s in the wake of the native title era. It started to be used to name in another, more 'Aboriginal' way those who had been designated the 'historical people'. It appears that the name was previously known to some people, and could be at times used to designate all Palm Islanders as belonging to the island. In its current use, depending on the context, Bwgcolman may have more or less inclusive connotations. At times, it specifically designates all those who are not the 'traditional owners', that is, the 'historical people', and their descendants. This is especially the case when Bwgcolman is used in contexts when the issue of Aboriginal land rights is discussed. But sometimes Bwgcolman refers to those who were born on the island only. However, it is also often used as a collective Aboriginal name for all Palm Islanders. There is also yet another meaning for Bwgcolman: 'all the tribes in one', or 'island of many tribes', a common Aboriginal identity based in the collective experience of displacement and of place-making on the island, and more precisely as part of the history of the 'tribal camps' in the Palm Island reserve.

## The 'Suburbs', the 'Wild' Areas and the 'Camps'

Today, some of the residential areas are still named after the former tribal camps, although it is mainly older people who possess detailed knowledge of where these used to be. The current residential areas, spread across a much larger space than during the reserve era, somehow form separate clusters, often named 'suburbs' and organized around what still constitutes a central area, often referred to by islanders of all ages as 'the mission' (and also including surrounding habitations). This central area, as with the former reserve, is constituted of administrative buildings, that of the local council as well as of various public service agencies, such as the social welfare centre, hospital, and supermarket, owned by the Queensland government. In the same area, Mango Avenue, the street along which Aboriginal people were forbidden to venture in the past, and in which most of the white staff lived, remains primarily inhabited by non-indigenous workers, who occupy most of the qualified positions at the hospital, police station and two schools. One end of Mango Avenue leads to Dormitory Drive, named after the three dormitories previously located there. Other streets are named after certain localities on the mainland – becoming 'tribal names' on the island – but also quite often after certain individuals and families who lived there – including a number whose current members still do. Individual and family histories are emplaced on the island, determining each one's particular relationship to certain places there. For instance, a young woman proudly told me that she 'remained' a 'Farm girl', although today she no longer resided at the Farm, one of the island's residential areas, named after the farm which operated during the reserve era. One particular street in this area was named after her family, numerous members of which, herself included, had resided there 'as one mob' after it was developed in the early 1970s. However, she also felt related to her new area of residence, closer to the central township, because this was where her grandfather had built his own house in 'the old days'. People's family histories of place-making on the island are thus somehow determinative of their belonging not only to the island but also to particular places on the island.

The largest surface of the island remains uninhabited, at least at first sight: wild pigs, as well as many wild horses (brought when the reserve was set up, and later 'gone wild'), can be found in or behind the hills, where dense vegetation grows. These areas are sometimes described as 'wild', and I was told on many occasions 'wild people' may 'still' live there: creatures, usually described as 'short' and 'hairy', as well as semi-human semi-spirits are said to perhaps 'descend from' the 'tribal people' who used to live on the island before the reserve was settled, and who managed to 'escape' to the hills. They are said to occasionally appear to, and scare, those who venture in these areas, including white people (in fact, many stories of 'wild' beings involve white people being scared off).

Away from the residential areas, around some of the island's beaches, islanders have established camping sites since the 1970s (when circulating freely outside of the reserve became possible). Some people go there for fishing, or to spend the night with family members, but others live there more permanently, often when they have no other place to stay or wait for government housing to become available to them. These camps of small self-built dwellings resemble the former 'tribal camps' I was told. Here, away from 'the settlement' and 'the mission' (that is, all the residential areas), people told me one is able to experience a life-style which is closer to the way in which the 'tribal people' used to live. One's family's particular history of place-making on the island matters in the manner in which camps have been settled around the island. One woman thus explained how the location of her camp depended on her family's former place of residence on the island. Other families, living in nearby residential areas, had also established camping sites near this extremity on the island, while those who had mostly lived in other areas had usually established them at another place, or on two small islands nearby. Although it was fine for her to visit some of her relatives or friends at another camping location, she didn't feel comfortable spending the whole night there: this would make her feel 'out of place', she insisted. 'This is how it was set up', she said.

## The 'Tribal Banner March'

Each year since the late 1990s on Palm Island, the 'tribal banner march' is held as part of the NAIDOC festivities – a week of national celebration of Aboriginal and Torres Strait Islander cultures.[18] In places where the celebrations are held, a march usually takes place, with participants holding the Aboriginal flag and/or the Torres Strait Islands flag, sometimes together with the Australian flag. On Palm Island, the march takes a particular form, since participants usually march with various other flags or variously decorated banners, which bear the names of the different 'tribes' with which the islanders identify themselves.

'This is for our future, for our children, so that they know […] how Palm Island was set up, and about our history, how our community is made of forty-plus different tribes. But you know today, we stand, and we all recognize, and see ourselves, as the Bwgcolman people'.[19] This was the short speech that the Palm Island council's mayor gave after the 2007 'tribal banner march'. The event is an occasion during which this 'history' is somehow commemorated, while offering participants the occasion to display, with some sense of pride, their belonging to particular tribal groups. Tellingly, for the NAIDOC celebrations and the tribal banner march, one woman had decorated a tee-shirt with the contours of Palm Island as viewed from above. Below this, she had written the name Bwgcolman, and inside the island she had placed the names of other tribes that she identified with, as if the corresponding tribes were somehow emplaced on the island. Another woman had also written several tribal names on the back of her tee-shirt, explaining that other names could well be added in the future, because these were only 'as far as I know, as far as I've tracked back the history'.

The event also takes the form of a contest for the best banner, and a jury is usually designated to select the winner based on the quality of design, each banner being very colourfully and beautifully decorated. However, banners are not always replaced on a yearly basis, and some may use the same ones for a number of years, only changing the date on it. Selection for the banner contest therefore seems to rely on diplomacy rather than the application of selective criteria. Interestingly, two non-Aboriginal individuals had been appointed judges at the last minute by the Palm Island councillors during the 2007 march. This, I was told by an Aboriginal resident, was partly motivated by the idea that most Aboriginal residents of the island would have made 'biased' judges because of their own connection to, and thus preference for, particular tribes. The Bwgcolman banner finally won the competition, with two runners-up. A young woman, whose banner came second, told me with disappointment that the Bwgcolman banner 'seemed to always win', even though, from her perspective, it was 'not really a tribe', but was 'made up to talk about everyone' in a way that prevented identification with a particular 'side'. Under different circumstances, however, she would call herself Bwgcolman. Her critique implied a sense of competing identities, one of which (Bwgcolman) risked appearing fabricated when placed in competition with other, and in her view more 'authentic', ones. I was told by another participant that the Bwgcolman banner was 'really more for the kids', because some of them did not yet know 'where they come from' and 'which way to go', and thus decided to walk with the Bwgcolman banner. She identified herself as Bwgcolman, however, since she was 'born here', as she stated, but she usually marched with her 'father's side's' banner.

The Palm Island mayor had walked behind the Bwgcolman banner too, on which it said in small characters 'Palm Island Council', whereas the previous year another Bwgcolman banner had as a subtitle 'Island of many tribes'. The mayor told me how she would usually walk with another banner, and that there were several different banners which she could choose to walk with. Her position as the council's mayor (she had been elected the previous year) partly motivated her choice in walking with the Bwgcolman banner this year, she admitted. Doing so, she sought to promote a sense of communal 'unity', while also remaining somewhat 'neutral' in not choosing a particular 'side'. In walking under the Bwgcolman banner, the mayor seemed also committed to showing the council as a unifying and diplomatic representative of the community. As she explained to me on another occasion, one of the difficulties of her role was being 'diplomatic', because 'there's all these different personalities, and you try to work on bringing everybody together, because we all want to see Palm Island developing, we want basic services'. 'Bringing everybody together' was thus a matter of being able to efficiently negotiate with the government for 'basic services', a diplomatic play somehow symbolically performed at the tribal march in front of the two non-indigenous judges. Interestingly, the latter were the council clerk and a representative of Queensland state's Department of Communities (which is notably in charge of 'Indigenous affairs'). In some sense, the position of these judges seemed to mimic the way in which the state regularly poses as judge of the authenticity and legitimacy of Aboriginal claims in native title cases, while it also reflected Aboriginal people's desires to be recognized by the state. But equally important was the performance and recognition of a 'well-functioning community', in which differences and rivalries were diplomatically negotiated.

Palm Islanders' 'imagination' of the community cannot be immune from the existence of 'community' as a 'bureaucratic category' (Kapferer 1995), and from its representation (and the representation of Aboriginality) in often derogatory terms, for instance as 'dysfunctional' (Garond 2012b, 2012c).[20] The 'imagination' of social tensions within the community in terms of tribes is not limited to 'mainland' representations of Palm Island, as Palm Islanders usually refer to 'outside' and generally non-Aboriginal representations of themselves. It also seems to be part of the way in which Palm Islanders tend to conceive of the social fabric, the community and its 'making'. For instance, reflecting humorously on conflicts among people in the community, a Palm Island woman told me that:

> family's going against family for who's going to be the best, but no one is gonna be the best! And they say that they're Bwgcolman people, but Bwgcolman people is one mob, we belong to the Bwgcolman tribe now! You know that's all the tribes in one, and you keep pushing that Bwgcolman people all the same, even though we come from these tribes but ... we all live on this island!

During a public meeting, one of the island's councillors declared, that 'government always tries to divide us. We have to show that we are unique, that even if we come from forty different tribes, we have a plan'. Interestingly, I was also told by one islander that what makes Palm Island 'special', and in a different sense 'unique', is that 'people come from all these different tribes'.

## Conclusions

Throughout this chapter, I have tried to describe how Palm Islanders' identifications, and in most cases multiple identifications, with various tribes relate to their historical experience of displacement and of place-making on the island, a former colonial reserve and now an Aboriginal community. By identifying themselves with particular tribal groups, Palm Islanders situate themselves as individuals and members of particular families in a network of relationships which somehow relate the island to many other places, be they experienced, remembered or imagined. At the same time, they situate themselves within a social fabric, conceived at times as made of a multiplicity of 'groupings', whose presence 'made' and 'makes' the community and the island as a place imbued with a particular history. A notion of 'cultural loss' (along with a desire to overcome such loss) and an objectified model of Aboriginality continue to impinge on the manner in which Palm Islanders identify as Aboriginal subjects, and on their sense of belonging – or not really belonging – to the models of authentic Aboriginality which they themselves value as such. However, there are particular Aboriginal senses of place and belonging which have been produced, rather than simply 'lost', throughout Palm Islanders' history of displacement and of making the island their place, and these particular senses of place and belonging in fact challenge an objectified model of indigeneity grounded in places of 'origin'.

## Notes

1. 'Murris' is a term used by many Aboriginal Queenslanders to designate themselves.
2. Palm Islanders commonly refer to the place where they live as an 'Aboriginal community'. The expression is also a bureaucratic term, designating localities at which a large majority of Aboriginal people reside, and which are administered by a local, Aboriginal council towards which particular state policies are directed.
3. Historian Mark Copland estimates that between 1918 and 1972 more than 4,200 people were removed to the Palm Island reserve (Copland 2005: 150).
4. I use the term 'origin', in 'places of origin' or 'histories of origin', to emphasize the importance which this seems to have for Palm Islanders, as a time and

place 'before' being displaced to the reserve, whether or not origin places and histories are actually known with precision. The term 'origin' (and 'original'), which Palm Islanders often use to refer to such places, also denotes a notion of 'authenticity' that plays a very significant role in relation to the value that Palm Islanders ascribe to tribal names, as we shall see.

5. Among the rich anthropological literature on the subject, see e.g. Myers (1986), Rumsey and Weiner (2001) and Poirier (2005).
6. But see Morris (1989), Trigger (1992), Merlan (1998), Cowlishaw (2004), Smith (2006), Babidge (2010) and Henry (2012).
7. The following quote from a 1913 report by a protector-in-chief is particularly revelatory: 'I think that any child whom the Protector considered should be separated from aboriginal conditions should be taken away as soon as possible so as to leave as little remembrance as possible of the camp in the child's mind' (William Bleakley, quoted in Blake 2001: 56).
8. Palm Island was chosen as a reserve for its remote location in order to serve especially as a penal settlement. Overall, administrators in charge of 'protection' policy could issue orders for removal to reserves or missions: 'illegal' employment, refusal or inability to work, the committing of any offence and poor health or disease were common reasons for removal, as well as being found 'destitute' or being categorized, for children and young women, as 'half-caste' (see Kidd 1997; Copland 2005; Watson 2010).
9. The policy led to what is now commonly referred to as the 'stolen generations': Aboriginal children and young adults who were separated from their families and placed in white foster homes and institutions (see Haebich 2000).
10. Among several other Palm Island songs, this short song, adapted from an original version from the Torres Strait Islands, evokes the island as a place of belonging and longing while one is separated from it: 'Old PI, my beautiful home / That's the place – or there's a place / Where I was born / And the moon and the sky that shine / Make me longing for home / Old PI, my beautiful home'. The variation 'there's a place' is often sang, notably by older Palm Islanders, who were born 'elsewhere'. See also Neuenfeldt (2002: 114).
11. The Sundowners are usually said to have mainly comprised people belonging to the Kalkadoon and the Waanyi tribes, with which many of today's islanders identify.
12. There are obvious parallels here to the Australianist anthropology of the early decades of the twentieth century (Merlan 1998).
13. In one of his texts, Archibald Meston, for instance, expressed his admiration for those he represented as the 'real wild warriors' (in Thorpe 1984: 59). In fact, looking at the abundant literature that they produced, it was towards a different category of Aboriginal people, especially those who lived near towns and were of 'mixed descent', that white experts were prone to show the most

visible disdain, although here again with some ambivalence: they tended to represent them as both more 'civilized' than the 'wild' or 'tribal' Aboriginal people, but often as having adopted the 'sins' of white society, while remaining ill-adapted to it. Those perceived as such were most at risk of being sent to the reserves.

14. The 'old people', on the other hand, as Palm Islanders commonly describe those (irrespective of age) who were removed to the island in the early decades of the reserve, are often referred to as having been 'very tribal people'; similarly, Aboriginal people living in remote parts of Australia, in particular in the central desert, are also referred to as 'very tribal', in the sense that they embody, for Palm Islanders, a living 'authentic culture' that they themselves experience as more or less partially (depending on their various perspectives on the matter) 'lost' or 'lacking'.

15. A few anthropologists have also started to use the term 'diaspora' to qualify more specifically Aboriginal people's attachments to the places from which they were removed and away from which they currently live (Rigsby 1995; Smith 2000, 2006; Weiner 2002).

16. The name Lorna is a pseudonym, as are other first names used in this chapter to identify Palm Islanders.

17. In this context, two definitions of Aboriginal attachment to land have been extensively used to demarcate certain attachments from others, identified in earlier anthropological accounts as 'historical' and 'traditional' (Trigger 1983). Following such definitions, almost all of Palm Island's population would be defined not as 'traditional' but 'historical' on two levels: in relation to the places from which they or their forebears were removed, and in relation to the island itself to which they or their forebears were removed.

18. NAIDOC (National Aboriginal and Islander Day Observance Committee) springs from one of the first major Aboriginal civil rights movements, the 1938 Sydney protest march, held on Australia Day (which then marked the 150th anniversary of the landing of the British fleet on Australian shores in 1788). It was only later, in the 1970s, that NAIDOC events started to be held regularly at a national level but on a different date to celebrate Aboriginal and Torres Strait Islander 'cultures', at a time when the notion of 'culture' started to be more consistently objectified as an object of national and state recognition.

19. Mention of the number of tribes which originally or which currently 'make' up the Palm Island community seems to originate in rather recent investigations into the early history of the reserve in the wake of the native title 'era', especially investigations into the data collected by the anthropologist Norman Tindale in the late 1930s, notably on Palm Island. Tindale collected many Aboriginal genealogies around Australia during this period, and he pursued a particular interest in identifying affiliations to 'tribes', which he

equated with Aboriginal language groups, and identifying these groups' geographical 'boundaries'. Tindale, with this 'old-fashioned' approach to social organization, produced a map of Australian Aboriginal tribes (Tindale 1974).
20. Ongoing national public debates on socio-economic and health issues within indigenous communities commonly feature the term 'dysfunctional', a generic term aimed at describing the 'problems' that indigenous communities face; what is generally described as 'dysfunctional' is the presence of unemployment, welfare dependency and alcohol abuse, together with a lack of 'leadership'. The term 'dysfunctional' was frequently used, at the time of the 2007 march, by political figures and journalists in reference to the highly mediatised events which took place in 2004 on the island: the 'riot' following the death of an Aboriginal man, Cameron Doomadgee, in the island's police station (on these events, see Hooper 2008; Glowczewski 2008; Garond 2012a). In many media accounts, Palm Island was subsequently portrayed as a typical 'dysfunctional' community, this dysfunction being brandished as cause of the 'riot' (rather than the death in custody itself). Interestingly, 'dysfunctionality' was often linked to an original 'tribal' heterogeneity, designated as a direct cause of the supposed endemic conflicts opposing the island's 'families', rendering any collective project, or the management of the community council impossible.

## References

Babidge, S. 2010. *Aboriginal Family and the State: The Conditions of History*. Farnham: Ashgate.

Barth, F. (ed.). 1969. *Ethnic Groups and Boundaries*. London: Allen and Unwin.

Bauman, T. 2006. 'Nations and Tribes "Within": Emerging Aboriginal "Nationalisms" in Katherine', *Australian Journal of Anthropology* 17(3): 322–35.

Bender, B. 2001. 'Introduction', in B. Bender and M. Winer (eds), *Contested Landscapes: Movement, Exile and Place*. Oxford: Berg, pp.1–18.

Bender, B. and M. Winer (eds). 2001. *Contested Landscapes: Movement, Exile and Place*. Oxford: Berg.

Blake, T.W. 2001. *A Dumping Ground: A History of the Cherbourg Settlement*. Brisbane: University of Queensland Press.

Butler, J. 1997. *The Psychic Life of Power: Theories in Subjection*. Stanford: Stanford University Press.

Casey, E.S. 1993. *Getting Back into Place: Towards a Renewed Understanding of the Place-world*. Bloomington: Indiana University Press.

Copland, M. 2005. 'Calculating Lives: The Numbers and Narratives of Forced Removals in Queensland 1859–1972', Ph.D. diss. Brisbane: Griffith University.

Cowlishaw, G. 2004. *Blackfellas, Whitefellas, and the Hidden Injuries of Race*. Malden, MA: Blackwell.

Feld, S., and K.H. Basso (eds). 1996. *Senses of Place*. Santa Fe, NM: School of American Research Press.
Fingleton, J., and J. Finlayson (eds). 1995. *Anthropology in the Native Title Era: Proceedings of a Workshop*. Canberra: Aboriginal Studies Press.
Foucault, M. 1977. *Discipline and Punish: The Birth of the Prison*. London: Allen Lane.
Garond, L. 2012a. '"There Is Lots of History Here": History, Memory and Subjectivity among the Aboriginal People of Palm Island, Australia', Ph.D. diss. Paris and Townsville: EHESS and James Cook University.
――― 2012b. 'The Values of Dysfunctionality, or Dysfunctionality as "Meaningful Difference"', unpublished paper delivered at the conference 'Values of Dominance and Difference', Cairns Institute, 9 August.
――― 2012c. '*L'émeute, le paradis perdu*, et la visite de Boney M: représentations médiatiques et subjectivité des habitants aborigènes de Palm Island', *Les Cahiers d'Anthropologie du droit* 2011-2012: 231-50.
Glowczewski, B. 1998. 'The Meaning of "One" in Broome: From Yawuru Tribe to Rubibi Corporation', *Aboriginal History* 22: 203-22.
――― 2008. *Guerriers pour la paix: La condition politiques des Aborigènes vue de Palm Island, avec la contribution de Lex Wotton*. Montpellier: Editions Indigène.
Haebich, A. 2000. *Broken Circles: Fragmenting Indigenous Families 1800-2000*. Fremantle: Fremantle Arts Centre Press.
Henry, R. 2012. *Performing Place, Practicing Memories: Aboriginal Australians, Hippies and the State*. Oxford: Berghahn.
Hooper, C. 2008. *The Tall Man: Death and Life on Palm Island*. London: Penguin-Hamish Hamilton.
Ingold, T. 2000. *The Perception of the Environment: Essays in Livelihood, Dwelling and Skill*. London: Routledge.
Kapferer, B. 1995. 'Bureaucratic Erasure, Identity, Resistance and Violence: Aborigines and a Discourse of Autonomy in a North Queensland Town', in D. Miller (ed.), *Worlds Apart: Modernity through the Prism of the Local*. London: Routledge, pp.69-90.
Keith, M., and S. Pile (eds). 1993. *Place and the Politics of Identity*. London: Routledge.
Kidd, R. 1997. *The Way We Civilize: Aboriginal Affairs – The Untold Story*. St Lucia: University of Queensland Press.
Massey, D. 1994. *Space, Place and Gender*. Cambridge: Polity Press.
Merlan, F. 1998. *Caging the Rainbow: Places, Politics, and Aborigines in a North Australian Town*. Honolulu: University of Hawai'i Press.
Morris, B. 1989. *Domesticating Resistance: The Dhan-gadi Aborigines and the Australian State*. Oxford: Berg.
Myers, F. 1986. *Pintupi Country, Pintupi Self: Sentiment, Place and Politics among Western Desert Aborigines*. Canberra: Australian Institute of Aboriginal Studies.

Neuenfeldt, K. 2002. 'Examples of Torres Strait Songs of Longing and Belonging', *Journal of Australian Studies* 57: 111–16.

Poirier, S. 2005. *A World of Relationships. Itineraries, Dreams and Events in the Australian Western Desert*. Toronto: University of Toronto Press.

Povinelli, A. 2002. *The Cunning of Recognition: Indigenous Alterities and the Making of Australian Multiculturalism*. Durham, NC: Duke University Press.

Rigsby, B. 1995. 'Tribes, Diaspora People and the Vitality of Law and Custom: Some Comments', in J. Fingleton and J. Finlayson (eds), *Anthropology in the Native Title Era*. Canberra: Aboriginal Studies Press, pp.25–27.

Rosser, B. 1985. *Dreamtime Nightmares*. Canberra: Australian Institute of Aboriginal Studies.

Rumsey, A. and J. Weiner (eds). 2001. *Emplaced Myth: Space, Narrative, and Knowledge in Aboriginal Australia and Papua New Guinea*. Honolulu: University of Hawai'i Press.

Smith, B.R. 2000. '"Local" and "Diaspora" Connections to Country and Kin in Central Cape York Peninsula'. Native Title Research Unit Issues Paper No. 2(6). Canberra: Australian Institute of Aboriginal and Torres Strait Islander Studies.

——— 2006. '"More Than Love": Locality and Affects of Indigeneity in Northern Queensland', *Asia Pacific Journal of Anthropology* (special issue) 7(3): 221–35.

——— 2008. 'Still Under the Act? Subjectivity and the State in Aboriginal North Queensland', *Oceania* 78(2): 199–216.

Thorpe, W. 1984. 'Archibald Meston and Aboriginal Legislation in Colonial Queensland', *Historical Studies* 21(82): 52–67.

Tindale, N. 1974. *Aboriginal Tribes of Australia: Their Terrain, Environmental Controls, Distribution, Limits, and Proper Names*. Canberra: Australian National University Press.

Trigger, D.S. 1983. 'Land Rights Legislation in Queensland: The Issue of Historical Association', in N. Peterson and M. Langton (eds), *Aborigines, Land and Land Rights*. Canberra: Australian Institute of Aboriginal Studies, pp.192–201.

——— 1992. *Whitefella Comin': Aboriginal Responses to Colonialism in Northern Australia*. Cambridge: Cambridge University Press.

Trouillot, M.R. 2001. 'The Anthropology of the State in the Age of Globalization: Close Encounters of the Deceptive Kind', *Current Anthropology* 42(1): 125–38.

Watson, J. 2010. *Palm Island: Through a Long Lens*. Canberra: Aboriginal Studies Press.

Weiner, J.F. 2002. 'Diaspora, Materialism, Tradition: Anthropological Issues in the Recent High Court Appeal of the Yorta Yorta'. Native Title Research Unit Issues Paper No. 2(18). Canberra: Australian Institute of Aboriginal and Torres Strait Islander Studies.

# 3

# Coconuts and the Landscape of Underdevelopment on Panapompom, Papua New Guinea

## Will Rollason

Panapompom is a small island in the Louisiade Archipelago of Milne Bay Province, a chain of islands running roughly north-west to southeast, somewhat to the south and east of the famous 'kula ring' (Malinowski 1922; Leach and Leach 1983). The island's population is some 500 people at any one time. North Panapompom has a population of about 360, of whom about 150 are adults and forty to sixty are active men.[1] A typical island community for the region, Panapompom people live from shifting horticulture, cultivating yams, cassava, bananas and sweet potatoes, and fish the lagoon that surrounds the island.[2]

Panapompom people are also keen participants in the money economy. Almost all of the money in circulation on Panapompom today comes from the collection and sale of bêche-de-mer, dried sea cucumber.[3] However, this is a recent development. Until the 1990s, almost all Panapompom men were involved in the production of copra (dried coconut) from plantations they maintained on the island.[4] The copra industry on Panapompom collapsed in the early 1990s, with important consequences not only for the economy of the island, but also for the identities and locations of Panapompom people.[5]

This chapter therefore considers how Panapompom people come to understand their place in a deeply interconnected postcolonial world as a position of underdevelopment. I am going to show how the copra industry of the colonial and immediately postcolonial periods simultaneously constituted Panapompom as a place of a particular kind, inhabited by people identified in, by and with the colonial order, and integrated into an economy that Panapompom people imagined as a network of vectors, flows and movements. In short, I argue that colonial Panapompom, at least as it is imagined by Panapompom people today, is constituted by a history of shifting assemblages (Collier and Ong 2005) of people, material and relationships. However, since the early 1990s, this assemblage has become both figuratively and literally derelict. This has been the result of the rapid collapse of the copra industry in the region and its replacement with marine-resource harvesting. The kinds of projects that Panapompom people pursued within the structure of the copra industry have been unhooked from their material and political concomitants, leaving Panapompom as a place whose location in the contemporary world is uncertain, inhabited by people who are not sure how they should act in order to resume the connections and movements on which their hopes for the future were based.

This chapter therefore seeks to engage with the themes of this volume by investigating ethnographically the genealogy of the way Panapompom people have imagined themselves to be people with a place in the world who are 'going somewhere'. In doing so, I hope to demonstrate how we might imagine contemporary Panapompom people in terms of the multiple and prospective movements, identifications and locations that put them where they are today and which enable and constrain their projects for the future.

## Prologue: Poiyaa 2006

It is 2006. The coconut plantation of Poiyaa that stretches away up the hill from the eastern shore of Panapompom, dividing the hamlets of Liliwaa and Pana-ewau, is dark, tangled and filled with the grumblings of pigs and the chatter of birds. The undergrowth is luxuriant, and the shadows under the trees are everywhere pierced with the sharp new shoots of young coconuts. These new palms are sprouting up in the shadow of their mother-palms, as well as their siblings of a few years' or months' growth. Despite the optimistic resurgence of the palms, however, this is a landscape of underdevelopment.

Until 1992, Poiyaa was the community plantation of Panapompom. The area covered by coconuts is very large, extending deep into the bush behind Liliwaa and covering the entire headland of Sui Bohuna (Coconut Point).

The older palms of the plantation are laid out in neat rows in a grid pattern, with several metres between each palm allowing space for their crowns to spread. Looked at from the sea, Poiyaa gives the impression of a corrugated forest, with creases in the canopy running up the hill and into the interior with orderly disregard for the features of the landscape.

The interior of the plantation today, however, reveals decay and the transgression of the grid that marks the land so forcefully when seen from the sea. Coconut palms have a relatively short lifespan, perhaps sixty years, and must be replaced regularly to maintain the productivity of a plantation. The regularly spaced palms have not been replaced for a long while, all are of more or less identical age, and they are at the end of their productive lives. To gather coconuts, the ground around the palms must be cleared so that the fallen nuts can be collected. It is clear from the luxuriant undergrowth that this has not been done systematically in a long while. Finally, the shoots of new palms are erupting where the nuts have fallen, and promise that in just a few years, as those new shoots attain their parents' height, the orderly grid a sailor in 2006 would have seen will no longer show its neat pleats, erased by a more random efflorescence of fronds.

In this chapter, I am going to explore some of the ways in which Panapompom people think about economic change in terms of the end of order and its replacement with disorder. This is apparent not just in the landscape – the principle productive resource for Panapompom people – but in the work that Panapompom people undertake, and the way in which they engage with their environment. Not all of the locations implicated by the disordering of work on Panapompom, however, are 'places' in the sense that Poiyaa is an intimately inhabited locale. Rather, the increasing disorder of Poiyaa stands as a pivot between Panapompom men and a wider world of linkages and flows. The processes in play constitute multiple places, more or less imaginary, associated with movements of considerable range and conflicting processes of identification. Panapompom's declining fortunes as a node in this world finds itself inscribed on the landscape, and known in the work of the men who inhabit this world.[6]

Nancy Munn has written: 'a mode of spacetime defines a form in terms of which the world is experienced by the agents whose actions produce it. However ... not only do the agents produce their world in a particular form, but they may also be seen as producing themselves, or aspects of themselves in the same process' (Munn 1986: 11). Munn's interest is in the qualities and vectors of movement, which constitute the relational world of kula traders, sailing between islands to the north-west of Panapompom (Munn 1983).[7] She is concerned first to understand how a moving body can constitute the quality of the space in which it moves – its time and distance, for example. Second, she is concerned with the ways in which movements, paths and vectors through spaces mediate and constitute relationships of particular kinds between actors (Munn 1973, 1983). Thirdly, she wants to understand how value is produced or made visible in the ways in which people, objects, stories and ideas circulate, and the qualities – speed and so on – of these movements. In creating a synthesis between place, movement, value and persons, Munn's project is cognate with others, both within the general region and further afield in Papua New Guinea (PNG) and the Pacific region at large.[8]

Intimate connections between people and land, and people and movements or flows, are not entirely surprising, of course, in an ethnographic context in which people are often thought of as being intimately connected to land, and especially the food that grows on it, and in which their worth is known in the circulation of goods that occurs in their names (Merlan and Rumsey 1991). Ethnographers of the highlands of PNG, for example, conceive of long-range exchange and the reproduction of foods – and therefore people – in terms of hydraulics. Death payments for casualties in war flow into pig exchanges and solidarity, which in turn convert seamlessly into more wars (Strathern 1971, 1972; Meggitt 1977; Strathern 1985); similarly, powerful fluids – semen, grease, blood or water (Strathern 1972) – circulate between men, women and the ground and its foodstuffs in the cycle of reproduction (Crook 2007).

The argument that I mount here builds on these idioms of flow and placedness. My concern is with the work Panapompom men undertake in primary resource industries as part of their ongoing engagement with long-range commodity economies. I am interested in the way the shifting form this work takes constitutes modes and media of relationships between Panapompom men and powerful others that they imagine as 'white people' (*dimdim*), who live in Australia, Singapore and other places (Rollason 2008b). These flows, movements and relations are seen, experienced and known, as Munn suggests, not only in abstractions or representations, but in the qualities of the working body and the spaces that it occupies (Munn 1986). In this case, underdevelopment is seen in the place and experienced in its decay.

In making this claim, I am at the same time intervening in the problem of 'the global'. The idea of the global, or of processes of globalization, entail tropes of scale or scope (Moore 2004) – an opposition, more or less explicit, between, for example, 'local' places and 'global' flows (Tsing 2000). The ethnography of PNG, indeed the Pacific more broadly, has very much been concerned with the constitution and documenting of a 'locality' – a site of socio-cultural specificity in which generalized and depersonalized commodities are converted into definite gifts (Gregory 1982; Miller 1987) which are intimately engaged in the constitution of persons (Mosko 2002;

Kuehling 2006; Leach 2006). Works that open the ethnography of PNG to the idea of the global are nevertheless important (e.g. Carrier and Carrier 1989; Carrier 1992; Foster 2002, 2008; Josephides 2008), but these have, on the whole, failed to retain localizing ethnographies' sense of the urgency and vitality of particular ways of life. As is frequently true, we are left with a choice between large-scale histories of movement and connection, and the fine, static detail of the 'ethnographic present'.

Part of the purpose of this chapter is to develop a project of connecting 'local' work with 'global' traffic, not as separate 'scales' of phenomena (Strathern 1995) but, on the model of Munn's 'spacetime', as a single manifold of movement and value, in terms of which the intimacies of work, place and identity can be known and judged alongside large-scale political vectors. That is, in 'suturing' (Baumann 2001) subjects to discourses and institutions of colonialism and global capital, work creates the conditions under which workers can be 'hailed' or 'interpellated' (Althusser 2008) into powerful assemblages, which simultaneously enable and constrain their projects. Place and the increasingly disordered coconuts of Poiyaa stand as such a suture between working people, their kin and friends, and the extended networks of demands, rulings and disciplines that motivate and compel work.[9]

## Coconuts and the Landscape of Underdevelopment

### The Poiyaa Dispute

The derelict state of the Poiyaa plantation embeds a series of memories for Panapompom people. It serves as a 'place/object of (or for) remembering' (Battaglia 1990: 8), *abanuwahikan* in the local vernacular. Just as Battaglia (ibid.: 11) shows for nearby Sabarl, Panapompom people are deeply concerned with memory, not merely as a source of knowledge, but a constituting feature of persons, as the stuff of relationships, which must be actively worked on in the course of everyday life if relationships are to be maintained.

The memories that the Poiyaa plantation embeds constitute Panapompom's evolving relationships with the colonial Australian government, especially following the Second World War, and the postcolonial national governments which succeeded it. In doing so, it charts the rise and fall of what Panapompom people call development, and gives evidence for judgements that Panapompom people pass on themselves as underdeveloped people. Here, I begin by explaining the history of Poiyaa and the copra industry on Panapompom, before examining what this history means for Panapompom people, their work, vectors and identities in long-range space-times of value and recognition.

The current derelict state of Poiyaa dates from 1992.[10] At this time the ownership of the plantation was disputed. Tuitui, the senior uncle of the men of Pana-ewau village (already dead when I began my fieldwork), had been responsible for the management of the community plantation. As the community plantation, Poiyaa was worked by cooperative members, often in communal working parties, gathering copra all together. In 1992, as a representative of the local cooperative, however, he went to the regional cooperative office in Bwagaoia, the local government centre, and closed the plantation, declaring that it belonged to his lineage. In the resulting disagreement and bad feeling, work there stopped altogether and has yet to be seriously resumed.

The arrangements for the ownership of the plantation, which was established under the colonial administration perhaps as late as 1973, had always been ambiguous. On Panapompom, all land is owned. Certain important areas – the school and mission plots, as well as the community plantation at Poiyaa – are problematic. This is because at one time or another they were expropriated by missionaries or colonial administrators. Although they were ultimately put at the disposal of the community at large, under the Organic Law of PNG permanently alienating land is difficult (PNG 1995). Hence these areas are always open to dispute as 'original' landholders assert their 'traditional' tenure against other users.

It was such a dispute that finally closed Poiyaa. The plantation lies between the hamlets of Liliwaa and Pana-ewau. Liliwaa was established in the early 1970s, probably in 1971, by Wesoweso, a man from Eiaus village on the island of Misima. Pana-ewau people come most recently from east Panaeati, across the lagoon from Panapompom, and before that from Misima and the village of Gulewaa. Like Liliwaa people, they appear to have arrived in numbers first in the late colonial period.

Poiyaa plantation appears to have been established principally by Liliwaa people. In common with people throughout this region, Panapompom people claim land on the basis of connections to places through ancestors, in stories which shade rapidly into legend and myth. Land disputes can be settled on the basis of competing narratives of connection and ownership of land.

Liliwaa people claim connection to Poiyaa through a distant, probably legendary, ancestress, and occasionally argue that the plantation belongs to them on that basis. However, while I was in the field, their most commonly adopted position was that Pana-ewau people were not effectively working Poiyaa and that it should return to 'the community'. Indeed, they went as far as to accuse Pana-ewau people of simply engaging in a land grab because they had failed to plant enough coconuts of their own when copra was thriving. For their part, in 2006, Pana-ewau people were either unable or unwilling to justify Tuitui's seizure of Poiyaa and were, in practice, allowing fairly open access to the plantation – with the important proviso, however, that this was evidence of their largesse.

In fact, most people agreed with the Liliwaa position. This was largely because of a fundamental change that land ownership had undergone during the colonial period. Colonial records show that the postwar Australian administration was active in encouraging copra production and supporting cooperative societies in this region as early as the 1950s. Before the war, expatriate owned plantations, mainly producing coconuts, dominated the economy of the province (CoA 1948; Connell 1997). Two such plantations were active on Panapompom throughout the postwar colonial period, and employed most people on the island at one time or another. Patrol reports for Misima suggest a copra cooperative operating on Panapompom by the end of the 1950s.[11]

Nevertheless, local accounts of the development of copra attribute enormous importance to a certain Mr Murray.[12] Murray appears to have been an agricultural extension officer working in the 1970s. Two independent sources date his visit to the island to 1973, a time when they were schoolchildren. The role of agricultural extension officers, especially on the eve of independence, was mainly to improve agricultural techniques and promote cash crops. Mr Murray, it seems, introduced pepper, chillies, certain kinds of trees for timber, a range of vegetables and perhaps coffee. Most importantly, however, he encouraged an enormous expansion in the capacity of Panapompom coconut plantations, especially those held by Panapompom people, outside the commercial estates.

In the early 1970s, there were two important population centres on Panapompom. On the south coast, and associated with the larger expatriate plantation at Nivani, was the village of Lalagela. On the north coast, the older, and by far the larger, village was Hoguguma, which included the church and later also the cooperative buildings. Hoguguma was divided into a number of hamlets or wards, which were owned by different clan and family groups. Large, concentrated villages of this sort were favoured by early colonial administrators, especially those belonging to the wartime military administration.

Hoguguma people, however, owned land on different parts of the island where they raised coconuts and made gardens. By local accounts, Mr Murray's contribution was first to encourage an enormous expansion in plantation capacity; second, he strongly advised people to go and live near to their plantations; third, and most importantly, he declared that wherever people made plantations on unused land, that land belonged to them – especially if they also went to live there.

Murray's intervention resulted in the break-up of Hoguguma, as the different groups of people who had constituted the village departed to create coconut plantations and live on them. In the process, completely new villages were established in both directions – east and north-west – of old Hoguguma. Often, it appears that these villages were created on land that was unclaimed and vacant in Mr Murray's sense. The dispute over Poiyaa, between two recently founded villages, works out the implications of Mr Murray's intervention. The terms of the debate are less about genealogy and ownership than about 'the community' and the rulings of a colonial administrator.

## The Making of 'the Community'

The notion of community is a pivotal one on Panapompom. Mr Murray's grant of land ownership to people who were essentially settlers was of deep significance; Panapompom people are almost all recent arrivals on the island. A patrol report of 1945 gives a population of between fifty and sixty people, all living at Hoguguma on the north coast.[13] This was put down to 'the original inhabitants having long since died'.[14] However, local tradition has it that the island was uninhabited until around the time of the Second World War. It had been a haunt of witches and monsters, and was in any case infested with crocodiles and mosquitoes. It was the establishment of the first commercial copra plantation at Nivani by a certain Mr Munt which seems first to have drawn people to the island. By 1956, the population had risen to seventy-five,[15] having been stable for at least three years,[16] but by 1961 it had increased to 103.[17] The 1961 figure appears to correspond to the foundation of the village of Lalagela on the south coast. Many of the people swelling the population of the island at this time were immigrants.

In the 1960s and 1970s, Panapompom was a regional economic hub. The island was served by seaplane as well as boats, and the Nivani plantation boasted a very large store, which was better stocked and more popular than those in Bwagaoia, the regional capital. Panapompom appeared to be a land of opportunity and attracted people from across the region to work and settle. These people ended up living on land where the genealogical and mythic connections were known and remembered not by the new residents, but by west Panaeati people, inhabitants of the larger island across the lagoon. This has rarely been a political problem for Panapompom people because the size of Panaeati has meant that there has been little pressure on land.[18] However, it meant that the population of Panapompom must have appeared as a collection of people standing at the ends of stories and migrations that linked them to Panaeati, Misima and the small islands to the south and east, Motorina, Brooker and beyond, rather than to the land where they were settled.

The difficulty for immigrants was that they lacked the sort of deep narrative connections to the land that longer residents might have had. Murray's fiat, granting ownership of land to those people prepared to develop it with cash crops, was important in this context in two ways. First, it removed the embarrassment of occupying other people's land. Local people often find themselves in this position, especially through marriage, where women usually end up making gardens on their husbands' lands. However, for men especially it is not a desirable situation, as it tends to recall the inferior status of the junior affine (*tovelam*), who owes duties and obedience to senior in-laws (cf. Battaglia 1990, 1992). Panapompom people argue that Murray, in his capacity as an officer of the colonial government, simply swept away the old patterns of ownership and replaced them with a shallow, rationalized pattern of rights (cf. Robbins 2007) based on work and exploitation of the land.

Second, Murray's intervention appeared radically to flatten the sorts of connections that Panapompom people saw themselves as having with other places. Hoguguma appears to have existed as a collection of hamlets which were essentially outstations of villages on Panaeati and Misima. Their genealogies connected them to their origins and the only land that they could claim to own. Murray was likely seen in this connection to be invoking a sort of rule typical of colonial governance, the law (*logugui*). He used this law to sweep away genealogy as a mode of connectedness to land, and to replace it with what Panapompom people now call 'the community'.

## Working for the Community

In 2006, the community (*kominiti*) on Panapompom was defined not as an organizational structure but by work. The work that defined the community was understood as an enactment of the law. It is necessary therefore to outline what work and law mean for Panapompom people.

Work (*tuwalali*) is a most important concept for Panapompom people in defining the sorts of people that they are and the values that they produce and operate with. Work is conceived of as a process demonstrating memory (*nuwahikan*). Both people and technical processes demand that people 'remember' their obligations. In the case of people, these are actual exchanges of gifts, support and so on – social life 'done properly'. In the case of work, the obligations exacted take the form of the demands a technical operation makes of a worker in terms of proper technique.[19]

The demands that work makes on a worker are generally called *logugui*, which Panapompom people gloss in English as 'law'. Law therefore becomes a particular aesthetic of work: how to work properly. Hence, for example, the 'law of the bush knife' (*kilepa ana logugui*), was described to me in terms of the ways in which a worker positions their body so as to avoid cutting themselves, the proper sharpening of the blade and maintenance of the handle, how the knife is properly carried and so on. Someone who ignores these rules acts 'without regard' or 'worthlessly' (*bwagabwaga*). Worthless acts (*ginol bwagabwaga*) are a problem; in the case of a twelve-inch bush knife, acting 'without regard' is liable to result in serious injury, which is painful and, just as important, will prevent a person from working for and with kin. It is the neglect of relationships that make *ginol bwagabwaga* problematic, an absence of respect that marks a person out as 'wicked' or 'irresponsible' (*sigasiga*). Thought about in a general sense, working in accordance with the law is therefore productive work – work that produces shared value – as opposed to 'worthless acts' and wickedness.

Law as a sort of rule established by the state is a particularly important class of *logugui*. It establishes particular processes or aesthetics of work that allow judgements of its quality and value in terms of demands that Panapompom people locate with 'the government' or with white people (*dimdim*). This is clearly seen when Panapompom people do 'community work' or, as they put it 'we do community' (*kominiti ha ginol*).

Community work takes place every Friday and Wednesday morning during the harvest season. Wednesdays are devoted to 'government' work, while Fridays are dedicated to the church. This arrangement is a relic of the colonial period (Berde 1976, 1979). First, missionaries enlisted local labour to clear mission grounds, and maintain the church, school and cemeteries. Later, as colonial patrolling became more intensive, local people were required to maintain paths and rest houses for patrols, and keep houses and village plazas in good order.[20] This arrangement persists today under the direction of officials, the ward councillor (*kaunsil*), who represents Panapompom in the Local Level Government, and his deputies, called 'committees' (*komiti*), who represent the *kaunsil* in their respective hamlets.

The establishment of community work, and therefore the community as such, is seen by Panapompom people as an act of law. Law appears in this aspect in terms of the time and motion of working bodies – Munn's 'spacetime'. The ideal for community work is that, in the early hours of the morning, a meeting is called in each of the hamlets where the work to be undertaken is described and tasks are assigned. After breakfast, the workers assemble wherever they are supposed to work. This, the Committees insisted, was at nine o'clock. The workers should begin to work simultaneously and continue to work all together until noon, whereupon, the task completed, they should disperse.

Working to this ideal presents a large number of problems, not least of coordinating work in terms of time in a community that lacks clocks. However, the idea that the law demands that people should work 'all together' was extremely powerful in explanations I was given of the law. Hence Lars, *komiti* for the north-western villages, described law to me in this way: 'The appearance of law is like this: the leader will say something, we show obedience as one, we work as one' (*Logugui ana awa i ola hiwe: tologugui ni ba, ta awatauwan, ta kululu pamiasena, ta tuwalali pamaisena*). The term *pamaisena* is deeply significant in this context. *Pamaisena* is formed of two linguistic elements: the prefix *pa-* means '(to cause) to be'; *maisena* means 'one', but not 'one' as an individual unit in a sequence of counted things. When people count, they use *etega* for 'one'. Rather, *maisena* indicates a singular unity, a 'whole'. Working 'as one' therefore conjures a singular unity, presents an image of oneness, which is, in light of the importance of ideas of time in community work, also an image of simultaneity. Obedience to the law appears to produce a sudden image of unity: people do not cleave to the law as the product of a history, as they might in the case of a genealogy, but in a way that establishes their unity in the absence of a temporal sequence – all at once.

To return to Poiyaa and Mr Murray's intervention in land-ownership on Panapompom, it is quite clear that his law, that lands could legitimately be held without appeal to genealogy – that is simultaneously with the act of occupation – belongs to the same pattern of practice as community work and shares a similar aesthetic. Both deny temporality and insist on a singular, one-off submission to a rule.

The simultaneity of the law means that social relations within the community, mediated by long-standing obligations of kinship and affinity, are hard to deal with in its terms. Indeed, Panapompom people explicitly deny that these kinds of obligations are the field of law. This is seen when, in community meetings, in-laws address one another publicly by name – something that would be unthinkably rude in other contexts. However, 'in the law' (*logugui eliyana*) the long-term obligations that name avoidance memorializes are not felt to be appropriate, and the resultant hierarchies are suppressed.

Moreover, the operation of law through community work establishes Panapompom as a new kind of place. When old men 'tell genealogy' (*lihu*) they paint a picture of Panapompom as a collection of people who have travelled from elsewhere to reach the island. Hence, Liliwaa people tell a story of ancestors who departed from Eiaus on the island of Misima and came, some by way of Panaeati, to Panapompom. These genealogies tie members of that kin group to gardens, cemeteries and villages on Misima. As each lineage on Panapompom tells its own story, the island as a meaningful location begins to break up, and it becomes increasingly difficult to think of Panapompom as a singular location. This is almost certainly the product of migration to the island in the recent past, as we have seen. These connections are mediated by the exchange of pigs, canoes, persons and valuables, particularly through funeral feasting – and by long skeins of memory and narrative.

The community, however, invokes different kinds of narrative, and suppresses memories of this kind. We can see this kind of narrative in the history of Poiyaa. The intervention Mr Murray is supposed to have made, and Liliwaa people's demand that the plantation return to the community at large, is based on the notion that law has cut off, suppressed or otherwise made connections and memories defined by kinship – it's space-time – redundant, or at least irrelevant in this case. Panapompom as a location that matters in itself appears at the point that this suppression takes place. The mechanics of local government in the form of the *kaunsil*, his officers and the work that they demand, make Panapompom people enact community in the motions of their bodies as they work 'as one', according to the law.

The effect of this redefinition of the place of Panapompom is that the relations that define the place, and in terms of which the qualities of work and workers are judged, are therefore not figured in terms of remembering genealogies or obligations between kin. Rather, they are thought of in terms of demands made by government. More specifically, Panapompom people continue to think in terms of demands made of them by the colonial government, and specifically white administrators like Mr Murray. Equally, whereas relations in kinship are essentially known through stories about land and relationships, the simultaneity of the law, or 'working as one', does not allow the same types of knowledge or value to exist. Rather, the qualities of lawfulness are seen in the appearance of places and people, not least in the orderly grid of the Poiyaa plantation, now under pressure from the encroaching bush.

## Development

Until the 1990s, most Panapompom men spent a large proportion of their time producing copra on plantations such as Poiyaa. Coconut plantations remain, as I have described, a very important aspect of the landscape of Panapompom and of other local communities. This striking impact on the 'appearance of places' (*panuwa ana awa*) is much remarked on by Panapompom people.

Coconut palms, although a striking feature of island landscape, are not the only elements in the geography of copra. On Panapompom, in Galowawaisana, the rump of the old village of Hoguguma, there is a leaky galvanized iron shed, sporting the remains of a solar panel, lights and a shortwave radio: the island's copra shed. Behind it in the bush are the remains of the capacious store previously run by the copra cooperative. Its corrugated iron roof was being slowly but surely cannibalized for other building projects. The coral-encrusted traces of concrete piles running out to sea mark the site of a long pier, where large cargo boats used to collect copra, but which fell into disrepair and, after being damaged by a cyclone, was not restored. Deeper in the bush, the hulks of copra smokers, built in steel and concrete, can be found, and older people remember the roads that were cut through the island by the expatriates to allow their trucks, even a motorbike, access to the plantations.

All of these elements of the contemporary landscape were the product of a particular moment in Panapompom people's relationship with the Australian colonial administration. Prior to the 1950s, the copra industry was almost exclusively in the hands of expatriate planters. However, by 1951, the administration was working to increase the proportion of Papuan copra produced by locals (CoA 1952), and to convert what had been the backbone of the plantation economy into the basis for a local money economy, ready for eventual independence. The strategy for achieving this goal was for the administration to support the foundation of copra producing cooperatives (CoA 1948). By 1955, officially registered cooperatives were operating on the Misima-speaking islands of the Louisiades,[21] and local copra production steadily increased relative to expatriate production, reaching 20 per cent of the total in 1953/54 (CoA 1954: 30), and 30 per cent in 1955/56 (CoA 1956: 29).

This period was very favourable to copra production, as Britain found herself starved of fats for cooking. In 1946, London signed an agreement with Canberra to purchase all of the copra Australia produced at a protected rate for nine years (CoA 1949: 31). This agreement mainly benefited the Territory of Papua and New Guinea. When the agreement expired in 1957, the administration agreed to continue to stabilize prices through a purchasing monopoly, the Copra Marketing Board or CMB (Jackman 1988). The effect of the colonial sponsorship of copra for communities such as Panapompom was an increase in production, and with it a rise in cash incomes. This led to desires for educational opportunities and mobility on the part of locals,[22] as well as changes in the appearance of Panapompom as a place, the remains of which are still visible.

What can the copra industry tell us about Panapompom people's place in a connective, valued world prior to the 1990s? Copra clearly had a profound impact on what Panapompom was like as a place, but it also placed the island in a larger – much larger – geo-political system. The CMB monopolized the purchase and export of copra, even after the expiry of the

Anglo-Australian agreement. In order to sell copra, Panapompom people told me, they had to have it transported to Alotau, the provincial capital, where it was purchased by agents of the CMB. From Alotau, it was shipped on, either to Port Moresby or to Australia.

Bwake, an older man and proud of his abilities as a copra producer, explained that when the copra was shipped, the bags it was packed in would be marked with an identifying number. This number identified the person or cooperative shipping the copra. He was proud to remember both his personal number and that of the cooperative, 200C529, of which he had been a leader. The bags of copra, with the numbers painted on, were loaded against a bill of lading, also marked with the producer's number. At Alotau, where the bags were weighed and the copra graded for quality, a receipt would be produced, attached to the money value of the copra, which was returned by cargo boat to the producers. Meanwhile, the copra, still in its numbered bags, Bwake imagined, was making its way to Australia.

The world of the copra economy was one of flows and connections, mediated by numbers, accounts and payments. At each step of the process Bwake recounted to me, he emphasized that he could be known and recognized as a copra man, and that the envelopes with receipts and money that returned with the boat were material demonstrations of that recognition. This was, we might say, the aesthetic of the copra economy, its law (*logugui*). The work that Panapompom people did on copra, and the landscape that they inhabited as a result of it, appeared to be fully integrated into a single, working system, extending far beyond their immediate social field. The well-laid-out plantations marching up the island's flanks were simply the beginning of a series of grids and tabulations through which numbers and names moved, and out of which money flowed (Lattas 1998, 2006; Scott 1998). Panapompom people found themselves sharing a context and project (Moore 1999, 2004) with colonial administrators and Australian merchants. Panapompom's place in this world of connections was an integral one, and the modifications to the Panapompom landscape reflected this.

What was the significance of the changes in the appearance of Panapompom for Panapompom people? The significance of these changes in what Panapompom looked like is tied up with what Panapompom people speak about as development. Development was very much a central feature of the ways in which Panapompom people – especially, but by no means exclusively, men – speak about the community and what they do as a group of people. I was frequently asked for advice, which I did my best to decline, on how development should be effected on Panapompom. When I probed what development meant to people, I found that a crucial idiom that people would use to gloss the notion was 'a change in the appearance of the place' (*panuwa ana awa ana sensi*).

In the context of development, the 'appearance of the place' (*panuwa ana awa*) was attached to many things. The sorts of buildings that people lived in and used, the sorts of clothes that people wore, how often they were able to light kerosene lamps and other physical features of 'what the place looked like' would often be mentioned. Other aspects of the place's appearance were less tangible, but importantly involved community work: how people worked together to clear paths and maintain village spaces and cemeteries affected how villages looked as a result. Working practices that emphasized simultaneous action and suggested central control of workers affected how Panapompom 'looked'. These are, clearly, the sorts of practices involved in *kominiti*, and which figure the law.

Panapompom people would say that with development their 'standard' would rise. 'Standard' here does not simply contract 'standard of living'. Rather, it repeats a colonial discourse on the 'standard of the people': their qualities, capacities and worth. The notion of 'standard' permeates the colonial patrol reports, both explicitly as 'the standard of the people', and implicitly, as administrators compare and contrast the various linguistic groups in the archipelago. All of this was linked to the paternalistic colonial aim of 'raising the standard' of the people, ultimately, as Australian rule was wound down, to prepare them for independence. Panapompom people know standards through their performance or demonstration of the law. This is the significance of the changing appearance of a place. It demonstrates the quality of that place, and through it the value of the people who live there, relative to the law.

Standards and development are racial concepts, a comparison which operates between people who have different types of skin and geographical origins: natives, who have black skin and come from PNG, and *dimdim*, 'white people' who have white skins and come from most other countries in the world, archetypically Australia. Social and economic outcomes are thought of as promoting development when they cause Panapompom to appear to be more like the 'homes of white people' (*dimdim panuwana*), and Panapompom people to be more like white people. Conversely, outcomes which evoke local custom or blackness are felt to be regressive and are despised as 'primitive'. Given the geography of race and development as an unequal distribution of skins and ways of life, development is thought of as a project that will promote a move to make PNG more like the homes of white people, especially in Australia and America, collapsing geographical and racial differences. This would be a marker of particular values and attributes, especially of an orderly or lawful, affluent, urban-style life.

These attributes in turn are figured in the places people inhabit. If Panapompom's appearance changes in this way, it would index the changed ethical capacity of the people to work and behave as white people. The discourses of law and development are therefore based on the ways in which Panapompom people imagine that white people value them; it is aimed at making Panapompom people into counterparts of white people in terms of colour and of wealth by placing them in the world as visibly equivalent.[23]

The sort of world or space-time that the copra industry allowed Panapompom people to imagine was one in which the product of their work, sponsored by *dimdim* in the administration, was taken in direct exchange for cash and the wherewithal to be developed. Indeed, the organization that produced this cash – the orderly circulation of numbers, paper and money – in itself suggests the visible orderliness that indexes law, and hence development, in the Panapompom political imagination. The dream was that natives could attain the same level of development as white people, exported to them as payment for their copra. White people, and their proxies in the government of the independent state of PNG, were seen openly to assist Panapompom people in their 'whitening' development goals.

The changes that people looked for in the appearance of Panapompom when they spoke of development were clearly very similar to the sorts of changes that the copra industry had brought, and that its decline and collapse had taken away. As such, the *logugui* or aesthetic of the copra economy instantiated not only a place, Panapompom as a location of simultaneous community work, but also people, law-governed, whitened citizens, identified with and within the colonial project, sharing a context – or relational 'spacetime' in Munn's (1986) terms – with white people. Panapompom and Panapompom people were in turn articulated to other, similar places and people by the movements of numbered bags, envelopes and money, which in turn instantiated the aesthetics of the law and their parity with *dimdim*.

## Return to Poiyaa

Poiyaa today is a landscape of deep ambivalence for Panapompom people. On one hand, the strict rows of the plantation, the serried ranks of palms marching into the bush, evoke the orderliness of law and development. On the other, the decay visible in the plantation demonstrates a decline in 'the appearance of the place'. Panapompom no longer looks like the thriving centre of the copra trade that it used to be.

At the root of the plantation's demise is a contest between the island as a community acting 'as one' – in accordance with the law and demonstrating development – and the sectional interests of a particular group, defined in terms of kinship – the people of Pana-ewau and their uncle, Tuitui. The problem of figuring the law in the bodies of workers here is obvious and acute. There are no longer communal, cooperative working parties on the plantation; rather, ownership is claimed and access granted by a specific lineage, people who expect recognition for granting these rights.

This is in many respects a product of the collapse of the global assemblage of the colonial and postcolonial copra economy. Although the Poiyaa dispute was primarily concerned with local political conflicts, the early 1990s was a period of general decline for the copra industry in PNG. This decline was linked to the closure of the Panguna mine on Bougainville in 1989, due to fighting with separatist forces there. Panguna's rich deposits had financed PNG's foreign exchange reserves. The country was rapidly thrown onto the mercy of the IMF and World Bank, and a series of structural adjustment and austerity programmes – both imposed and home grown – followed. State subsidy and protection for copra was wound up. As a result, the law by which Panapompom people worked copra in order to access development has ceased to be effective. That assemblage of material, people, places and flows has become as derelict as the leaking copra shed and the broken-down pier.

Copra has now been replaced as a source of income for Panapompom people by harvesting marine resources, specifically bêche-de-mer. While the bêche-de-mer trade in these waters is old, in its current form the industry is of a piece with the monetarist economic policies that proved to be the downfall of copra. Most notably, state support and efforts to integrate local producers as stakeholders in the industry, so important in the colonial development of the copra economy, have evaporated. The market in bêche-de-mer is regulated to encourage sustainable use, but the relations between grassroots producers, buyers and exporters are not controlled. What regulations exist – primarily limits on export licences – serve mainly to exclude grassroots people from the high-earning sectors of the industry, which are dominated by urban capitalists.

Panapompom men today scour the seas looking for edible sea cucumbers to process into bêche-de-mer, and sell their product to buyers from urban export companies. However, the relationships that constitute this economy are not visible in the way the relationships constituting the copra industry were. Rather, from a Panapompom perspective, they are disordered, truncated, violent and unknown (Rollason 2010). Panapompom divers today express a deep uncertainty about how they can secure development through diving for bêche-de-mer: the law of this work and the standard that is demanded are profoundly unclear.

'There are many of us who live worthlessly' (*Ama ha gewi ha mi-bwaga-bwaga*) was the comment of Bole, a younger man. To live without value in terms of Panapompom notions of work is to live without due regard for standards. That is, to live without regard for others in whose eyes one can be judged. The failure of the copra economy represents one moment in which Panapompom people failed to live up to standards they located in a context they shared with white people and in which they had invested a great deal. The bêche-de-mer industry does not offer the same explicit laws and standards to which people can work. Panapompom people can now think of themselves as worthless in this connection; Bole's comment expresses a deep regret and an uncertainty about the future.

None of this, of course, is to say that Panapompom has ceased to be a place, or to argue that Panapompom people are not continuing to negotiate powerful identifications within and against the world they inhabit. My argument is that to understand Panapompom as a place – a place in some ways dominated by the melancholic palms of Poiyaa – and to understand who Panapompom people are and where they are going, we need to understand Panapompom's location within shifting assemblages of material, people and relationships. The making of Panapompom as a place and the constitution of Panapompom people as subjects has to be understood through this genealogy of movement and historical change.

## Notes

1. A highly mobile population makes definitive estimates problematic. These estimates are based on the local church records.
2. General ethnographic details for Panapompom and the region are provided in Berde (1974), Battaglia (1990) and Rollason (2008a, 2008b, 2008c).
3. See Foale (2005) for a good overview.
4. See Gregory (1979), who offers an overview of the industry.
5. In this regard, my argument here is similar to others advanced by the likes of Knauft (2002a, 2002b) and Robbins (1998a, 1998b, 2005), drawing on Sahlins (2005).
6. It is important to recognize that on Panapompom it is men who dominate talk about development. Women do speak about these issues, but are much more likely to frame their ideas in terms of religion. In public contexts, including in church, it is men's views which are most often expressed. Women speak on these issues much more rarely.
7. Munn's concern is related to the work of Hau'ofa (1994) and others who see the Pacific less in terms of emplacement and fixity than motion and connection.
8. For general accounts, see Thune (1989) and Battaglia (1990); for further afield in Papua New Guinea, see Weiner (1991), Hirsch (2001a, 2001b), Leach (2003) and Bashkow (2006); for accounts from the Pacific region at large, see Hviding (1996), Toren (1999), Rumsey and Weiner (2001) and Scott (2007).

9.  Battaglia (1990) notes that such points of connection and turning are highly significant on neighbouring Sabarl, where they are referred to as 'elbows'. She is especially concerned with the productive return of gifts and people towards their origins and movements. These are figured in local wealth items: the two halves of a shell necklace (*bag*) and the L-shaped handle of a greenstone axe (*giam*).
10. Local informants are generally only slightly interested in chronology; this date is approximate, but was independently volunteered by a number of informants.
11. Misima No. 4 (1955/56). B.N. Teague. 'Deboyne and Reynard Census Division: 18 June 1956–25 June 1956'. The colonial patrol reports I refer to here are housed in the National Archives of PNG. I consulted the microfiche copy held at the Don Tuzin Archive at the University of California, San Diego. The reports are referenced by patrol station (here Misima) and their place within the sequence of patrolling in a given government year (hence Misima No. 4). The references give the government year (here 1955/56), the patrolling officer and a summary description of the movements of the patrol. These details correspond to those found on the reports' cover and index sheets as they were originally archived.
12. White people of the colonial era are always known as 'Mr'.
13. Misima No. 2 (1944/45). F.I. Middleton. 'Rossel, Sudest, Calvados: 26 August 1944–16 September 1944'.
14. Misima No. 1 (1946/47). J.S. MacLeod. 'Panapompom, Panaeati, Brooker, Misima: 16 May 1946–27 May 1946'.
15. Misima No. 4 (1955/56).
16. Misima No. 4 (1952/53). F.V. Esdale. 'Paneati, Panapompom: 14 May 1953–29 May 1953'.
17. Misima No. 8 (1960/61). R.A. Deverell. 'Calvados, Misima: 24 February 1961–10 March 1961'.
18. There are indications that this situation is changing. A lawsuit claiming almost all of Panapompom for a Panaeati family was pending at the time I left the field.
19. These two aspects of memory – social and technical obligations – are intertwined. Most work is a social affair, requiring the support of kin, affines and friends. As such the proper technique for clearing a garden or building a house is indistinguishable from the obligations involved in persuading workers to assist. Where memory in either sense fails, major works are impossible.
20. Misima No. 2. (1946–47). W.J. Johnston. 'All Misima Villages: 16 May 1946–[end date not given]'. This was true even on islands like Panapompom, where in fact such paths and houses were rarely used by patrols arriving by boat.
21. Misima No. 3 (1954/55). J.S. MacLeod. 'Calvados and Deboyne Sub-Divisions, Selections Misima and Sudest Islands: 4 April 1955–6 April 1955, 12 April 1955–4 May 1955'.

22. Misima No. 2 (1955/56). B.N. Teague. 'Part Misima (South and West): 6 March 1956–20 March 1956', comments.
23. As such, it is a type of ethical work, as highlighted by Laidlaw (2002) as an application of Foucault's notion of 'the care of the self' (Foucault 1994a, 1994b)

## References

Althusser, L. 2008. *On Ideology*. London: Verso.

Bashkow, I. 2006. *The Meaning of Whitemen: Race and Modernity in the Orokaiva Cultural World*. Chicago: University of Chicago Press.

Battaglia, D. 1990. *On the Bones of the Serpent: Person, Memory, and Mortality in Sabarl Island Society*. Chicago: University of Chicago Press.

———— 1992. 'The Body in the Gift: Memory and Forgetting in Sabarl Mortuary Exchange', *American Ethnologist* 19(1): 3–18.

Baumann, Z. 2001. 'Identity in the Globalising World', *Social Anthropology* 9(2): 121–29.

Berde, S. 1974. *Melanesians as Methodists: Economy and Marriage on a Papua and New Guinea Island*. Pennsylvania: University of Pennsylvania.

———— 1976. 'Political Education in the Rural Sector: A Comparison of Two Papua New Guinea Island Communities', *Journal of the Polynesian Society* 85(1): 87–98.

———— 1979. 'Impact of Christianity on a Melanesian Economy', *Research in Economic Anthropology* 2: 169–87.

Carrier, J.G. (ed.). 1992. *History and Tradition in Melanesian Anthropology*. Berkeley: University of California Press.

Carrier, J.G., and A.H. Carrier. 1989. *Wage, Trade, and Exchange in Melanesia: A Manus Society in the Modern State*. Berkeley: University of California Press.

CoA. 1948. 'Territory of Papua: Annual Report 1947/48'. Canberra: Australian Government Publishing Service, Commonwealth of Australia.

———— 1949. 'Territory of Papua: Annual Report 1948/49'. Canberra: Australian Government Publishing Service, Commonwealth of Australia.

———— 1952. 'Territory of Papua and New Guinea: Annual Report 1951/52'. Canberra: Australian Government Publishing Service, Commonwealth of Australia.

———— 1954. 'Territory of Papua: Annual Report 1953/54'. Canberra: Australian Government Publishing Service, Commonwealth of Australia.

———— 1956. 'Territory of Papua: Annual Report 1955/56'. Canberra: Australian Government Publishing Service, Commonwealth of Australia.

Collier, S., and A. Ong. 2005. 'Global Assemblages, Anthropological Problems', in J. Collier and A. Ong (eds), *Global Assemblages: Technology, Politics and Ethics as Anthropological Problems*. Malden, MA: Blackwell, pp.3–21.

Connell, J. 1997. *Papua New Guinea: The Struggle for Development*. London: Routledge.
Crook, T. 2007. *Exchanging Skin: Anthropological Knowledge, Secrecy and Bolivip, Papua New Guinea*. Oxford: Oxford University Press.
Foale, S. 2005. *Sharks, Sea Slugs and Skirmishes: Managing Marine and Agricultural Resources on Small, Overpopulated Islands in Milne Bay, P.N.G.* Canberra: Australian National University.
Foster, R.J. 2002. *Materializing the Nation: Commodities, Consumption, and Media in Papua New Guinea*. Bloomington: Indiana University Press.
———— 2008. 'Commodities, Brands, Love and Kula: Comparative Notes on Value Creation in Honour of Nancy Munn', *Anthropological Theory* 8(1): 9–25.
Foucault, M. 1994a. 'Preface to *The History of Sexuality*, Vol. 2', in P. Rabinow (ed.), *Ethics, Subjectivity and Truth: The Essential Works of Michel Foucault*, Vol. 1. London: Allen Lane, pp.333–39.
———— 1994b. 'Sexuality and Solitude', in P. Rabinow (ed.), *Ethics, Subjectivity and Truth: The Essential Works of Michel Foucault*, Vol. 1. London: Allen Lane, pp.175–84.
Gregory, C.A. 1979. 'The Emergence of Commodity Production in Papua New Guinea', *Journal of Contemporary Asia* 9(4): 389–409.
———— 1982. *Gifts and Commodities*. London: Academic Press.
Hau'ofa, E. 1994. 'Our Sea of Islands', *Contemporary Pacific* 6(1): 148–61.
Hirsch, E. 2001a. 'Making Up People in Papua', *Journal of the Royal Anthropological Institute* 7(2): 241–56.
———— 2001b. 'New Boundaries of Influence in Highland Papua: Culture, Mining and Ritual Conversions', *Oceania* 71(4): 298–312.
Hviding, E. 1996. *Guardians of Marovo Lagoon: Practice, Place, and Politics in Maritime Melanesia*. Honolulu: University of Hawai'i Press.
Jackman, H.H. 1988. *Copra Marketing and Price Stabilization in Papua New Guinea: A History to 1975*. Canberra: Australian National University.
Josephides, L. 2008. *Melanesian Odysseys: Negotiating the Self, Narrative and Modernity*. New York: Berghahn.
Knauft, B.M. 2002a. *Exchanging the Past: A Rainforest World of Before and After*. Chicago: University of Chicago Press.
———— 2002b. 'Trials of the Oxymodern: Public Practice at Nomad Station', in B.M. Knauft (ed.), *Critically Modern: Alternatives, Alterities, Anthropologies*. Bloomington: Indiana University Press, pp.105–43.
Kuehling, S. 2006. *Dobu: Ethics of Exchange on a Massim Island*. Honolulu: University of Hawai'i Press.
Laidlaw, J. 2002. 'For an Anthropology of Ethics and Freedom', *Journal of the Royal Anthropological Institute* 8(2): 311–32.
Lattas, A. 1998. *Cultures of Secrecy: Reinventing Race in Bush Kaliai Cargo Cults*. Madison: University of Wisconsin Press.

――― 2006. 'The Utopian Promise of Government', *Journal of the Royal Anthropological Institute* 12(1): 129–50.

Leach, J. 2003. *Creative Land: Place and Procreation on the Rai Coast of Papua New Guinea*. New York: Berghahn.

――― 2006. '"Team Spirit": The Pervasive Influence of Place-generation in "Community Building" Activities along the Rai Coast of Papua New Guinea', *Journal of Material Culture* 11(1/2): 87–103.

Leach, J.W., and E.R. Leach (eds). 1983. *The Kula: New Perspectives on Massim Exchange*. Cambridge: Cambridge University Press.

Malinowski, B. 1922. *Argonauts of the Western Pacific: An Account of Native Enterprise and Adventure in the Archipelagos of Melanesian New Guinea*. London: Routledge.

Meggitt, M.J. 1977. *Blood Is Their Argument: Warfare among the Mae Enga Tribesmen of the New Guinea Highlands*. Palo Alto, CA: Mayfield.

Merlan, F., and A. Rumsey. 1991. *Ku Waru: Language and Segmentary Politics in the Western Nebilyer Valley, Papua New Guinea*. Cambridge: Cambridge University Press.

Miller, D. 1987. *Material Culture and Mass Consumption*. Oxford: Blackwell.

Moore, H.L. 1999. 'Whatever Happened to Women and Men? Gender and Other Crises in Anthropology', in H.L. Moore (ed.), *Anthropological Theory Today*. Cambridge: Polity Press, pp.151–71.

――― 2004. 'Global Anxieties: Concept Metaphors and Pre-theoretical Commitments in Anthropology', *Anthropological Theory* 4(1): 71–88.

Mosko, M.S. 2002. 'Totem and Transaction: The Objectification of Tradition among the North Mekeo', *Oceania* 73(2): 89–110.

Munn, N.D. 1973. *Walbiri Iconography: Graphic Representation and Cultural Symbolism in a Central Australian Society*. Ithaca, NY: Cornell University Press.

――― 1983. 'Gawan Kula: Spatiotemporal Control and the Symbolism of Influence', in E.R. Leach and J.W. Leach (eds), *The Kula: New Perspectives on Massim Exchange*. Cambridge: Cambridge University Press, pp.277–308.

――― 1986. *The Fame of Gawa: A Symbolic Study of Value Transformation in a Massim (Papua New Guinea) Society*. Cambridge: Cambridge University Press.

PNG. 1995. 'Constitution of the Independent State of Papua New Guinea'. Port Moresby: Papua New Guinea Government Press.

Robbins, J. 1998a. 'Becoming Sinners: Christianity and Desire among the Urapmin of Papua New Guinea', *Ethnology* 37(4): 299–317.

――― 1998b. 'On Reading "World News": Apocalyptic Narrative, Negative Nationalism and Transnational Christianity in a Papua New Guinean Society', *Social Analysis* 42(2): 103–30.

――― 2005. 'Humiliation and Transformation: Marshall Sahlins and the Study of Cultural Change in Melanesia', in H. Wardlow and J. Robbins (eds), *The Making of Global and Local Modernities in Melanesia: Humiliation, Transformation and the Nature of Cultural Change*. Aldershot: Ashgate, pp.3–22.

———— 2007. 'Continuity Thinking and the Problem of Christian Culture', *Current Anthropology* 48(1): 5–38.

Rollason, W.H. 2008a. 'Black Skin, White Yacht: Negotiating Race Opposition in Panapompom Tourist Encounters', *Tourism, Culture and Communication* 8(2): 109–22.

———— 2008b. 'Counterparts: Clothing, Value and the Sites of Otherness in Panapompom Ethnographic Encounters', *Anthropological Forum* 18(1): 17–35.

———— 2008c. 'Football and Postcolonial Subjectivity, Panapompom, Papua New Guinea', Ph.D. diss. Manchester: University of Manchester.

———— 2010. 'Working out Abjection in the Panapompom Bêche-de-mer Fishery: Race, Economic Change and the Future in Papua New Guinea', *Australian Journal of Anthropology* 21(2): 149–70.

Rumsey, A., and J. Weiner (eds). 2001. *Emplaced Myth: Space, Narrative, and Knowledge in Aboriginal Australia and Papua New Guinea*. Honolulu: University of Hawai'i Press.

Sahlins, M. 2005. 'The Economics of Develop-man in the Pacific', in J. Robbins and H. Wardlow (eds), *The Making of Global and Local Modernities in Melanesia: Humiliation, Transformation and the Nature of Cultural Change*. Aldershot: Ashgate, pp.23–42.

Scott, J.C. 1998. *Seeing Like a State: How Certain Schemes to Improve the Human Condition Have Failed*. New Haven: Yale University Press.

Scott, M.W. 2007. 'Neither "New Melanesian History" nor "New Melanesian Ethnography": Recovering Emplaced Matrilineages in South-east Solomon Islands', *Oceania* 77(3): 337–54.

Strathern, A. 1971. *The Rope of Moka: Big-men and Ceremonial Exchange in Mount Hagen, New Guinea*. Cambridge: Cambridge University Press.

———— 1972. *One Father, One Blood: Descent and Group Structure among the Melpa People*. London: Tavistock.

Strathern, M. 1985. 'Discovering "Social Control"', *Journal of Law and Society* 12(2): 111–34.

———— 1995. *The Relation: Issues in Complexity and Scale*. Cambridge: Prickly Pear Press.

Thune, C. 1989. 'Death and Matrilineal Reincorporation on Normanby Island', in F.H. Damon and R. Wagner (eds), *Death Rituals and Life in the Societies of the Kula Ring*. DeKalb: Northern Illinois University Press, pp.153–68.

Toren, C. 1999. *Mind, Materiality, and History: Explorations in Fijian Ethnography*. London: Routledge.

Tsing, A. 2000. 'The Global Situation', *Cultural Anthropology* 15(3): 327–60.

Weiner, J.F. 1991. *The Empty Place: Poetry, Space and Being among the Foi of Papua New Guinea*. Bloomington: University of Indiana Press.

# 4

# Invisible Villages in the City

## Niuean Constructions of Place and Identity in Auckland

◆●◆

### Hilke Thode-Arora

I can only stay in New Zealand for one week, then I want to go home. If you go to New Zealand, the clock is always your boss. Here, doing handicraft, I am my own boss.
—Tuleimanogi Puletama Tupuolamoui, 2003

Do you know that song 'Rivers of Babylon' by Boney M? That line 'How can we sing the Lord's song in a strange land?' That is exactly how we felt here in New Zealand: How can we *weave* in a strange land?
—Matafetu Smith, 2003

The above quotations from interviews with women from the Polynesian island of Niue evoke two associations connected with the city of Auckland in New Zealand: a place where one is controlled by events and one cannot be autonomous regarding one's time and work, and even a place which bears all the baleful connotations, including cultural uprooting and powerlessness, of biblical Babylon and the Babylonian captivity – a potent image when used by a speaker who, like all middle-aged and elder Niuean women, knows her Bible. These quotations serve as examples of the variety of ways in which Niueans living (temporarily and permanently) in Auckland construct place and identity in the city, the subject that forms the focus of this chapter, based on eighteen months of fieldwork among the Niuean community in Auckland, and on Niue between 2002 and 2005.

## Auckland

Pre-European Māori settlements in the area of today's Auckland were the origin of what would develop into the country's biggest city in the twentieth century. Made New Zealand's capital (which it is no longer) by the British in 1840, Auckland increasingly extended southward from its natural harbours in the north over the next 165 years, becoming a city with a high degree of urban sprawl. Covering about 6,000 square kilometres and home to more than 1.3 million inhabitants – more than a third of New Zealand's total population – Auckland is the country's largest and most cosmopolitan city. Until the 1950s, New Zealand's policy favoured Anglo-Saxon immigration, although there had been Dalmatian, Chinese and Continental European entrants since the 1870s. Shortage of labour led to a liberalization of immigration laws between 1950 and 1975, especially as far as 'racial' boundaries were concerned, bringing in more and more immigrants from South-East and East Asia, Central and Southern Europe, and from Polynesia.

Scholars of urban anthropology have shown that the physical and visual appearance of a city, its public space with buildings, monuments, street names and the like, as well as media coverage in newspapers, radio and TV programmes, or tourist brochures, can be taken as representations in which dominant ideologies are reflected. Consequently, these appearances and media coverage allow assumptions on social constellations of power, for example hierarchies, some groups' power of interpretation, and on the conscious or unconscious in- or exclusion of certain parts of the population (see e.g. Donald 1992; Zukin 1995, 1996; Dürr 2000; Brumann 2004). Examining Auckland in this regard, older areas of the city in particular reveal New Zealand's links to Great Britain and Pākehā/palagi descendants: streets are called Queen Street, King Edward Street, Symonds Street, Sandringham Road, for example; urban districts have names like Morningside, Henderson, Ponsonby, St Luke – most of them referring to persons from or events in colonial British and New Zealand history.[1] Among Aucklanders and non-Aucklanders, the city has the reputation of being the commercial centre of the country, manifest in the Central Business District with its new and expensive high-rise buildings, a fast-paced, hectic metropolis with traffic chaos and rowdy drivers, as well as with a high crime rate.[2]

On the other hand, a number of smaller streets, outer districts and especially younger urban development areas, mostly (though not exclusively) in the south, bear Māori names: Te Atatu, Papatoetoe, Otahuhu, Manukau, Otara,[3] reflecting not only the historical development of the city, but also New Zealand's new official policy and self-image. Since the Treaty of Waitangi Act of 1975, and with the Māori Language Act of 1988, New Zealand has started a process of recognizing her dual Māori and Pākehā/palagi heritage. This is as visible in Auckland as it is in other cities: public buildings and letterheads are labelled in English and Māori; a number of institutions, for example educational centres and universities, have their own Māori *marae*; there is now a Māori TV channel; the curriculum of pre-schools and schools must encompass elements of Māori culture and language; and New Zealand's national anthem is in both languages.

Pacific Islanders make up about 14 per cent of the population of Auckland Region, while the Māori comprise about 11 per cent.[4] Niueans make up 8 per cent of all resident Pacific Islanders in New Zealand, and probably about the same percentage of Auckland Region's population.[5] Pacific Islanders are part of official discourse about Auckland, but not in the same way as Māori are. It is mentioned with pride that Auckland is the city with the largest Polynesian population in the world.[6] At Auckland's airport, apart from a carved Māori gate which every arriving passenger passes through, a large-screen film in the entrance hall shows Pacific Islanders of different origins performing dance in an infinite loop. Once a week, a TV programme called *Tagata Pasifika* brings news and features on people of Polynesian origin in New Zealand and on the islands. Inaugurated in 2004, the Fale Pasifika, an impressive building modelled on a Sāmoan house, stands opposite Auckland University's Faculty of Arts, serving as an official multi-purpose hall and used for many functions involving Pacific Islanders.[7] The annual open-air events of the Pasifika Festival and the Polyfest, with their music and dance performances, food and handicraft stalls, draw millions of visitors (Moyle 2002: 104–5; Taouma 2002: 136–37).

As the few examples given above highlight,[8] people from the Pacific are certainly part of official representations of contemporary Auckland, but the discourse concerning relations between Pākehā/palagi and Māori is the dominant one, despite the fact that Pacific Islanders make up a larger part of the city's population.

## Niue and the Niueans

Niue is a small, central Polynesian island state with an area of only 260 square kilometres. Annexed in 1901 by New Zealand, Niue became independent in 1974, but chose the status of being in free association with New Zealand. As a consequence, every Niuean has the option of New Zealand citizenship.

Niuean soils are riddled with limestone and partly exhausted by slash-and-burn agriculture, as well as ill-advised agricultural programmes of the past. The island is without surface fresh water and comparatively poor in natural resources; consequently, toiling in the plantations is hard work, although the majority of the population lives from the land. Every few years, cyclones represent additional hazards. Jobs in the administrative, tourist and education sectors are scarce. Since the mid nineteenth century, labour migration has been part of most men's life histories, and from the 1950s emigration has gained momentum (see Terry and Murray 2004). Worldwide, there are about 24,000 Niueans; however, only about 1,200 live on the island. Apart from small communities in Australia and the United States, the overwhelming majority of Niueans have settled in New Zealand, about 80 per cent alone in the Auckland region (SNZ 2007).

There are some conspicuous characteristics of present-day Niuean culture and social structure.[9] First, as the demographic situation shows, this is a community which, in social practice though not necessarily in the ideals adhered to in actors' discourses and narratives, is overwhelmingly urban. Second, it is a truly translocal community, with frequent visits, interactions and transactions made between Niueans living in New Zealand and on Niue.[10] Many of today's Niueans in fact spend different phases of their lives, encompassing several years, alternating between New Zealand and Niue, as well as sometimes Australia and other places (cf. Hauʻofa 1994). Third, only about 30 per cent of all Niueans worldwide are able to speak the Niuean language – about the same percentage of Māori who speak the Māori language. Significantly, as the census data show, the island-born Niueans – that is, the older generation – contains a much higher proportion of Niuean speakers, while young, New Zealand-born people of Niuean origin are not as prone to mastering the language of their forefathers. Fourth, the most striking part of Niuean society is a person's strong ties to and solidarity with their village of birth and/or residence in Niue. Apart from kinship, most elements of the social structure on Niue are organized by village; village identity is in many respects more important than identity as a Niuean. As a consequence, there is a strong tie of loyalty to one's village of origin and/or village of postnuptial residence. Fifth, in contrast to other Polynesian societies, even in pre-European times, Niuean society has never had an inheritable or stable institutionalized hierarchical structure: there has never been anything like nobility, inheritable chiefly rank or *matai*, the ranked Sāmoan titles (cf. Ryan 1977). Although powerful warriors in pre-European times could gather followers and thus exercise power, and although in the post-mission era pastors enjoy a lot of respect and have been very influential in the social sphere, respect and social standing among one's fellow Niueans have to be earned by using one's material and social resources to the good of other Niueans. Only then will a person be able to gather supporters and followers around themselves; but this leadership is not eternal and does not go unchallenged. There is a deep mistrust among many Niueans towards the idea that one of them should be of superior rank or have privileges merely by holding a political office in the administration or even in the Church.

## Theoretical Considerations

This sketch of some social and cultural patterns among the Niuean community is the setting for what I wish to explore. Given that the overwhelming majority of Niueans live in New Zealand and not on the island or in their village of origin, and also given that most of them do not speak Niuean, how do Niueans living in New Zealand constitute themselves as an ethnic group in a society dominated by Pākehā/palagi, and what role do places on Niue and in Auckland play in this process?

A number of scholars, having done fieldwork in places as different as Amazonia, Roti, Fiji, Australia, Papua New Guinea and East Anglia, have pointed out that identities, space and time, manufactured through social practice and narration, are dimensions of the same social process (see Gow 1995; Morphy 1995; Toren 1995; Casey 1996; Frake 1996; Kahn 1996; Fox 1997). Drawing on some of the issues highlighted in this work, I would argue that space on Niue is created through the narratives older people relate to younger ones, which are filled with details of kin and place, often depending on the simultaneous presence of a speaker and hearer in a place where the traces of ancestors' or spirits' movements and agency can be pointed out. In Niue, land rights and kinship create a 'sociocentric mapping' (Morphy 1995: 199) affecting where one can go and what one can do in particular places, whether they are potentially dangerous or safe. As Fox puts it, 'a landscape of places forms a complex structure of social memory' (Fox 1997: 7).

However, if knowledge of a 'landscape' – understood here as a process (see Hirsch 1995: 22) – comes 'partly through moving through it', and land, with all its Niuean connotations of local ancestors and spirits, is an aspect of kinship (cf. Gow 1995: 47), how can Niueans in New Zealand relate to Niuean and New Zealand places? One aspect of my fieldwork focused on the place-making and spatial self-positioning of Niueans in Auckland, especially that of Niuean women.[11] Another important focus, closely connected with the first, was that of ethnic identity or identification. This is a central concern for many Niueans as the overwhelming majority lives in New Zealand, and only a third still speak the Niuean language.[12]

Let me postulate two basic assumptions. First, the symbolic order of a place – or in this context, a city – is construed and interpreted quite differently by different actors. Second, as a consequence, actors have individual 'mental maps' which are formed through interactions and concepts as well as spatial manifestations. Keeping this in mind, to structure my fieldwork data I used the insights of Lefebvre (1991) and Harvey (1989), who divide spatiality into three dimensions.[13] First, space as experience or spatial practice: this includes settlement structure, the physical use or forming of space. Second, space as perception: this encompasses representations of space, its cognitive and symbolic 'control' and 'handling'. Third, space as imagination: this means as vessel or bearer of socio-cultural ideas or as a symbol for normative structures – or, to cite Feld and Basso, I tried 'to describe and interpret some of the ways in which' Niueans 'encounter places, perceive them, and invest them with significance' (Feld and Basso 1996: 8).

The methods applied in exploring these three dimensions of space and their relationship with Niuean ethnic identifications were biographical interviews, participant observation and statistical analysis using data drawn from Auckland Region and New Zealand. The research focused on egocentric mappings, Niuean narratives relating to place and to whether there are 'Niuean places' (or 'non-places') in Auckland. Clifford asks: 'How do diaspora discourses represent experiences of displacement, of constructing homes away from home? What experiences do they reject, replace or marginalize?' (Clifford 1997: 244). Important actors in formulating or even manipulating meaning in this context turned out to be Church officials, elders and especially elder women.

## Space as Experience and Spatial Practice

As for settlement structure, there are no Niuean suburbs, quarters or blocks. Due to economic reasons, most Niueans have applied for subsidized housing, and the New Zealand authorities take great care in mixing ethnic groups in order not to create ethnic ghettos. Reflecting the historical development of Auckland over the last few decades,[14] there is a certain concentration of Niueans, along with other Pacific Islanders and Asian immigrants, in the city's southern suburbs, but there are substantial numbers of Niueans living in the central and western parts of the city as well (SNZ 2007). Efforts of early Niuean migrants to establish the chain migration of co-villagers to the same suburbs in Auckland failed in the long run.

Owing to this residential dispersal, central meeting and organization points have become of great importance. Starting in the 1950s, the earliest of these have been churches, especially the Pacific Islander Church (PIC) in a small street off Auckland's Karangahape Road near the Central Business District. Similarly, in other suburbs there are a number of churches of different denominations offering Niuean-language services. All these churches are shared with other ethnic groups, although they have a time slot for the Niuean-language service. In contrast to more hierarchically organized ethnic communities, for example Tongans and Sāmoans, the dream of a Niuean-owned church building used only by Niueans has yet to be fulfilled, although some people are working towards that aim. Most Niueans belong to the LMS-based Ekalesia Niue and to the Church of the Latter-Day Saints (Mormons), but, irrespective of their denomination, churches regularly gather substantial numbers of the Niuean migrant community for services and life-cycle events. As one interviewee put it:

> We want to live in family units and village units in Auckland or New Zealand, but it's very hard to do because you have to go and apply for a state house, and the house that you are given, you got to take it. You don't have any say. Whether you like it or not. [...] And that is another thing, that we don't always see our families here because we are scattered in Auckland. And the only best place for us, time for us to go and see each other, is during funerals, during weddings, hair cuttings,[15] or any [...] special occasions. (Lino Nelisi, woman, aged 52)

During the last thirty years, among middle-aged and older women, other meeting and organization points have been created in the form of weaving or women's groups.[16] A typical female Niuean migrant biography, as established in my interviews, included decades of very busy years in the New Zealand labour market just after arrival in the 1950s to 1970s, aggravated by the double bond of family: three jobs per day, often from early morning, five or six o'clock, till late at night, and at the same time caring for families with up to nine children. This left hardly any time for meaningful cultural activities – perhaps apart from church labour – like weaving. Accordingly, many women actively tried to embrace the new life in an industrial society and to leave certain Niuean ways behind. Matafetu Smith, the founder of the first Niuean weaving group in Auckland recalls:

> Some would laugh and say, 'That's what we do back home, we don't weave in New Zealand'. They referred to when you dampen your finger to handle the pandanus leaf. They would say, 'We don't lick fingers and pull pandanus in New Zealand, we knit here in New Zealand'. Some who used to say that are now some of the top weavers today. (Quoted in Pereira 2002: 84)

At the same time, weaving was painfully missed in those years by a great number of women. Only when the majority of them reached their late fifties in the early 1980s, when their active participation in the labour market came to an end and their children were grown, did they have enough leisure time to restart this activity. This was difficult, however, as pandanus and coconut, the plants that provide the most important raw materials for weaving in Niue, do not prosper in New Zealand's moderate climate, and pandanus grown and prepared on other Pacific islands, which is sometimes available in Auckland, does not meet the women's high quality standards. It was precisely at this time that, triggered by the New Zealand government's new policy of more support for Māori as the *tangata whenua* ('people of the land') and, to a certain degree, Pacific Islanders, a workshop of Māori and Pacific weavers was set up. The Māori women showed the Pacific weavers the technical and ritual use of New Zealand flax, which has been the traditional Māori weaving material for centuries, and they authorized the Pacific women to make use of this knowledge. This kick-started a vibrant renaissance of Pacific Islanders' weaving in Auckland and in New Zealand; and soon the process of inventing, experimenting with and borrowing patterns and types of woven items spread all over New Zealand and even back to the Pacific islands, where old and new inputs from pandanus and coconut weaving have occurred. For the Niuean women, as well as for many other Pacific island women, this boosted a development which has had social and spatial implications as well. In every Auckland suburb with a Niuean population, weaving groups came into existence, facilitated by a funding system for socio-cultural groups by city councils and cultural organizations.

As Pereira (2002: 88) has pointed out, the term 'weaving group' is a misnomer. Most of the weaving groups are also self-help groups for social or medical problems, for example running Niuean-language pre-schools, older-people support groups, diabetes and asthma groups.[17] Some groups have organized emergency housing for newcomers, others help their members by running a savings club, accumulating surplus money for Christmas, or by supporting them in filling in complicated administrative forms. One day per week is reserved for weaving, however. Weaving groups never meet at members' houses, but always in public halls like church or community centres. As with the churches, these centres are shared with other ethnic groups, and as with a church, the initiative to found an exclusively Niuean cultural centre has been unsuccessful till now.

At Auckland's large Pasifika Festival, a huge annual open-air festival of Pacific island groups in a park, drawing several thousands of visitors over two to four days (see Moyle 2002: 105), every Pacific Islander group is allocated a certain area called a 'village' (Sāmoan village, Niuean village, etc.). Niuean women – as with the weaving groups, it is women who basically run the activities for this festival – are not only found in the Niuean 'village', however, but have their stalls all over the park. This is partly due to the highly contested space and limited number of stalls in the Niuean 'village'. However, a number of women or groups would like to set themselves apart due to village and group rivalries. Some Auckland parks are used for Niuean sport events in summer, such as inter-village cricket games, *tika* throwing, touch or netball. These are usually male or joint male and female activities.

Public space, like a park, church or community hall, is thus occupied by Niueans in a rather temporary and unobtrusive way. As Niuean ethnic identification is signalled only very subtly by dress (or rather accessory) codes only known to the adept – such as certain kinds of hat or necklace accompanying European dress – the use of public space by Niueans is often not even apparent to other users from different ethnic groups, and Pākehā/palagi are especially prone to classify Niueans unspecifically as 'Polynesians'.

A non-Niuean place which at first sight could be perceived as a Niuean one, as it is closely linked with Niuean skill and art, is the Kermadec Brasserie in Auckland's Viaduct Harbour. Its interior is meant to mimic the aesthetics of a Pacific canoe: large wooden poles, reminiscent of masts, carry 'sails' of huge, finely woven flax mats made by Niuean expert weavers, and made of canvases painted by John Pule, an artist of Niuean origin who borrowed heavily from Niuean *tapa* (bark cloth) motifs in that phase of his oeuvre. Still, and in contrast to the Fale Pasifika – which also incorporates Polynesian elements into its architecture and design, but hosts many Pacific functions – the Kermadec Brasserie is not a Niuean place as it lacks Niuean spatial practice: Niuean customers usually do not frequent this restaurant. As in most public spaces where Niueans are involved, the majority of guests are probably not even aware that the impressive ceiling decoration has been made by Niueans.

## Space as Perception

> How are you going to make your living on Niue? What are you going to eat? Can you top taro with taro? Better a modest living in New Zealand than only taro in Niue. I tell everyone to come here to New Zealand.
> —Lagi Viliko, 2003

A number of older Niuean interviewees described how they perceived Auckland as a very dangerous city when they first came from Niue. There were repeated narratives of how, as newcomers, they had shut themselves in and did not open the door, or did not dare to leave the house alone in the beginning. Interestingly, this is in striking contrast to newer narratives about Sydney, a city which objectively seems to be much more dangerous than Auckland, and where an emerging Niuean community is coming into existence. Sydney is idealized as a place full of chances and beauty. These narratives might reflect different generations of (potential) immigrants: most young people of Niuean origin are either living in New Zealand and see the Australian metropolis as a more fast-paced and exciting place, or, when living on Niue, they are quite comfortably familiar with New Zealand from visits. The broadcasting of Australian soap operas in Niue is probably responsible for creating an idealized picture. New Zealand was where the older immigrant generations first lived away from the island, however, and they must have experienced the big city of Auckland as quite frightening.

Apart from these first impressions, Auckland is seen as a city with good opportunities to earn money and lead a life of abundance, even luxury, and a place that is full of entertainment options. Connected with this is a perception of Auckland as a place with high potential for education, and thus for upward socio-economic mobility. The overwhelming majority of interviewees stressed the potential of a better education for their children as their main reason for migration. Young people, but also the generation over sixty, are enrolled in university and education programmes to a large degree, and graduate as social workers, nurses, pre-school teachers and lay preachers, to name just the most frequently chosen professions, and they also enter many other fields and gain other qualifications.

Correspondingly, a number of places frequented by Niueans are assigned representations linked with economic and educational activities. This is obvious, of course, with buildings which house educational institutions used by Niueans, and factories, offices and the like where Niueans work. Furthermore, many women are weavers and have regular stalls at weekend markets or at annual cultural festivals, even in those suburbs where few Niueans live. Till about thirty years ago, weavers who wanted to cut New Zealand flax had to ask the permission of the Māori *iwi* ('tribe') on whose land the flax grew. Today, flax weaving among Pacific Islanders has grown to such a degree that Auckland's city council gives out written permissions for cutting flax which have to be carried and shown to city officials controlling the parks. On Niue, weavers have their own secret methods and preferences for certain kinds of pandanus growing in special places; similarly, in Auckland each woman prefers certain varieties of flax grown at selected places for her own weaving. In contrast to corresponding locations on Niue, these places in Auckland are not perceived as mythically charged, but seen merely pragmatically.

Quite a number of Niuean weavers declared their aim of making NZ$1,000 profit during the annual Pasifika Festival. But this does not mean necessarily that the articles, materials and colours of weaving or the set-up of the Niuean 'village' are made to suit Pākehā/palagi tastes. Weavers who enjoy working with bright colours and plastic strands instead of ecru and organically coloured pandanus do not change their style for the festival. Similarly, Niuean music, dance and cultural performances are usually for a Niuean target group: there are no deliberate attempts to draw a Pākehā/palagi audience, for example by having young girls dancing and thus enforcing old stereotypes of beautiful, young Polynesian dancers (cf. Taouma 2002: 134). Old women do the dancing and fashion shows, and the presenter announces the programme and gives their comments in Niuean: the Niueans of the 'village' seem to celebrate themselves.

As the example of the Niuean 'village' at the Pasifika Festival shows, economically relevant locations can be places of fun and entertainment at the same time. In a similar way, weaving groups and markets, where one can meet compatriots acting in the same cultural reference system, also have a social apart from their economic function. The same holds true for the casino in Auckland's Sky Tower, which is frequented by many Polynesians. The chance of gains from playing the slot machines, the fun of gambling and a shared visit to one of the Sky Tower's restaurants catering to Polynesian tastes, combining financial gains with pleasure, is part of a number of autobiographical narratives, and makes the Sky Tower one of the Niuean places in Auckland, albeit again shared with other ethnic groups. In the male sphere of life, there are comparable places like pubs, and TABs where horse betting is done.

Diaspora in Auckland, with its educational and economic opportunities, comes with a price, however. Apart from initial and sometimes long-lasting feelings of the loss of culture and personal autonomy, as verbalized in quotations at the start of this chapter, migrants' 'belonging' to Niue, which some of them refer to as 'back home' even after thirty-five years of living in New Zealand, is contested by those who have stayed on or returned to the island. A common discourse among some Niuean politicians (and quite a number of Niueans on the island, even if they have spent years in New Zealand, and might do so again) is the contrasting of 'true' Niueans living from the land under difficult conditions with those who have given in to the 'lure of the golden city lights' and chosen a 'life of luxury'. Land rights seem to be the most controversial subject in the debate over 'belonging' between Niueans on the island and overseas. Niuean land rights are complex: allocation by an extended family group (*magafaoa*) – basically defined through common interests in land tenure – and/or its elected representative, the actual use and cultivation of the land, as well as the explicit bequeathing by a relative who possessed rights to a certain plot, all play a part (Crocombe 1977). In April 2007, Niue's premier declared that he had sealed off recourse to Niue's land claims court. Those Niueans who had been overseas for more than twenty or thirty years without reclaiming their houses, land or having 'touched base with their relations' would run risk of losing their ancestral land: 'You will have to come back and prove yourself, that you belong to this family, that you own this land, that you are part of it', Niue's premier Young Vivian said (Manning 2007). Niueans in New Zealand, however, at least of the first generation of immigrants, symbolically replicate Niuean spatial patterns, as I will show, and go to great lengths to validate their belonging.

## Space as Imagination

> Village comes first in New Zealand and being Niuean second.
> —Interviewee quoted in E.T. Kay, 'Honoured in the Observance'

On Niue, space is highly and consistently charged with socio-cultural ideas: every individual has a close relationship to their village and the land rights they possess in it. Going to other villages, except to the capital Alofi, was uncommon: only a few decades ago, young men entering the territory of a different village without permission risked violent attack, and one of Kay's informants remembered her joy and amazement when, travelling around the island as a young nanny with her new palagi employer, she saw other Niuean villages for the first time (Kay 1989: 163). Traditionally, a newborn baby's placenta is buried on family land,[18] as are the dead, often in the front garden of houses the deceased lived in. The spirits of numerous ancestors remain linked to land and certain places, and consequently it can be potentially dangerous to trespass on land not connected to one's family.

In Auckland, however, supernatural connotations like this seem rather associated with persons than with land. Apparently, individuals carry the implications of their Niuean village and family land with them. For example, medical and supernatural practitioners can be found in many parts of the city; the ingredients they require are brought to them from their Niuean home villages by visitors. Pastors and church elders possess *mana* through their office, but not through the space around their church: as the PIC, the most important Niuean church in Auckland, is found off Karangahape Road (an area also known for a long time for its pubs and red-light district), the awe-inspiring numinous space of a Niuean village green in front of a church, which requires a respectful demeanour, cannot exist around the PIC building.

Still, Niuean villages are reproduced in a strictly spatial way in Auckland. In the PIC, for example, Niueans sit in village groups,[19] and there is no 'neutral' way to sit apart from this order. Each village group sings a separate hymn which has a special slot during the liturgy. Elders are elected from every village group, and represented by the village *ulumotua*, a senior church elder who ideally is in close contact with the *ulumotua* of the actual village in Niue. Village groups in the PIC compete over the church collections, and in the performance of hymns during the liturgy.[20] Ambitious *ulumotua* commit their village group to regular choir rehearsals to outdo other village groups, and bad performances by other village groups are openly ridiculed during the church service. Ideally, the PIC *ulumotua*s try to stay in close touch with their counterparts on Niue. They validate their parishioners' belonging to their home village by actively taking part in village affairs, often expressed by fund raising and donations:

> Our forefathers brought the Liku church bell from Pago Pago. In 1908. How did they bring that bell to Niue? Nobody knows. It is down and has to be put up again. If we ring that bell, we remember our forefathers. But in Liku, they wanted to buy a new bell. I'd like to see the old bell ringing every Sunday and every time remember our forefathers. We raised 4,000 dollars. And we sent them to Liku. We've got the power to say because we raised the money that they asked for and said they needed to put it up. (Esau Noue, male PIC *ulumotua* for Liku village, aged 62)

Concordantly, the island discourse about 'desertion' and non-belonging of migrant Niueans is deeply resented. As another PIC *ulumotua* said angrily: 'We paid for the floor, the windows, the chairs and many other things. Not a single church in Niue would look the way it looks without our money'.[21]

A symbolic recreation of Niuean villages as spatial and normative patterns is also found in summer cricket games, which take place in some of Auckland's parks on a regular basis, usually between village groups. Remarkably, inter-village cricket games have ceased on Niue, but they are carried on in the diaspora. Niuean weaving groups in Auckland are another example. While some groups combine members from different Pacific islands or are linked to churches, at least two-thirds of those weaving groups attended and run by Niuean women are village-based. To the adept, this is apparent in many of the names these groups have given themselves, referring to places, narratives of mythical heroes, animals, flowers and the like, which are linked to certain places on the island.[22] Most weaving-group members in Auckland are willing to travel long distances to join a group linked with and comprised of members of their village. Others, however, especially in the older age groups and impaired by decreasing mobility, prefer to attend a group which is close by, even if it is not associated with their village. It is in this context that the spatial role of a certain tree in the park of Western Springs, in the area where the Niuean 'village' during the Pasifika Festival is located, has to be interpreted. The tree symbolizes neutral territory where women of different weaving groups, and thus different village groups, meet to discuss matters on a super-ordinate level.

A second principle at work in the Niuean diaspora, apart from village loyalty, and at the same time supporting and undermining it, seems to be status rivalry. Status rivalry of course is a classic topic in the study of Polynesian societies, and has its special dimension in Niuean society, which is basically egalitarian. Similar to the process in which a Polynesian nobleman of a bygone era would have gathered followers around him and left his island of origin after a conflict about status to sail away and found his own realm on another island, it is quite common in Niuean village, church and weaving groups that rivals for status challenge each other and clash, often resulting in one gathering their followers and joining another village group in the PIC – due to Niuean cognatic kinship structure there are always family links to other villages as well – founding their own group among a different Christian denomination, or their own weaving group. As a consequence, there are, for example, several weaving groups representing the same village.

While the recreation of Niuean village structures is found among first-generation Niuean immigrants, it is the generation born in New Zealand that seems to have closer links to their school or suburb in Auckland than to a remote Niuean village they might never have seen. Even for those actively aiming at reviving cultural skills by learning and using the Niuean language, criticism by the elders is an issue here, as observations and narratives of young and middle-aged New Zealand-born Niueans show.[23] Rivalry at this level apparently is usually between schools and suburbs, as at Polyfest, for example, a huge school competition involving dancing and singing by different Pacific Islander groups. Similarly, at Niuean functions there are occasional music and dance groups who organize themselves according to Auckland suburbs rather than Niuean villages – apparent in the suburb name they have printed on their uniform. This might be an indication that suburbs could gradually start replacing Niuean villages as spatial points of reference in the years to come. A few Niuean house owners have buried the placentae of their children in their Auckland gardens, thus confirming their connection with their new place of residence, but this is far from being a majority or consistent pattern yet. On the other hand, there seems to be a reorientation towards Niuean village structure when young people get married and have children, a tendency which has been shown for other Pacific Islanders as well (e.g. Anae 2001: 111–12). The oscillation between Niuean and Auckland points of reference is also seen with old people, who, when they tend to be less mobile, also gravitate towards attending a nearby church and weaving group, even if these are not those of their denomination or village. Active leaders of village-centred PIC or weaving groups, however, take extra care to visit and pick up these old people on a regular basis to make sure that they stay in touch with and feel cared for by their village group.

## Concluding Remarks

This chapter is based on fieldwork among the Niuean community in Auckland, and inspired by the framework provided by Lefebvre and Harvey, as well as Feld and Basso's reformulation, postulating three dimensions of space: spatial practice, space as perception and space as imagination. At the city-wide level of spatial practice, Niueans have not been able to appropriate connected spaces, being spread out all over Auckland and consequently dependent on central meeting points. Among the most important weekly meeting points are churches and weaving groups. At the level of space as perception, Auckland overwhelmingly represents a place of education and work opportunities, and for newcomers it is also a threatening place. Niuean women have managed to appropriate economic niches partly through weaving, which holds the double advantage of offering economic and symbolic gains in the Niuean and in the New Zealand system of reference. At the level of space as imagination, a reconstruction of Niuean villages as an important element of social structure is evident in Auckland, as can be seen with the PIC and weaving groups.

This analysis of Niuean place-making is closely linked to findings about ethnic marking among Niueans. Ethnicity is signalled quite discreetly towards non-Niueans and especially Pākehā/palagi in the Auckland context; it is more a pan-Polynesian identity which is signalled – and understood – here. On the other hand, Niueanness, overlaid with village identity, is very strongly signalled intra-ethnically – towards Niueans from Niue and towards other Niueans in Auckland. This might be connected with the Niuean concern with cultural loss, which seems to make it more urgent to signal and stress ethnic identity towards members of one's own ethnic group.

As Kahn (1996) has aptly pointed out, as places involve complex constructions of social histories, personal and interpersonal experiences and selective memories, they can be powerful metaphors for social relations and obligations, and thus highly 'emotional territory', where human relationships, inclusion and exclusion are constantly negotiated. Power relations as reflected and negotiated in place-making and in identifications occur at several different levels for Niueans in Auckland. At a political and demographic level, Niueans live in a city whose official discourse is dominated by Pākehā and Māori, although Pacific Islanders, mainly from Polynesia like themselves, are part of that discourse. Living scattered over the large sprawl of the city, and due to their egalitarian social structure, Niueans as a group lack a position of power in Auckland's polyethnic setting. As shown by their non-exclusive use of churches, meeting halls for weaving and participation at the Pasifika Festival, they share territory, in the spatial and symbolic sense, with others. In public spaces, a down-playing of ethnic identification as Niueans, something which is only subtly marked, or even the signalling of belonging to a pan-Polynesian community, expresses this position.

In intra-Niuean contexts, however, the symbolic dimension of space and belonging is immensely important and can be highly contested. Here, the observations made by Hermann, Kempf and Van Meijl in the introduction to this volume are salient: the power of definition is negotiated between actors and may claimed to be 'true' on the basis of performance in skills. The question what makes a 'true' Niuean is at the centre of many debates and social practices. Although the overwhelming majority of persons identifying themselves as Niueans live in New Zealand, the discourse of most Niueans dwelling on the island labels them as deserters who have preferred the temptation of an easy and luxurious life to the hardship of making a living from their own soil, thus forsaking their (land) rights on Niue. New Zealand Niueans, on the other hand, go to great lengths to validate their belonging, most often through the raising of large amounts of cash, which is spent on family, village and church matters on the island. Positions of power are here negotiated between those having influence because they are present on Niue, and those who have a say because of their ability to raise crucial funds.

The identification of first-generation Niuean immigrants with their respective villages is recreated in a number of ways in Auckland, as can be seen in the sitting arrangements in the PIC, in village-based weaving groups and in cricket. This generation of migrants is now middle aged and older, most of them having come to New Zealand a few decades ago. According to Niuean conventions, it is this generation which is highly respected, influential and has a say over the lives of younger, unmarried people. As census data show, the over-forties are more prone to be island-born, proficient in the Niuean language, with higher proportions of formal education and employment. As a consequence, what they define as a 'true' and respected Niuean identity is often very different from that of young people.[24] Again, power relations and social practices are linked to place-making and ideas of belonging here. Low-income neighbourhoods, schools with a mainly Polynesian intake and pressures to speak English seem to invite the embracing of pan-Polynesian urban identifications. Furthermore, elders have the power to criticize young people and make them feel their lack of competence in things they consider Niuean: the correct and elegant use of language or certain dress codes, for example. Being unable to perform adequately according to these definitions, even when trying hard, young people's first choice is to identify themselves as pan-Pacific urbanites. It remains to be seen whether in the future, and in which forms, identification as Niueans will be handed down to or embraced by the younger generation, a matter of deep concern for a number of older people. Many Niueans spend several phases of their lives alternating between New Zealand and Niue, and the oscillating and negotiating between Auckland and island spaces of imagination will remain an issue for the generation born in New Zealand as well.

## Acknowledgements

My research was started and took place under the auspices of the Ethnological Museum, Berlin, Germany, and was funded by the German Research Foundation (Deutsche Forschungsgemeinschaft). An honorary affiliation with the Women's Studies Programme and Department of Anthropology at the University of Auckland provided ample organizational support. The assistance of all these institutions is gratefully acknowledged. Many thanks to Markus Schindlbeck, Phyllis Herda, the late Roger Neich, the late Mick Pendergrast, Fulimalo Pereira, and Thomas Ryan for their valuable support and exchange of ideas on this project. *Fakaaue lahi mahaki* to Ahi Cross, the late Sialemoka Eveni, Senuola and Sefeti Fatiaki, Mele Heketoa, Maihetoe Hekau, Molie Huka, Reverend Falkland Liuvaie, the late Lineahi Lund, TaniRose Lui, Mary Magatogia, Lino Nelisi, Esau Noue, Lekei Palemia, Eseta Patii, Moliama and Fata Pihigia, Lisa Punu, Mahele Siakimotu, the late Esi Sipeli, Sifa Siuhani, Matafetu Smith, Herman Tagaloailuga, Maryanne Talagi, Sāmoa Togakilo, Shane Tohovaka, Malo Tulisi, Tuleimanogi Puletama Tupuolamoui, the late Tapu Vaha, Sina Vemoa, the late Lagi Viliko, Joanna Vilitama and Reverend Matagi Vilitama; to Niue's former premier Young Viviani; to all those interviewees who preferred to stay anonymous; to the ladies of the groups Falepipi He Mafola, Huanaki, Mumuafi, Pine mo Luku, Tufuga Mataponiu a Niue and Tukuofe; and to the ladies in the women's groups of Makefu, Liku, Avatele and Hakupu. Without their kind and invaluable help, conversation, input, encouragement, patience, generous sharing of insights and warm welcome, this research would not have been possible.

## Notes

1. The tendency is not as marked in Auckland as in some other New Zealand cities, however. Christchurch, for example, hosts a number of neo-gothic buildings and a statue of Queen Victoria in its centre, reminiscent of Oxford and Cambridge.
2. The slang term Jafa reflects some of the antagonisms between Aucklanders and non-Aucklanders; cf. http://en.wikipedia.org/wiki/Jafa.

Niuean Constructions of Place and Identity    111

3. There are contesting interpretations of whether Auckland's central Karangahape Road has a Māori name connected with a chief called Hape, or whether the name, like that of the Bombay Hills south of Auckland, refers to colonial British involvement in India.
4. Auckland Region includes Auckland and the adjacent settlements of Waitakere and Manukau. For a critical evaluation of the statistical category 'Pacific islanders', see e.g. Bedford and Didham (2001).
5. Data on Pacific ethnicity in Auckland have not been published by New Zealand Statistics, but Niueans cluster in Auckland in the same proportion as all New Zealand's Pacific islanders (SNZ 2007).
6. There are about 178,000 Pacific islanders living in the Auckland Region according to the 2006 census (SNZ 2007).
7. See Refiti (2002) for more examples of Pacific architecture in Auckland.
8. This is not a systematic survey of official representations of Māori, Pākehā/palagi and Pacific people in the city.
9. See Thode-Arora (2009: 70–156) for a more detailed analysis.
10. For summaries and discussions of different theoretical approaches towards diaspora, translocalism and transnationalism, and their connection with ethnic identities, see e.g. Gupta and Ferguson (1997: 1–51); Spickard, Rondilla and Wright (2002: 8–21), Morton (2003: 1–7) and the introduction to this volume. See also Clifford on the need to 'consider circuits, not a single place' (Clifford 1997: 37).
11. Being a female ethnographer, and having as the main focus of my fieldwork the mostly female activity of weaving and its role in Niue and in the Auckland diaspora, it has to be kept in mind that I had easier access to women, so there is a certain female bias in my results. I thus have less to say about pubs and cricket as Niuean places and activities than I have about more female places and practices. See Clifford (1997: 5, 6) on the importance of articulating gender differences in migration histories.
12. This number is even smaller among young people.
13. I found Harvey's refinement of Lefebvre's three-fold framework (Harvey 1989: 220–21) particularly suitable for structuring empirical data referring to space, and linking them with other domains found during my fieldwork (cf. Spradley 1974). This does not mean that I embrace these authors' neo-Marxist approach in my analysis.
14. From the 1950s to the 1970s, districts like Ponsonby, Grey Lynn, Arch Hill, Onehunga, West Tamaki, Mt Wellington, Otara, Otahuhu and Mangere offered affordable housing for Pacific immigrants, Niueans among them (Walsh and Trlin 1973: 69). Since the mid 1970s, about half the Pacific population has relocated to the new suburb of Manukau, which developed out of a colony of Polynesian builders working on the construction of the city's main power station (Colchester 2003: 169–70, 174). Walsh and Trlin's (1973: 71)

findings, that in the early 1970s people tended to settle in village groups, were not confirmed by my data.
15. Most Niuean families let their oldest (or several) son's hair grow and first cut it when the child is between five years and a teenager. This is done in an elaborate ceremony (*hifi ulu*) where family members and guests of honour cut strands of the boy's hair, giving speeches, blessings and presents, and invited guests bring money donations for which they are given certain kinds of food in return. The scaling of the amounts of cash and of the kinds and quantities of food is highly strategic, taking into account former and future ceremonies as well as the creation or claiming of reciprocal duties between the actors. *Hifi ulu*, like other life-cycle events, thus has an important role in consolidating social relations (see Thode-Arora 2009: 96–103).
16. The correct technical term for the techniques used (interlacing, twill weave and half-hitch-coiling) is 'plaiting' (see Pendergrast 1984; Seiler-Baldinger 1991). As the term 'weaving' is widespread in Anglo-Saxon publications, and as the Niuean women doing fibre handicrafts prefer the term 'weaving', I will stick to this usage here.
17. These 'language nests' (*kohanga reo* in Māori) originally started with Māori children (Morton 2003: 112). As many children of Niuean parentage grow up in exclusively English-speaking surroundings, with their parents actively embracing English or being unable to speak (good) Niuean themselves, a number of older Niuean women are concerned about language loss and have started to run these pre-schools, which receive funds from the city council.
18. This is expressed in the Niuean word *fonua*, which means both 'land' and 'placenta' (Sperlich 1997: 83).
19. In smaller Niuean-language congregations and churches, this has not been observed and is probably impossible due to sheer lack of numbers. See also Toren (1995: 166) for an example from Fiji where seating in church reflects social structure.
20. There is a certain order to which village follows which in singing hymns. Every Sunday, the village which begins rotates, so that over time each village group will be the first to sing during the service. Niuean village rivalry has been described many times by European chroniclers (Becke 1897: 88–104, 294–95; Thomson 1984: 138; Pointer 2000: 48–49). There are certain hymns typical to each village, and the way of singing them is so characteristic that a latecomer to church can tell which village group is singing just by listening while still outside the church.
21. There is continuity in these dynamics. Nineteenth-century palagi missionaries frequently complained about the selfish motives and sinfulness of labour migrants who came back with new ideas and money from overseas jobs. Still, a lot of this money was used to erect and embellish the village churches, and to enhance a person's prestige by making donations to the church (see

McDowell 1961: 175–76, 196, 198–201; Tukuitonga and Head 2001: 1883, 1889).
22. It was only after many months of acquiring a sound, though far from complete, knowledge of Niuean place names, and after a number of biographical interviews, that I came to understand this. Many Niuean place names are not found on maps but are well known to people living on the island or in a particular area. Mythical narratives are usually linked to certain places and not always shared with outsiders from different families or villages. As a consequence, the name of a flower or animal might have an instant association with a local myth for someone from this area, but not for an outsider.
23. This is especially so for those New Zealand-born young people who have tried to include Niuean texts in songs or other pieces of art. Elders have been observed several times to comment scornfully on younger people's awkward and inelegant use of the Niuean language.
24. This antagonism has also been described by Anae (2001: 105–18) for Sāmoans, as well as by Morton (2003: 151) for Tongans living in the diaspora, and by Van Meijl (2006) for Māori.

## References

Anae, M. 2001. 'The New "Vikings of the Sunrise": New Zealand-borns in the Information Age', in C. Macpherson, P. Spoonley and M. Anae (eds), *Tangata O Te Moana Nui: The Evolving Identitites of Pacific Peoples in Aotearoa/New Zealand*. Palmerston North: Dunmore Press, pp.101–21.

Becke, L. 1897. *Wild Life in Southern Seas*. London: Fisher Unwin.

Bedford, R., and R. Didham. 2001. '"Who Are the Pacific Peoples?" Ethnic Identification and the New Zealand Census', in C. Macpherson, P. Spoonley and M. Anae (eds), *Tangata O Te Moana Nui: The Evolving Identities of Pacific Peoples in Aotearoa/New Zealand*. Palmerston North: Dunmore Press, pp.21–43.

Brumann, C. 2004 'Der urbane Raum als öffentliches Gut: Kyoto und die Stadtbildkonflikte', *Zeitschrift für Ethnologie* 129(2): 183–210.

Casey, E. 1996. 'How to Get from Space to Place in a Fairly Short Stretch of Time', in S. Feld and K.H. Basso (eds), *Senses of Place*. Santa Fe, NM: School of American Research Press, pp.13–52.

Clifford, J. 1997. *Routes: Travel and Translation in the Late Twentieth Century*. Cambridge, MA: Harvard University Press.

Colchester, C. (ed.). 2003. *Clothing the Pacific*. Oxford: Berg.

Crocombe, R. 1977. 'Traditional and Colonial Tenure in Niue', in S. Kalauni et al. (eds), *Land Tenure in Niue*. Suva: Institute of Pacific Studies, University of the South Pacific, pp.14–24.

Donald, J. 1992. 'Metropolis: The City as Text', in R. Bocock and K. Thompson (eds), *The Social and Cultural Forms of Modernity*. Cambridge: Polity Press, pp.417–61.

Dürr, E. 2000. 'Perzeption und Funktion von städtischem Raum im multikulturellen Kontext', in W. Kokot, T. Hengartner and K. Wildner (eds), *Kulturwissenschaftliche Stadtforschung: Eine Bestandsaufnahme*. Berlin: Dietrich Reimer Verlag, pp.301–21.

Feld, S., and K.H. Basso. 1996. 'Introduction', in S. Feld and K.H. Basso (eds), *Senses of Place*. Santa Fe, NM: School of American Research Press, pp.3–11.

Fox, J. 1997. 'Place and Landscape in Comparative Austronesian Perspective', in J. Fox (ed.), *The Poetic Power of Place: Comparative Perspectives on Austronesian Ideas of Locality*. Canberra: Research School of Pacific and Asian Studies, Australian National University, pp.1–21.

Frake, C.O. 1996. 'Pleasant Places, Past Times and Sheltered Identities in Rural East Anglia', in S. Feld and K.H. Basso (eds), *Senses of Place*. Santa Fe, NM: School of American Research Press, pp.230–57.

Gow, P. 1995. 'Land, People and Paper in Western Amazonia', in E. Hirsch and M. O'Hanlon (eds), *The Anthropology of Landscape: Perspectives on Place and Space*. Oxford: Clarendon Press, pp.43–62.

Gupta, A., and J. Ferguson (eds). 1997. *Culture, Power, Place: Explorations in Critical Anthropology*. Durham, NC: Duke University Press.

Harvey, D. 1989. *The Condition of Postmodernity: An Enquiry into the Origins of Cultural Change*. Oxford: Blackwell.

Hau'ofa, E. 1994. 'Our Sea of Islands', *Contemporary Pacific* 6(1): 148–61.

Hirsch, E. 1995. 'Introduction', in E. Hirsch and M. O'Hanlon (eds), *The Anthropology of Landscape: Perspectives on Place and Space*. Oxford: Clarendon Press, pp.1–30.

Kahn, M. 1996. 'Sharing Emotional Landscapes in Wamira, Papua New Guinea', in S. Feld and K.H. Basso (eds), *Senses of Place*. Santa Fe, NM: School of American Research Press, pp.167–96.

Kay, E.T. 1989. 'Honoured in the Observance: Retention of Portable Customs as an Affirmation of Niuean National Identity, Revealed through Life History Studies', M.A. diss. Auckland: University of Auckland.

Lefebvre, H. 1991. *The Production of Space*. Oxford: Blackwell.

McDowell, D.K. 1961. 'A History of Niue', M.A. diss. Auckland: University of Auckland.

Manning, S. 2007. 'Niue Premier Calls Expats to Return Home', *Scoop Independent News*, 12 April. Retrieved 12 April 2009 from: http://www.scoop.co.nz/stories/HL0704/S00186.htm.

Morphy, H. 1995. 'Landscape and the Reproduction of the Ancestral Past', in E. Hirsch and M. O'Hanlon (eds), *The Anthropology of Landscape: Perspectives on Place and Space*. Oxford: Clarendon Press, pp.184–209.

Morton, H.L. 2003. *Tongans Overseas: Between Two Shores*. Honolulu: University of Hawai'i Press.

Moyle, R.M. 2002. 'Sounds Pacific: Pacific Music and Dance in New Zealand', in S. Mallon and P.F. Pereira (eds), *Pacific Art Niu Sila: The Pacific Dimension of Contemporary New Zealand Arts*. Wellington: Te Papa Press, pp.103–15.

Pendergrast, M. 1984. *Raranga Whakairo: Maori Plaiting Patterns*. Auckland: Coromandel Press.

Pereira, P.F. 2002. 'Lalaga: Weaving Connections in Pacific Fibre', in S. Mallon and P.F. Pereira (eds), *Pacific Art Niu Sila: The Pacific Dimension of Contemporary New Zealand Arts*. Wellington: Te Papa Press, pp.76–89.

Pointer, M. 2000. *Tagi Tote e Loto haaku – My Heart is Crying a Little: Niue Island Involvement in the Great War 1914–1918*. Suva: Government of Niue and Institute of Pacific Studies, University of the South Pacific.

Refiti, A. 2002. 'Making Spaces: Polynesian Architecture on Aotearoa New Zealand', in S. Mallon and P.F. Pereira (eds), *Pacific Art Niu Sila: The Pacific Dimension of Contemporary New Zealand Arts*. Wellington: Te Papa Press, pp.208–25.

Ryan, T.F. 1977. 'Prehistoric Niue: An Egalitarian Polynesian Society', M.A. diss. Auckland: University of Auckland.

Seiler-Baldinger, A. 1991. *Systematik der textilen Techniken*. Basel: Wepf for Ethnologisches Seminar der Universität und Museum für Völkerkunde.

SNZ. 2007. 'Niuean People in New Zealand: 2006', Statistics New Zealand-Tatauiranga Aotearoa. Retrieved 3 March 2010 from: http://www.stats.govt.nz/Census/about-2006-census/pacific-profiles-2006.aspx.

Sperlich, W.B. 1997. *Tohi Vagahau Niue: Niue Language Dictionary*. Alofi/Honolulu: Government of Niue/University of Hawai'i Press.

Spickard, P., J.L. Rondilla and D.H. Wright (eds). 2002. *Pacific Diaspora: Island Peoples in the United States and across the Pacific*. Honolulu: University of Hawai'i Press.

Spradley, J.P. 1974. *Participant Observation*. New York: Holt, Rinehart and Winston.

Taouma, L. 2002. 'Getting Jiggy with It: The Evolving of Pasifika Dance in New Zealand', in S. Mallon and P.F. Pereira (eds), *Pacific Art Niu Sila: The Pacific Dimension of Contemporary New Zealand Arts*. Wellington: Te Papa Press, pp.133–45.

Terry, J.P., and W.E. Murray (eds). 2004. *Niue Island: Geographical Perspectives on the Rock of Polynesia*. Paris: International Scientific Council for Island Development.

Thode-Arora, H. 2009. *Weavers of Men and Women: Niuean Weaving and Its Social Implications*. Berlin: Dietrich Reimer.

Thomson, B.C. 1984 [1902]. *Savage Island: An Account of a Sojourn in Niue and Tonga*. Papakura: R. McMillan.

Toren, C. 1995. 'Seeing the Ancestral Sites: Transformations in Fijian Notions of the Land', in E. Hirsch and M. O'Hanlon (eds), *The Anthropology of Landscape: Perspectives on Place and Space*. Oxford: Clarendon Press, pp.163–83.

Tukuitonga, V.P., and R.B.W.L. Head (eds). 2001. *Niue: Ko e motu ofania/Niue: The Island of Love*. Alofi: Government of Niue.

Van Meijl, T. 2006. 'Multiple Identifications and the Dialogical Self: Urban Maori Youngsters and the Cultural Renaissance', *Journal of the Royal Anthropological Institute* 12(4): 917–33.

Walsh, A.C., and A.D. Trlin. 1973. 'Niuean Migration: Niuean Socio-economic Background, Characteristics of Migrants, and Settlement in Auckland', *Journal of the Polynesian Society* 82(1): 47–85.

Zukin, S. 1995. *The Cultures of Cities*. Oxford: Blackwell.

―――― 1996. 'Space and Symbols in an Age of Decline', in A.D. King (ed.), *Representing the City: Ethnicity, Capital and Culture in the Twenty-first Century Metropolis*. New York: New York University Press, pp.43–59.

# 5

# Migration and Identity

## Cook Islanders' Relation to Land

◆●◆

### Arno Pascht

For Cook Islanders today, travel to New Zealand or Australia in order to work, study, visit relatives or for other purposes is a normal occurrence. Movement of this kind is an integrated aspect of everyday life for many of them, and influences their thoughts and actions. David Chapell accordingly considers Cook Islanders, together with Niueans and Tokelauans, as 'perhaps the most transnational peoples of Oceania' (Chapell 1999: 282). Like many other inhabitants of Oceania, they are engaged in a process that Epeli Hau'ofa called 'world enlargement' (Hau'ofa 1994: 151, 155). Whereas the population of the Cook Islands in 2007 was 11,800, the New Zealand census of 2006 lists 58,011 Cook Islanders, assumedly permanently resident in New Zealand (Pascht 2009). The most recent figure for the population of Cook Islanders in Australia is 40,000.[1] In New Zealand, the situation for Cook Islanders is especially favourable, since they all automatically have New Zealand citizenship, and thus are allowed to go there and stay without restrictions; they are also entitled to social security benefits. Compared to most other migrants, both in the Pacific and elsewhere, they therefore constitute an exceptional case.

All those Cook Islanders staying in foreign countries still have rights, or at least potential rights, to land on the islands of the Cook group – irrespective of where they are currently living. This situation is the result of the specific history of land tenure and the plurality of legal notions and practice concerning land rights in the Cook Islands. Today, land tenure in the Cook Islands is characterized by state rules, norms and practices on the one hand, and 'family' rules, notions and practices, with pre-colonial roots, on the other.

Here I focus on the question of what role relations to land and land rights play in the identification processes of Cook Islanders who stay for longer periods of time or permanently overseas. To do this it is central to look closely at the phenomenon of 'absentee landowners' – persons who own land but do not live on it or use it directly.

During fieldwork on Rarotonga I often heard complaints about 'absentee landowners'. Rarotongans told me that Cook Islanders who live 'overseas' – mainly in New Zealand and Australia – are often very 'greedy'; I was told that although many of them have good lives in those places, they nevertheless also try to secure use rights for a piece of land in Rarotonga. Rarotongans complained that these 'absentee landowners' often do not actually use their piece of land, which thus lies idle, while Rarotongans at home are prevented from using it for agricultural or tourist purposes. Ultimately, 'absentee landowners' are even blamed for hindering the economic prosperity of the island. However, I was told by Cook Islanders, and I also observed myself, that in practice many of the pieces of land 'owned' by absentees are used – mainly by Cook Islanders living on Rarotonga – for instance as land for growing short-term crops, and that houses of absentees are in a number of cases used as places of residence for their family members.

According to Zygmunt Baumann, in modern conditions, identity – or, better, identification – has to be chosen by individuals rather than being a given. For Baumann, identification is a 'never-ending, always incomplete, unfinished and open-ended activity in which we all, by necessity or by choice, are engaged' (Baumann 2001: 129). Cook Islanders who have migrated to New Zealand or Australia are part of the globalizing and individualizing processes that Baumann sees as the basis of modern notions of identification. In New Zealand, Cook Islanders' identity is not a given – in fact they can (and do) engage in a variety of identification processes – as 'Pacific Islanders', 'New Zealanders', 'Rarotongans', and so on. Some individuals may decide not to become involved in matters of family and land in the Cook Islands, and to refuse to identify as Cook Islanders.[2] But others choose to engage in an active process of identification with their home island, their home land and their family. In contrast to Baumann's claim that people who live in individualizing conditions, for whom identity 'sprouts on the graveyard of communities' (ibid.: 129), for Cook Islanders who engage in this process, identity is also connected to community – mainly to the family. It has to be specified that this community is largely a 'virtual community', in the sense that it is maintained to a considerable degree by means of communications media such as telephone and the internet.

In order to interpret and explain the role of land and the phenomenon of 'absentee landowners' with regard to the 'identity' of Cook Islanders, I will initially describe some general principles of land tenure in Rarotonga and then continue with the topic of land and identity. Subsequently I then turn to examine the situation of Cook Islanders in New Zealand and their connections with their home islands, and finally I offer an explanation for the phenomena initially presented.

## Legal Orders and Absentee Landowners

Here I will illustrate the background of the specific land tenure situation by describing the different legal orders in the Cook Islands that are relevant for land rights, with a particular focus on 'absentee landowners', and offer some interpretations of it. I will begin by briefly sketching out the general background of the topic of absentee landowners.

### The Basic Principles of the State Land Tenure System

The legal order of the state and of its main institution concerning land issues – the Land Division of the High Court of the Cook Islands – has its origins in the colonial court established in 1902 by the New Zealand administration. The judge at the time considered the most important task to be that of determining who the landowners were (with a focus on Rarotonga). Thus, in the following years, the names of those persons who convinced the judge that they were the 'rightful owners' of existing land sections were recorded in a Register of Titles. Officially, this determination of owners of land titles was carried out according to the customary principles of the Cook Islands Māori.[3] The result was that several owners were found for most of the sections (in most cases, five to ten persons) and they were treated prospectively as tenants in common (Browne 1994: 207). This means that pieces of land in the Cook Islands were not allocated to individual owners, but rather that individuals formally owned a share of a section, that share being neither localized nor of a determinate size. Today, the process of registering owners of land sections has almost been completed for Rarotonga, though the situation is different for other islands of the Cook group. Although registration was characterized by mistakes and injustices, the majority of Cook Islanders accept it today pragmatically as the basis of the state system for determining rights to land.

The colonial judges soon introduced an influential practice that is still valid today, and which has consequences for all, especially for absentee landowners: bilateral succession of land ownership. In the case of the death of one of the owners of a land section, all their children have a right of succession and a right to be registered as co-owners of the land(s). This means that today in general the number of registered co-owners of a land section is significantly higher than the original five or ten: it is not uncommon for there to be more than a hundred registered co-owners of a single section.[4] Another important principle is that in the Cook Islands land, or more precisely the fee simple of that land, cannot be sold.[5] A result of these rules and related practices, the allocation of pieces of land among co-owners is a crucial topic today. Because the area of a land section is, in many cases, relatively small, it is not sufficient for sensible utilization by all the co-owners. Due to the multiple ownership of land sections, and to the fact that many Cook Islanders live overseas, this situation is not as problematic as it may appear. In the course of time, legislation was passed to create options which now allow formalized allocation of land at state level to individuals or couples; the most important of these, for the purposes of private use, is the so-called 'occupation right'.[6] This is the right of one or more persons to use a piece of land that is registered in the Register of Titles. The way in which the land is utilized – in most cases for residential or agricultural purposes – is also registered. In order to allocate pieces of land according to this legislation, normally a meeting is held (usually called a 'family meeting') at which preferably all recognized holders of rights to the respective land section are present, and either a consensus is reached or a vote takes place. After the meeting, a judge from the Land Division of the High Court has to confirm the procedure so that the occupation right can be registered. The High Court does not usually refuse to register the occupation right (although it has the discretion to do so) when the majority of the co-owners present at the meeting agree.

**Non-state Principles of Land Tenure**

Rules of land tenure that have their roots in pre-colonial time are mainly passed on within the various families (*ngāti*) of Rarotonga.[7] In the 1970s a commission of traditional authorities tried to put the most important of these principles into writing. The aim was that these would finally be included in state law. Although there have been several attempts since then (Koutu Nui 2001), these rules have not yet been codified (Pascht 2007). Nevertheless, notions and practices that are subject to these rules do play an important role today, mainly in guiding matters of land ownership within families, but also, in a number of cases, they have been important at court hearings. Although state institutions such as the High Court are widely accepted – and are referred to in certain formal aspects of land administration, as well as for managing conflicts of a certain kind – many Cook Islanders' present ideas and notions are nevertheless rooted in 'traditional' ones. The land rights of individuals here depend on recognized membership in a family that is connected with a specific sub-district. Rarotongans believe that the warriors Tangiia and Karika divided the whole land, bestowed individuals with *tā'onga* (title names), and gave parts of the land to the holders of the *tā'onga* and their descendants (*ngāti*) twenty-eight generations ago. Since then, the *ngāti* and the holders of the *tā'onga* of the *ngāti* as their representative hold the rights for the totality of the members of the *ngāti*. As a recognized member of a *ngāti*, a person generally has the right to use land held by that group. Family membership, and thus the right to land, can be considered cognatic, and is therefore very flexible. Membership depends first on genealogy: one's identity as a descendant of the ancestor, the first holder of the *tā'onga*, must be acknowledged. Descent in this case is recognized in both the male and female line. In order to have a recognized right to use a piece of land, however, this alone is not sufficient. A person also has to demonstrate membership through active commitment in family affairs, by making contributions to family feasts and by subordinating themselves to family rules, and this demonstration of membership must be acknowledged by the other family members.

My fieldwork revealed that the two kinds of legal orders – that of the state, and that of families – play varying roles depending on the families involved and the specific case in question. Some families follow principles modelled on 'traditional' legal ideas in their organization of land rights, land transactions and the utilization of land notions, while other families follow the state system. In some families, for example, in order to limit the numbers of landowners of land sections, only some of the potential holders of rights are registered. This practice is closer to the cognatic inheritance system that existed in pre-colonial times than the bilateral principle introduced by the Court.

## Implications of Land Tenure Principles for Absentee Landowners

Put simply, both state and 'family' notions and rules are valid for all Rarotongans, irrespective of their place of residence. Cook Islanders who live overseas have several kinds of rights concerning land based on the legal order of the state. First, they have the right to be registered as co-owner when one parent dies. Second, when they have been registered they have the right to decide, together with the other co-owners, about the use of the land, especially regarding who has the right to use it (today, use rights mainly take the form of an 'occupation right' or a lease). And third, they have the right to apply for use rights to a piece of land themselves.[8] In this case they have to convince the High Court that they intend to come back to the Cook Islands to use the land, for example to build a house or for agricultural purposes. Thus, people who have neither lived on nor used the land in question for a long time (if at all) have the opportunity to claim legal rights to it, and in some cases they actually do so.

According to the state system, therefore, three different categories of Cook Islanders can be distinguished concerning their land rights. First: persons whose parents are still living, or who have not (yet) registered their rights; according to the state system, these do not have the right to decide about land matters in meetings. Second: persons who have registered their rights, and are thus acknowledged at the state level as co-owners of one or – more usually – several sections of land; they have the right to vote in meetings. And third: persons who applied for and were granted use rights to a piece of land.

It is mostly only persons of the third category who are referred to as 'absentee landowners' if they do not live on their piece of land, but sometimes the term is also used to refer to persons of the second category who do not live on their land, since they have legal rights and can therefore influence decisions about who obtains use rights. There have been some attempts by the state to limit the power of 'absentee landowners' in this category. For example, although only 25 per cent of a land section's co-owners are required to be present at a meeting in order for decisions to be made, many of the absent co-owners return for meetings or grant powers of attorney to other landowners living in the Cook Islands to vote as proxies. The result is that, in practice, the power of these absentee landowners remains high (Crocombe, Araitia and Tongia 2008: 160).

In fact, there are many Cook Islanders who apply for rights to a piece of land before they migrate (ibid.: 162), and a number of Cook Islanders in New Zealand have applied for an 'occupation right' to a piece of land. In the cases when the latter kind of application was successful, various different developments have taken place: some of them have not come back at all and the land has lain idle; others have begun to build houses, but they have not finished them. On Rarotonga one can see numerous houses, or the shells of houses, at different stages of construction; some are already partly overgrown. Yet others have handed over use of their piece of land to friends or relatives, who commercially plant short-term crops. Others still have built houses and moved to the Cook Islands, but then moved back to New Zealand or Australia after a few years. Only a few have stayed permanently in the Cook Islands – mainly those who have started an enterprise or, as in a number of cases, those who work as government employees. Some of the consequences of the existence of 'absentee landowners' are thus quite visible on the Rarotongan landscape. Not only are the partly finished houses striking, but so is the fact that the pieces of land around them are mostly kept in good condition; they are usually cleared and the grass is mowed. The same is true for some pieces of land where no house has (yet) been constructed. Some well-kept empty plots, planted with ornamental flowers and hedges and with perfectly mowed lawns, are evident. The pieces of land that are used for crop cultivation by relatives or friends of the holder can usually not be distinguished from other agricultural land. They are planted with short-term crops, but this is not unusual on Rarotonga, where short-term crops like tomatoes and cabbage can be found, as well as long- and mid-term crops such as taro, pawpaw and bananas. Also notable are the finished houses that are used not by holders of use rights but by their relatives. Many of the pieces of land held by absentee landowners are used in some form, or at least cared for. The underlying reason is that if this is not done people worry that other family members will claim the land (Pascht 2006: 283–84).

According to the state legal code, occupation rights can return to the co-owners of a whole section if the holder does not use the land within five years. But this doesn't happen very often; I heard of only a very few cases. Rarotongans differentiated between 'good families' and 'bad families': the former would never demand a piece of land back, even when it is not used.

The number of absentee landowners in Pouara, a sub-district of Rarotonga, may serve as an illustration. In this rather rural sub-district, fifty pieces of land were allocated to specific persons or couples in 2001. Nineteen persons were classified as 'absent'.[9] So, more than one third of the allocated pieces of land were allocated to absentee landowners.[10] Roughly one half of these are not in permanent use. This situation can be seen as typical for the whole island, although there are local variations in some (sub-)districts.

## The Meaning and Role of Land for Rarotongans

Land is one of the most discussed topics in Rarotonga. Cook Islanders explained to me that '*mana*[11] is land', and that the size of one's land is important for one's *mana*. Land is not only related to *mana*, however, but also to other principles that Irving Goldman (1970) found to be important for Polynesian status systems, and which Richard Feinberg (2002), for example, has used to explain Oceanian systems of leadership. Of importance are the notions of honour, *tapu*,[12] *mana*, *aloha* (the Cook Islands form is *aro'a*[13]), and descent. Because the last three of these are especially closely connected to the topic of this article, I will return to them below.

## Individuals, Groups and Land

Cook Islanders' relationships to land at the individual level are closely connected with that at the group level. I begin with the former. For Cook Islanders, land is strongly connected with individual success: possessing land means, for example, that one is able to plant, to build a house and rent it to tourists or to use it in other ways. As a result it is possible – or even expected – that one might redistribute some of the benefits (mainly) to one's family. It is expected that land will be used, and thus individual success – and *mana* – is enhanced.

In order to explain Cook Islanders' relationships to land at the group level, it is necessary to briefly outline the already mentioned Rarotongan oral tradition, which has been identified as a kind of mythical 'charter' by several authors (e.g. Gilson 1980: 7). According to this narrative, the warriors Tangiia and Karika established a stable spatial and political order on Rarotonga when they came to the island. They erected a certain number of *marae* (ceremonial places), invested a certain number of persons with title names (*tā'onga*), divided the land of the whole island and distributed the portions to the *tā'onga* to be used by their families. This basic structure still exists today, although a number of political aspects have since been transferred to the modern state. But still, the spatial order of districts and sub-districts is seen as a material manifestation of the oral tradition, the 'mythical charter' of Rarotonga. The way that ownership of land is ordered here implies a certain timelessness and fixity. Thus it can be seen as a 'landscape' in the sense of Eric Hirsch (1995: 22), and also as a 'complex structure of social memory' (Fox 1997: 7). The arrangement of districts and sub-districts, and the title names that are directly connected with them, symbolize and at the same time authenticate the basic structures of Rarotongan society – especially the status of holders of title names. The order that was established in the past is thus manifested spatially, and this spatial order indicates both that history happened in a specific way, and that the order that was thereby established remains valid.

As with other examples in which land and kinship are mutually implicated (Hirsch 1995: 9, 18–19), on Rarotonga the political order is also involved as an additional aspect. A Rarotongan family that is accepted as owning a certain area of land and possessing a title name is recognized and identified as being descended from a certain ancestor who had originally been given a title name by Tangiia and Karika. Thus the family is part of this larger historical order: they have a certain status, and they are seen as human.[14] Only descent from a 'chiefly' ancestral family with a title ensures others' recognition of one's human status. A person is identified as a member of a certain family that is part of this order, and is thus distinguished from members of other families.

If a family possesses a *tā'onga*, the family has a history, *mana* and land. Specifying the role of land in this respect, I have previously shown that, using concepts developed by Annette Weiner (1992), land, as an inalienable possession, functions as a way of authenticating one's family ties, history and origin (see Pascht 2006). Weiner and, in a similar vein, Maurice Godelier (1999), stress that inalienable possessions are important for the identity of groups and individuals. An inalienable possession implies myths of creation and origin (ibid.: 190), and this 'affirms the difference between one person or group and another' (Weiner 1992: 43). Although Weiner concentrates on material objects when she speaks of 'inalienable possessions', she mentions in several places that land, land rights or ownership of land can also be forms of inalienable possession (e.g. ibid.: 11, 26, 33, 38–39). Although I do not deal with the subject of exchange here, in my opinion it makes sense to apply her concept to the possession of land in the Cook Islands, since many of the characteristics of inalienable possessions that Weiner mentions can be applied in this context, and the concept makes the role and meaning of land, and its connection with identity, more understandable. Weiner says, 'an inalienable possession acts as a stabilizing force against change because its presence authenticates cosmological origins, kinship, and political histories' (ibid.: 9). This is true for land in Rarotonga, which is divided into districts and sub-districts as a result of a specific history that authenticates the division and order of land, titles and families. Ownership of this land was transferred from one generation to the next, and remained in the possession of one family (*ngāti*). What Weiner states more generally (ibid.: 10) is true of Rarotonga: identity and status are legitimized by ownership of an inalienable possession – in this case the land of a certain district and sub-district. Land in Rarotonga cannot be sold. Despite the norms and practices of the High Court today, in many contexts land is still considered to be owned by specific families. It is seen as the property of these families and the right to use it is usually transferred to the children of the owners. Furthermore, the land was given to Rarotongans by Tangiia and Karika – thus imbuing it with a status similar to that of Godelier's 'sacred objects': 'To a Cook Islander, land is a gift from the ancestors. So to own a piece for living on is a must', writes the Cook Islander Paiere Mokoroa (n.d.: 12). In Rarotonga, land can be seen as an inalienable possession of a family, one that defines the family, and legitimizes it; it establishes that family's position in the Rarotongan social universe, and at the same time it is an expression of the identity of that family.[15]

Land is thus closely connected with the family, and Rarotongans identify with their family as they do with the associated land (Pascht 2006: 321, 323). Identity as a family member is not a static condition: Rarotongans are engaged in a constant process of maintaining relationships or creating new ones, by engaging in family affairs, contributing to family projects and so on. Thus, ties to a specific family can be strengthened. An example is provided by Ati, the son of the sister of the present holder of the Terangi title.[16] Ati used to use the family name of his father, but in recent years he became involved in the family affairs of the Terangi family: he did research concerning the history of the family, and he is included in their decision-making, and even chairs meetings for the family. For a while now he has been using Ngāti Terangi as his family name. He is accepted within the family, and I even heard people wondering if he will be the successor to the Terangi title. Because ties to family and land are not stable, but rather must be actively maintained and created, and thus identity in this case is not original, unified and unchangeable, Rarotongan 'identity' is obviously processual in Baumann's (2001) terms. Thus it is more appropriate to use the concept 'identification', as Stuart Hall (1996) and others have suggested.

It is useful to differentiate between two levels of identification: that of the group, and that of the individual. Whereas a family is seen as being closely connected with a specific area (normally specific places within a sub-district of the island), this is often not the case for individual persons. For an individual, it is important to be recognized as a member of a family and thus to have a recognized connection to an area. If this is the case, a person's right to use one or more pieces of land in the area held by this specific family is recognized at the 'family legal level'. The family's area represents the place of origin and the place of belonging: the place is a visible manifestation of the collective identity of the family. It is tied to the history of the family, and at the same time to the history of the whole island.[17] In pre-Christian times history, family, title names (*tā'onga*) and land – indeed, the whole spatial order of the island – were connected with specific *marae* erected by Tangiia and Karika. *Marae* were ceremonial places where important rituals were conducted, and were believed to be the homes of gods.

## Land Conflicts

Conflicts over land were and are very frequent in the Cook Islands, and can play an important role in the identification processes of individuals and families. As an example I will describe one particular conflict concerning a whole sub-district (*tapere*) of Rarotonga. This conflict is a very old one – it began in the early twentieth century and took on several forms (Pascht 2006, 2011). After years of preparation, it was brought to the High

Court again in 2000. The parties involved in the conflict both referred to themselves as 'family', or sometimes as Ngāti X. Represented in court by lawyers, they tried to assert their claim to a huge piece of land by attempting to prove that their ancestors had originally received the land from Karika or Tangiia. One family invested much of their energy and time during the trial in trying to prove that the family once owned a title name (*tā'onga*), and that its past holder was originally given the land from Tangiia. To varying degrees, for both families the preparation for the lawsuit involved researching the family's history, identifying members and non-members, conducting meetings and settling intra-family conflicts. For a number of individuals, being a member of one family or the other took on a deeper meaning than it had previously. The result was that both families did their best to prove their status and identity as a 'real' family of Rarotonga – one that held a valid, chiefly title name, and thus had requisite ancestral and legal rights to own land.

## Cook Islanders in New Zealand

Having outlined the basics of land tenure in the Cook Islands, and the meaning and role of land in the lives of Rarotongans in general, I next turn to examine the situation of Cook Islanders who live for longer periods in New Zealand. After a short sketch of some important characteristics of migrant life, especially with regard to identity and connections to the Cook Islands, I then outline the role land plays in the lives of these migrants.

### Important Characteristics of Migrant Life

Cook Islanders in New Zealand may identify themselves as Pacific Islanders, Polynesians or New Zealanders – and also as Cook Islanders, as Rarotongans, or as member of a specific family. 'For many Cook Islanders, the foundation of their group identification is … a fundamental sense of belongingness', Fitzgerald (1989: 275) says of Cook Islanders living in New Zealand. He does not examine this belongingness in detail, but he mentions the importance of community and especially that of belonging to a family (ibid.: 267). Similarly Terrence Loomis concludes that the most important common interests and reference points of the 'Cook Islands migrant community' in New Zealand are kinship and, especially, the extended family (*kōpū tangata*), although the community is also divided by multiple interests and identities (Loomis 1991: 47–48). Two other very important reference points are church communities and so-called '*enua* associations'. Loomis calls *enua* (land) associations 'the focus of Cook Island ethnic identity' (ibid.: 176). They are based on one's village, district or island of origin and have social, cultural and recreational functions (Loomis 1990: 176–80). Loomis stresses that cultural performances of *enua* associations 'rely upon and thus serve to reproduce the customary reciprocity system of assistance and exchange' (ibid.: 180). Both *enua* associations and kinship ties are important not only for relations among Cook Islanders in New Zealand but also for relations among Cook Islanders who live in other countries (ibid.: 185). Ilana Gershon (2007) has shown in a recent article on Oceania in general that family networks and exchange practices enable migrants to maintain long-term connections across long distances. This is also true for Cook Islanders who stay in New Zealand.

Mobility and exchange between the islands and New Zealand (or Australia or the USA) is very common. In a recent article, Kalissa Alexeyeff (2004) has shown the importance of contacts and especially of exchange between Cook Islanders at home and those living overseas. She stresses the importance of reciprocal relationships among kin and the wider community, and the role of *aro'a* in these relationships. *Aro'a* is sometimes translated as love, sympathy or affection, and can also mean aid or assistance (see Feinberg 2002: 25). Alexeyeff shows that there is a gift economy that is much more comprehensive than that indicated by an examination of financial remittances alone. The exchange of goods and ceremonies between New Zealand and the Cook Islands is in fact very much alive. Remittances and material goods are sent or brought personally, and groups travel regularly from the Cook Islands to New Zealand and vice versa (Loomis 1984, 1990; Alexeyeff 2003).[18] Family ceremonies play an important role in this respect, such as the haircutting ceremony.[19] One such ceremony I attended when I was in Rarotonga took place mainly because the boy's grandmother – who lived in New Zealand – insisted that it was held.

Loomis (1990) states that there are a number of typical commitments that Cook Islanders make to their homeland (see below). He interprets these commitments mainly as ways of investing in the future by fulfilling absent people's obligations to their homeland (ibid.: 52–53, 211) due to the uncertainty among migrant workers in New Zealand over their economic and political future. To Loomis, this uncertainty is an important factor in the maintenance of the links to the islands. Loomis also identifies the dependent economic conditions of the islands as another reason for the maintenance of these links (ibid.: 185).

**The Role of Land**

In Oceania, one way in which those that remain on their home islands reciprocate the gift of remittances sent from absentee relatives abroad is by maintaining the land. For those who went away, the fact that they still have a homeland strengthens 'their bonds, their souls, and their identities' (Hau'ofa 1994: 157). For Cook Islanders who have moved away from their home islands, this tie to land can be important in several respects. Loomis identifies five main typical 'commitments' of Cook Islanders to their homeland: knowledge of land rights; registration of land rights; building a house on the land; high frequency of visits to the homeland; plans to return one day (Loomis 1990: 52).[20] Land clearly plays a major role in these commitments. The great importance of land and place in the identities of first-generation migrant Cook Islanders living in New Zealand is also stressed by Fitzgerald, who terms land the 'mother of identity' (Fitzgerald 1989: 272). In their recent article about absentee landowners, Crocombe, Araitia and Tongia mention that land is 'highly valued as a source of identity and confidence' (Crocombe, Araitia and Tongia 2008: 163),[21] and they state that more than two-thirds of a sample of Cook Islanders residing in Auckland 'felt their land rights should never be affected by how long they stayed away' (ibid.: 164). Land plays a prominent role in the explanations that Cook Islanders in New Zealand give for the importance of maintaining contact with their homeland. During an interview with Makiuti Tongia, a Cook Islander who lived in New Zealand in 2001, he told me:

> Cook Islanders [in New Zealand] ... maintain contact and keep the fire burning via trips to the homeland, phone calls, fax messages and emails. They speak the language and dance the dance ... They write, talk and sing to their relatives in the homeland. They maintain contact to the land. They contribute to the developments of the family land. They fight over their rights with the others. They remain Māori.[22]

Here it is clear that land is a central aspect of identification not only for Cook Islanders 'at home' but also for those living in New Zealand, although it must be stressed that this does not mean that it is the only important aspect. As Loomis's statements above show, Cook Islanders in New Zealand also engage in other practices of identification – such as church groups.[23]

Makiuti Tongia's remarks indicate not only the general importance of land but also the fact that a person's identity as a Cook Islands Māori living in New Zealand is not a given that is valid forever, but rather has to be actively maintained through a continuing process that individuals engage in. The imagination of a homeland is constantly recreated and re-established by the activities Tongia mentions.[24] The nature of people's relation to the land, it seems, is principally the same for Cook Islanders at home and in New Zealand.

One example of a conscious effort to maintain or re-establish a connection to land is that of the *marae* in Rarotonga; today most of these are overgrown and not visible as such.[25] Recently, however, traditional authorities have made efforts to clear places once more and mark them as *marae* – partly for the benefit of members of the younger generation living overseas. As one traditional leader explained to me, 'We have to show [them] where they come from'.

There are various ways to actually 'maintain contact to the land', and thus with the place of origin. The main way, as stressed by Tongia, is by maintaining contact with the family, in order to maintain kinship ties and thus ensure one's belonging to a community. Since along with these family ties, one's ties to the land are also maintained (or created), they include rights to land at the legal level of the family. A specific example of this is the family situation of Kopu. When I talked to her in 2001, Kopu had lived for twenty years together with her husband in Auckland. They both had well-paid jobs and could afford to visit Rarotonga quite often. She explained: 'When we retire we go back to Rarotonga. We have a piece of land in Arorangi from the family of my husband. We [have] already started building a house [...] I have also started to build a house for my family in Rutaki together with [my sisters and brothers]'. The house in Rutaki is not a house for herself but will be a 'family home' where members of the family can stay and come together. 'So the family has always a place where we can go', Kopu said. It is being built on the piece of land where her parents are buried. Kopu contributes in many ways to family affairs. I met her on a number of occasions during my fieldwork on Rarotonga: at a ceremony in connection with the erection of a headstone of a relative, at a haircutting ceremony of one of her nephews, and at a funeral of one of her family members. Kopu stressed her emotional relation to her homeland, and said that keeping in contact with her family on Rarotonga is very important for her. She often talked about her intention to return to the island in later years, and stressed that she never forgot where she came from – which family and which land.

Paiere Mokoroa, a Cook Islander who has written about absentee landowners, also stresses the deep relationship Cook Islanders have with their land:

> To the Cook Islanders, the 'rights' to land is always awaiting for them. They could leave at any time and would return if it suits them. There is very little or none of any Cook Islander that I have heard of has changed his nationality. This is because that the Cook Islanders beleive [sic] that they have a 'home' *ipukarea* to live on. (Mokoroa n.d.: 9)[26]

In my opinion, this implies that belonging to a place can counterbalance feelings of dislocation and displacement (Lovell 1998: 5).

Clearly not all Cook Islanders who intend to return after retiring actually do so. But there are a number of returnees, like an elderly couple I met in

Mangaia. They had lived in New Zealand for more than twenty years, and came back to Mangaia five years before I spoke to them. 'We always knew when we retire we have a piece of land in Mangaia where we can plant. This piece of land is enough. We can live from this land [...] The people in the Cook Islands have a different life. They are not as greedy as people in New Zealand. You don't need much to live here'. For them to have a piece of land meant security during their life in New Zealand. It also meant that they were part of a society that matches their notion of an ideal society – at least more so than that in New Zealand. Connell states that the returned nurses he interviewed said that they had returned mainly for social reasons – for instance, because of the way of life in the Cook Islands, the possibility of owning land and a house, to be close to their families, and for the sense of being 'at home' (Connell 2005: 341). For many of the Cook Islanders of the first generation living in New Zealand with whom I talked, the topic of returning to their home island at some time was important. Staying in New Zealand was seen as temporary, and a plan to return usually existed – sometimes as only a vague idea, but in a number of cases as a project on which they had been working for some years, such as by building a house on their home island.

To have land rights in the Cook Islands also has another meaning for absentee landowners. Many times I heard the statement 'I am a landowner', especially from Cook Islanders in New Zealand or those who had recently returned to their home island. To be a landowner in Rarotonga has various cultural meanings; in particular it means that an individual is legitimized as part of the Rarotongan social order, because to have such rights their family has most probably lived on the island for a long time, and that family's original title holder was given a share of land from the founding ancestors Tangiia and Karika. Even in cases in which individuals did not have specific use rights, the connection to land was often evoked in statements like: 'My family owns land in Rarotonga. The land reaches from the mountains to the sea. It is the land where my family has always lived'.

The importance of the exchange of goods – both material and immaterial – between Cook Islanders in different places is shown by both Alexeyeff (2004) and Fitzgerald (1989: 263). The concern of the latter, however, is on those with direct Cook Islands ancestry who are born in New Zealand. He stresses that they tend to continue to identify as 'some form of "Cook Islander"' (ibid.: 264), and concludes that although places in the Cook Islands do have significance for them, those places are somewhat less important than they are for Cook Islanders of the first generation – they lose their significance as points of reference in everyday life. The result is that the place has no 'real' aspect, but is mainly imagined. He concludes that the consequence is a 'misplaced' identity (ibid.: 264). In my opinion,

Fitzgerald overemphasizes the importance of 'real' places: all kinds of places are only meaningful for people if they have an imagined meaning.[27]

In a number of cases, contact with land and family is maintained or established at a different level. For a number of Cook Islanders who have left their homeland, ties to their family have become weak or even nearly disappeared. Nevertheless, some wish to be registered as landowners, or even, for various reasons, wish to obtain use rights over a piece of land. It is not unusual that in such cases they refer to the right that is defined by the legal order of the state. This means that they do not consult the family but instead apply to the Land Division of the High Court for establishing use rights directly. In a number of cases the consequence of this procedure is a serious conflict with that person's family members 'at home' who consider the family as the rightful holder of the respective piece of land. These conflicts can eventually end up before a Land Division judge. Because the judges normally do not decide for applicants in cases where the family does not agree, the conflict is then 'handed back' to be settled out of court. The consequence is that the applicants have to talk to their families, and thus enter into or revive a dialogue with them. Conflicts can thus be a way to strengthen or revitalize bonds between migrants and Cook Islanders at home through a process of arguing that is at the same time one of learning about the history and traditions of the island and their family.

Belonging in these cases is made visible and tangible first by engaging in argument, and eventually by gaining the legal right to use land in one's homeland. It is important to note that I did not hear of any case where such an application was not finally accepted by the family. Family members feel morally obliged to give a piece of land to the applicant once they accept them as a member of their family, but this acceptance is reached through a process of a conflict and its management. Conflict can thus contribute to a process in which a group identifies an individual as a recognized member of that group, and the individual identifies themselves as a member.

The connection between land rights and belonging to a family is visible in the 'written traditions' collected by the traditional authorities mentioned above. In the part of these 'written traditions' that covers the land rights of absentees, it is recorded that for 'a member of a tribe who leaves the tribe to reside with and become a member of another tribe', use rights in land are 'secured to the members of the tribe who have remained within the tribe' (Koutu Nui 2001: 4). Rights to hold and use land and membership of a 'tribe' are closely linked here.

As already mentioned, many of those Cook Islanders living in New Zealand or elsewhere who have acquired a right of occupation on the island do not, in the end, return to their home island. In some cases their land is used by their descendants or by other relatives, and in other cases by persons who are not related to them. In the latter case, the land is almost always used in order to plant short-term cash crops.[28] When there is a dwelling house on the land, in an increasing number of cases this is used as tourist accommodation, and friends or relatives organize the rental of the property. Although the judges of the Land Division of the High Court have tried, at least since 1978, to avoid this kind of 'absentee ownership' (David 1987: 167), numerous 'occupation rights' are in the hands of absentees; despite complaints about 'greedy' absentee landowners, these people are then accepted as family members and thus their right to occupy the land is also accepted. It must be stressed in this context that in many districts of the Cook Islands land is not particularly scarce. This means that family members or co-owners who need land normally get it – although in some cases not as much as they want.[29]

Applications for land rights can be interpreted as an identification process in which the place of origin of the applicant is maintained or re-established at a 'legal' level. The process actively involves two sides: the applicant and the family both have to negotiate the question of whether an individual belongs to a certain group, and deal with the consequences of this belonging. Because of the connection of people's places of origin with the social order of Rarotonga, places serve as a reminder of this order, a reminder of basic principles and of stability. In this context it is important not to dichotomize between nature and humans as, Lovell (1998: 8), for example, reminds us. I have shown elsewhere that the strong interconnections between land, social order, *mana* and history mean that in many contexts Rarotongans do not view the relationship between land and humans as a subject–object relationship (Pascht 2006: 325).[30] This does not mean that other motivations are totally excluded from individuals' efforts to maintain contact with their land and families. Economic considerations also play a role, as well as others, such as the desire 'to have a holiday place for our children', as one Cook Islander told me.[31] Because connection to and identification with land is re-established in a different manner from that which Cook Islanders at home have, it also includes elements related to notions that are common and accepted in New Zealand society: a registered piece of land in a beautiful location.

The role and meaning of land for both migrant Cook Islanders and for those who still live on the land differs in some respects: for migrants it usually has little meaning in their everyday lives in comparison with the significance it has for many Rarotongans 'at home'. For a number of Cook Islanders in New Zealand, however, one basic form of identification is the process of maintaining a link with their place of origin, to the land and to their family which is connected with it. Fitzgerald (1989: 272) mentions that it can take on the image of a nostalgic island paradise. This may be true in some cases, but in my opinion the term 'paradise', which I did encounter in a number of cases when Cook Islanders in New Zealand talked about their homeland, can also have other implications. When one returnee told me, 'I came back to Rarotonga because it's paradise here', and I asked him what this meant, he explained, rather as had the couple in Mangaia mentioned above: 'you don't have to buy everything, things are shared [...] family members care for one another'. So 'paradise' has become a metaphor for life and society on the islands, and for an ideal social and moral order. For some Cook Islanders in New Zealand, this 'paradise' is actually accessible, as they know they have rights to land there, and they try to actually realize this possibility by maintaining contact with it and by attempting to gain use rights.

## Conclusions

In order to illuminate the role of land in the identification of Cook Islanders I have offered several different perspectives on the phenomenon of 'absentee landowners'. Firstly, residents of the islands interpret the actions of the absentees in moral terms: they are seen as greedy, as infected by *papa'ā* values;[32] as not caring enough for their families, but instead only caring for themselves. This view on the part of Cook Islanders – that it is 'greed' that leads absentees to register use rights on the islands – is, in my interpretation, the expression of a sense that the absentees have disregarded an important value in the Cook Islanders' world-view, which is also related to family, land, *tā'onga* and *mana*, namely the aforementioned *aro'a*, which in this context is best translated as aid or assistance (for the family). Greed can be viewed as the antithesis of *aro'a*, and to say that migrants are 'greedy' implies that they have forgotten the value of *aro'a* for the family – especially the family that has remained on the land – and that they have neglected to engage in activities that are expected of them: participating in family affairs, engaging in exchange, sending money. Ultimately, when they are 'greedy' they are not acting appropriately as members of the family, and thus do not have rights to family land. Because they do not conform to local cultural values – especially that of *aro'a* – their identification as family members is refused.

Secondly, Loomis (1990) views the registering of land rights and the building of a house as ways of investing in the future, in response to the inherent uncertainty of many migrants' situations, and thus portrays it as an economically motivated act. My interpretation does not exclude that offered by Loomis, but in my opinion a very strong motivation for migrants to try to obtain use rights on their home island is identification: the process of maintaining their ties to their homeland, and at the same time with their family, the ancestors and the basic order of life, since all of these are deeply connected with land and land rights. In my interpretation, these ties can be maintained not only through the exchange of goods and by communication or family visits, but also by acquiring a use right in land. Conflicts can be an important aspect in this respect, because in the course of the attempt to come to a settlement, identities are challenged, created, strengthened and rebuilt. Land is not only important for Cook Islanders 'at home' who use it directly, but also for those who have moved away. Although ultimately only a small percentage of Cook Islanders living in New Zealand have actual use rights at home, most still maintain a connection with their homeland, not only for their own benefit, but also, indirectly, for that of their relatives.

The process of actively creating and maintaining relationships with one's family that are embodied in (rights to) land is not only significant for Cook Islanders in New Zealand; it is also important for Cook Islanders who live 'at home'. Individuals must show their affiliation to a group by actively engaging in group affairs (Pascht 2006: 281). This also allows the possibility of shifting one's affiliation from one family to another.

In my opinion, these considerations are important for any attempt to understand cultural change and the identities of Cook Islanders who live away from the Cook Islands themselves. Although their relation to land and place on their islands of origin is not necessarily important in daily life, and the meaning of land changes for them – and especially for those who are born there – it is misleading to call their sense of identity 'misplaced' as Fitzgerald (1989: 264) does. For Cook Islanders, identification with a place is part of the whole process of identification, and can take various forms. One way of identifying is to actually apply for use rights to a piece of land. Identification is also always closely connected to notions of kinship and family. Other aspects that may be relevant in this context are *tā'onga*, the myth of settlement of the island, the history of the family, *mana* and performances. In this process, the memory of place serves as a memory of social and political organizing principles, of morals and of stability (cf. Lovell 1998: 15).

## Acknowledgements

This chapter is based on thirteen months' fieldwork in 2000 and 2001 in the Cook Islands and New Zealand, sponsored by the German Research Foundation. My research focused on the island of Rarotonga, where I spent about eleven months. I would especially like to thank the Cook Islanders who helped me during my research, as well as Thomas Bargatzky, Marianne Hartan and Michaela Haug, who gave me valuable comments on the text.

## Notes

1. This figure is taken from Crocombe, Araitia and Tongia (2008: 156). They also mention that 65,000 Cook Islanders now live in New Zealand. They do not cite sources for these figures, however.
2. In Fitzgerald's interviews, for example, 17 per cent of second-generation Cook Islanders in Wellington see themselves as 'New Zealanders' and not as 'Cook Islanders' (Fitzgerald 1989: 264). Statistical material from New Zealand shows that 34 per cent of the persons who identified with one of the Pacific ethnic groups also identified as 'New Zealanders' (SNZ 2006: 10). For other combinations, see also Bedford and Didham (2001: 25–26).
3. In practice, a variety of motivations and aspects were responsible for the judge's decision as to who is registered and who is not. One result is that a number of conflicts today have their origins in these processes at the beginning of the twentieth century.
4. Crocombe, Araitia and Tongia (2008: 161) refer to two surveys from 2005 to show the high degree of fragmentation of land today. In the first example the number of owners of a section has risen from the original six to 170. If the register had been up to date, they suppose that the number could be 1,000 or more today.
5. This law was established with the Cook Islands Act (1915). There is the possibility of buying and selling leases in certain contexts, so that in practice land can be 'alienated' for up to sixty years (inclusive of all rights of renewal). An agreement to lease is only effective if the lease comes into effect within a year of the agreement. Since 1976, in addition to the approval of the landowners and the Land Division of the High Court, the approval of a Leases Approval Tribunal is required before a lease will be recognized in law.
6. This was established with the Cook Islands Amendment Act 1946 (§ 50).
7. In this article I use the term 'family', as Cook Islanders also do, in a very broad sense including *ngāti* and *kōpū tangata* (see below).
8. Although any Cook Islander can apply for occupation rights, it is usually granted only to people who are acknowledged co-owners of the respective land section.
9. Six lived in other places in Rarotonga, thirteen overseas. On nine of the nineteen pieces of land, a dwelling house has been built, of which five were in permanent use and four were not, or were only in temporary use.
10. One of the recent case studies of Crocombe, Araitia and Tongia (2008: 163) from 2005 shows an even higher percentage: about sixty per cent of the allocations were to absentees.
11. *Mana* is usually translated as 'power'. Shore specifies in his discussion of this important concept that for 'Polynesians, *mana* manifests the power of the gods in the human world' (Shore 1989: 164).

12. *Tapu* is an extremely complex term. Bradd Shore explains: 'As an active quality, *tapu* suggests a contained potency of some thing, place, or person. In its passive usage, it means forbidden or dangerous' for people who are not *tapu*. *Tapu* 'seems to combine contradictory properties, suggesting on the one hand sacredness, reverence, and distinctiveness and, on the other, danger, dread, and pollution' (Shore 1989: 144).
13. The term *aro'a* can be translated variously as, 'Kindness, sympathy, sorrow (for [somebody] in trouble), love (i.e. divine love, or loving kindness, not love between sexes…)' (Buse and Taringa 1995: s.v.).
14. To'u Ariki, the present president of the House of Arikis, explained to me in 2009: 'If you don't come from a chiefly family, from a chiefly title, that means you belong to the horse or to the dog or to the pig. As Cook Islanders, we come from a chiefly family. If not from a chiefly family, from a *mataiapo* [sub-chief] family. You don't come from the horse'.
15. This is not only true for Rarotonga. For example, Kingdon and Ward (1995: 46) point out that the role of land for identity in Oceania has been an important topic for decades.
16. Because of the sensitivity of the topic of land rights, I have used pseudonyms for the examples used in this chapter.
17. Not only places of origin, but also places that people have relations with in general may become bases for identity (Nero 1997: 446). For Rarotongans, many places are connected with their families.
18. Loomis (1990: 51–53) states that remittances do not decrease when migrants stay in New Zealand for longer periods.
19. A haircutting ritual is conducted today for boys at the age of about six to eight years. It was probably invented by the first missionaries (Loomis 1990: 199–202). For the ceremony, the boy wears his long hair in many thin plaits. The guests each hand over a present and cut one of the plaits. Normally this ritual is performed for the eldest son of a family, but many parents today decide against performing it.
20. This is not meant to imply that all Cook Islanders in New Zealand share the same world-view and the same identifications. As with other Pacific peoples in New Zealand (see Macphershon 2001: 72; Macphershon, Spoonley and Anae 2001: 13), Cook Islanders show great variety and diversity in this respect.
21. Unfortunately they do not elaborate on this topic.
22. Note that Cook Islanders refer to themselves as 'Māori'. This statement originates from an interview, during which Makiuti Tongia also wrote down his explanation for me and asked me to cite it from the written document.
23. I do not take into account the identification of Cook Islanders with their specific home islands here. To be a Rarotongan or an Atiuan can be important in certain contexts. Also, national identities that initially did not play a primary

role as an element in the complex personal identities of Pacific peoples have become more and more important for them (Macpherson 2001: 70–71); additionally, new identities that focus on a shared Polynesian origin ('P.I.'s,' 'Polys,' *tangata Pasefika* or 'Pasifikans') have recently become important for New Zealand-born Cook Islanders, Sāmoans and Niueans (Macphershon 2004: 143).
24. The general importance of new media and travel opportunities for migrants is mentioned by Spoonley (2001: 86–89).
25. Today, *marae* play a central role mainly when holders of traditional title names are invested. In certain situations they can symbolize the history and basic structure of the society.
26. Buse and Taringa give *ipukarea* as, 'Inherited land, homeland, ancestral home' (Buse and Taringa 1995: s.v.).
27. It remains unclear what Fitzgerald actually implies with the term 'misplaced'.
28. Concerning the reasons for planting various crops, see Hartan (2008).
29. It must be mentioned that, because of multiple ownership, the process of allocation of pieces of land becomes increasingly complicated if there is no established way to solve the allocation at the family level.
30. For a more general discussion of this topic for Polynesia, and especially Sāmoa, see Bargatzky (2001: 630).
31. Crocombe, Araitia and Tongia (2008: 165) stress that by the 1990s the monetary value of land rights had become more important.
32. The term *papa'ā* is Cook Islands Māori for 'white man, European' (Buse and Taringa 1995: s.v.).

## References

Alexeyeff, K. 2003. 'Dancing from the Heart: Movement, Gender and Sociality in the Cook Islands', Ph.D. diss. Canberra: Australian National University.
―――― 2004. 'Love Food: Exchange and Sustenance in the Cook Islands Diaspora', *Australian Journal of Anthropology* 15(1): 68–79.
Bargatzky, T. 2001. 'Die Weltanschauung der Polynesier unter besonderer Berücksichtigung Samoas', in H. Hiery (ed.), *Die deutsche Südsee 1884–1914: Ein Handbuch*. Paderborn: Ferdinand Schöningh, pp.607–35.
Baumann, Z. 2001. 'Identity in the Globalising World', *Social Anthropology* 9(2): 121–29.
Bedford, R., and R. Didham. 2001. 'Who Are the "Pacific Peoples"? Ethnic Identification and the New Zealand Census', in C. Macphershon, P. Spoonley and M. Anae (eds), *Tangata o te Moana Nui: The Evolving Identities of Pacific Peoples in Aotearoa/New Zealand*. Palmerston North: Dunmore Press, pp.21–43.

Browne, T.P. 1994. 'Traditional Rights and Customary Usage in the Cook Islands', in R. Crocombe and M. Meleisea (eds), *Land Issues in the Pacific*. Christchurch/Suva: Macmillan Brown Centre for Pacific Studies/Institute of Pacific Studies, pp.205-19.

Buse, J., and R. Taringa (eds). 1995. *Cook Islands Maori Dictionary*. Rarotonga: Ministry of Education, Government of the Cook Islands.

Chappell, D.A. 1999. 'Transnationalism in Central Oceanian Politics: A Dialectic of Diasporas and Nationhoods?' *Journal of the Polynesian Society* 108(3): 277-303.

Connell, J. 2005. 'A Nation in Decline? Migration and Emigration from the Cook Islands', *Asian and Pacific Migration Journal* 14(3): 327-50.

Crocombe, R., T. Araitia and M. Tongia. 2008. 'Absentee Landowners in the Cook Islands: Consequences of Change to Tradition', in AusAID (ed.), 'Making Land Work, Vol. II: Case Studies on Customary Land and Development in the Pacific'. Canberra: AusAID, pp.153-71.

David, R. 1987 [1984]. 'Cook Islands: Occupation Rights', in B. Acquaye and R. Crocombe (eds), *Land Tenure and Rural Productivity in the Pacific Islands*. Rome: FAO, pp.163-74.

Feinberg, R. 2002. 'Elements of Leadership in Oceania', *Anthropological Forum* 12(1): 9-44.

Fitzgerald, T.K. 1989. 'Coconuts and Kiwis: Identity and Change among Second-generation Cook Islanders in New Zealand', *Ethnic Groups* 7(4): 259-81.

Fox, J.J. 1997. 'Place and Landscape in Compararative Austronesian Perspective', in J.J. Fox (ed.), *The Poetic Power of Place: Comparative Perspectives on Austronesian Ideas of Locality*. Canberra: Research School of Pacific and Asian Studies, Australian National University, pp.1-21.

Gershon, I. 2007. 'Viewing Diasporas from the Pacific: What Pacific Ethnographies Offer Pacific Diaspora Studies', *Contemporary Pacific* 19(2): 474-502.

Godelier, M. 1999 [1996]. *Das Rätsel der Gabe: Geld, Geschenke, heilige Objekte*. Munich: Beck.

Gilson, R. 1980. *The Cook Islands 1820-1950*. Wellington, Suva: Victoria University Press, Institute of Pacific Studies of the University of the South Pacific.

Goldman, I. 1970. *Ancient Polynesian Society*. Chicago: University of Chicago Press.

Gupta, A., and J. Ferguson. 1992. 'Space, Identity, and the Politics of Difference', *Cultural Anthropology* 7(1): 6-23.

Hall, S. 1996. 'Introduction: Who Needs "Identity"?' in S. Hall and P. Du Gay (eds), *Questions of Cultural Identity*. New York: Columbia University Press, pp.3-17.

Hartan, M. 2008. 'Landwirtschaft in Polynesien zwischen Tradition und Moderne: Aspekte des lokalen Wissens zum Anbau von Nutzpflanzen auf den Cookinseln', Ph.D. diss. Bayreuth: University of Bayreuth.

Hau'ofa, E. 1994. 'Our Sea of Islands', *Contemporary Pacific* 6(1): 148-61.

Hirsch, E. 1995. 'Landscape: Between Place and Space', in E. Hirsch and M. O'Hanlon (eds), *The Anthropology of Landscape: Perspectives on Place and Space*. Oxford: Clarendon Press, pp.1-30.

Kingdon, E., and R.G. Ward. 1995. 'Land Tenure in the Pacific Islands', in E. Kingdon and R.G. Ward (eds), *Land, Custom and Practice in the South Pacific*. Cambridge: Cambridge University Press, pp.36-64.

Koutu Nui. 2001. 'A Report by the Koutu Nui of the Cook Islands on Lands and Traditional Titles of the Indigenous People of the Cook Islands'. Rarotonga: Koutu Nui.

Loomis, T. 1984. 'The Politics of Cook Islands Culture-troupe Performance', in P. Spoonley et al. (eds), *Tauiwi: Racism and Ethnicity in New Zealand*. Palmerston North: Dunmore Press, pp.128-41.

―――― 1990. *Pacific Migrant Labour, Class and Racism in New Zealand: Fresh off the Boat*. Aldershot: Avebury.

―――― 1991. 'The Politics of Ethnicity and Pacific Migrants', in P. Spoonley, D. Pearson and C. Macpherson (eds), *Nga Take: Ethnic Relations and Racism in Aotearoa/New Zealand*. Palmerston North: Dunmore Press, pp.37-50.

Lovell, N. 1998. 'Belonging in Need of Emplacement?' in N. Lovell (ed.), *Locality and Belonging*. London: Routledge, pp.1-24.

Macphershon, C. 2001. 'One Trunk Sends Out Many Branches: Pacific Cultures and Cultural Identities', in C. Macphershon, P. Spoonley and M. Anae (eds), *Tangata o te Moana Nui: The Evolving Identities of Pacific Peoples in Aotearoa/New Zealand*. Palmerston North: Dunmore Press, pp.66-80.

―――― 2004. 'From Pacific Islanders to Pacific People and Beyond', in P. Spoonley, C. Macphershon and D. Pearson (eds), *Tangata Tangata: The Changing Ethnic Contours of New Zealand*. Southbank: Dunmore Press, pp.135-74.

Macphershon, C., P. Spoonleyand and M. Anae. 2001. 'Pacific Peoples in Aotearoa: An Introduction', in C. Macphershon, P. Spoonley and M. Anae (eds), *Tangata o te Moana Nui: The Evolving Identities of Pacific Peoples in Aotearoa/New Zealand*. Palmerston North: Dunmore Press, pp.11-15.

Mokoroa, P. n.d. 'Absent Landowners', MS.

Nero, K. 1997. 'The End of Insularity', in D. Denoon et al. (eds), *The Cambridge History of the Pacific Islanders*. Cambridge: Cambridge University Press, pp.439-67.

Pascht, A. 2006. 'Das Erbe Tangiias und Karikas: Landrechte auf Rarotonga', Ph.D. diss. Bayreuth: University of Bayreuth.

―――― 2007. 'Die Macht der Traditionen: "Maori Custom" und Landrechte auf den Cookinseln', *Zeitschrift für Ethnologie* 132(1): 59-76.

―――― 2009. 'Cook Islands', in A. Dittmann, W. Gieler and M. Kowasch (eds), *Die Außenpolitik der Staaten Ozeaniens: Ein Handbuch von Australien bis Neuseeland, von Samoa bis Vanuatu*. Paderborn: Ferdinand Schönigh, pp.107-9.

_____ 2011. 'Land Rights in Rarotonga (Cook Islands): Traditions and Transformations', *Pacific Studies* 34(2/3): 195–222.

Shore, B. 1989. '*Mana* and *Tapu*', in A. Howard and R. Borofsky (eds), *Developments in Polynesian Ethnology*. Honolulu: University of Hawai'i Press, pp.137–74.

SNZ. 2006. 'Profile of New Zealander Responses, Ethnicity Question: 2006 Census', Statistics New Zealand. Retrieved 15 May 2009 from: http://www.stats.govt.nz/NR/rdonlyres/EA0F8124-619C-47B3-ADB7-CBB28F44AE85/0/ProfileofNewZealanderCensus2006.pdf.

Spoonley, P. 2001. 'Transnational Pacific Communities: Transforming the Politics of Place and Identity', in C. Macphershon, P. Spoonley and M. Anae (eds), *Tangata o te Moana Nui: The Evolving Identities of Pacific Peoples in Aotearoa/New Zealand*. Palmerston North: Dunmore Press, pp.81–96.

Weiner, A.B. 1992. *Inalienable Possessions: The Paradox of Keeping-while-giving*. Berkeley: University of California Press.

6

# Protestantism among Pacific Peoples in New Zealand

Mobility, Cultural Identifications and Generational Shifts

◆●◆

Yannick Fer and Gwendoline Malogne-Fer

According to the United Nations Population Fund, Oceania has the largest concentration of immigrants in its population (15.2 per cent) of any region, most of them living in Australia and New Zealand. Auckland – which includes 67 per cent of the 266,000 Pacific islands migrants – has thus become the largest Polynesian city in the world. Considering the particular strength of Christian faith on their home islands, and the fact that contemporary Polynesians tend to consider Christianity as a pillar of their cultural or 'traditional' identity, the establishment of several Polynesian churches in New Zealand may at first glance be interpreted as an attempt to restore a place of stability to a lifestyle disrupted by migration. Indeed, this was often the purpose of New Zealand Christian churches that have tried to accommodate Polynesian migrants. From these churches' perspective, religion has to serve as the 'ideological, practical and symbolic apparatus' described by Danièle Hervieu-Léger, enabling migrants to maintain and develop their sense of belonging to a 'chain of memory' (Hervieu-Léger 1993: 119). Linking the first migrants to their past life in the Pacific islands, churches also contribute to the intergenerational transmission of cultural and religious identities, which takes on a specific dimension in the migration context. This understanding of religion as a guardian of memory is partly relevant, but it may underestimate migrants' capacity to elaborate new forms of religious life, fostered both by their inclusion into the New Zealand context and by enduring transnational links with the islands. Memory is indeed caught in conflict between competing ideals of cultural and religious authenticity, and the 'children of the migration' do not always easily identify with their parents' churches.

This chapter aims to explore aspirations, dynamics and conflicts within Protestant Polynesian churches in New Zealand. After a general presentation of New Zealand's Polynesian communities, the chapter considers the extent to which 'historical' Polynesian Protestant churches have helped migrants to find their own place in New Zealand society by strengthening cultural identification, promoting political commitment and maintaining transnational links with families and 'mother' churches in the Pacific islands. Following this, the chapter looks at the trajectories of young New Zealand-born Pacific peoples converted to evangelical Protestantism, and at the alternative articulations between self-identification, cultural belonging and Christianity that are emerging from this conversion.

## The Establishment and Organization of Polynesian Communities in New Zealand

### Historical Overview and Demography

The expressions 'Pacific Islanders' and 'Pacific peoples' designate migrants from the Pacific islands, mostly Polynesian islands (Sāmoa, Tonga, Cook Islands, Tuvalu and Niue), living in New Zealand. They numbered about 2,000 following the Second World War, 167,000 in 1991 and 266,000 in 2006 – that is, 6.9 per cent of the population, a 60 per cent increase in fifteen years.[1] The migration of Pacific peoples to New Zealand is part of a larger process comprised of both increasing internal migration (rural depopulation) and external migration (from Micronesian and Polynesian islands to New Zealand, Australia and the United States, especially Hawai'i and California) (Rallu 1997). Except for Tongan migrants, all Pacific peoples come from countries formerly or currently placed under New Zealand administration. Sāmoan and Tongan entry into New Zealand is ruled by visa and quota schemes, while no restrictions apply to the entry of migrants from the Cook Islands or Niue (in free association with New Zealand since 1965 and 1974 respectively), or from Tokelau, a New Zealand territory.

To explain this migration, Pacific peoples mention their desire for a better life, through salaried jobs and opportunities to achieve a better education for themselves and their children. Kinship plays an important role, as family members already living in New Zealand are in charge of preparing for arrival and the establishment of close relatives (Macpherson 2004: 137–38). This system – which puts kinship at the core of migration networks – partly explains the strength of continuing links between communities that are geographically distant. This strength is illustrated by the significant amount of remittances from Polynesian migrants to their families on the islands, by information exchanges facilitated by media (TV, newspapers) and newer means (internet, e-mail), by holidays spent on the islands, and by the exchange of goods (taro, fish, art and craft items).[2] The organization of specific, often religious events – baptisms, birthdays, weddings and burials – also presents opportunities to gather together the scattered members of a family. For all these reasons, Paul Spoonley has suggested the concept of 'transnationalism', rather than diaspora, to underline the enduring links between communities (Spoonley 2001: 82). Helen Morton Lee, analysing overseas Tongan communities, adds that transnationalism entails that individuals feel 'at home' both in their nation of origin and in the host society (Lee 2004: 135–36).

Images that transnational migrants mentally associate with their two countries play a significant role in this process. 'For me', says Pastor Tourangi, 'I came here [in 1958] because of what I heard about New Zealand, a lot of money, a land of honey and all these things'.[3] At the same time, the strong link between first-generation migrants and their home island nurtures dreams of a return that is not always realized, as many close relatives have also settled in New Zealand. Aso Saleupolu also points out a recent evolution in funeral practices:

> I have a case in this church. Next month there will be a family trip to Sāmoa to exhume their mother and bring her to New Zealand, because now all the family's children are in New Zealand. I think ten years ago, every parent wanted to go back and die in Sāmoa. It's not the same now: people come here and their children look after them until they die. And when they die, they want to be buried where the children are.[4]

## Institutional Classification and Self-Identification: From Pacific Islanders to Pacific Peoples

The debate on the use and meaning of the expression 'Pacific Islanders' throws light on a construction of identity influenced both by self-identification and the perceptions of others. This expression has been criticized for fifteen years. Melani Anae in particular has underlined the fact that it is primarily an imposed identity construct, assuming a 'unity' or 'community' that has never existed. Moreover, in the mid 1970s, a time of economic crisis during which Pacific Islanders were accused of contributing to the increase in unemployment in New Zealand, the expression took on a pejorative connotation (Anae 1997). However, Anae also acknowledges the relevance of the expression, as in arts and sports, for young New Zealand-born Polynesians. This is congruent with the observations of Cluny Macpherson (2004: 139–43), which point to the fact that within Pacific Islander communities, new forms of differentiation tend to be less cultural than inter-generational. The children of first-generation migrants, whether from the Cook Islands, Sāmoa or Tonga, have 'grown up in extended families, lived in similar homes in the same suburbs, attended the same schools and churches ... played in the same rugby and netball teams, learned the same songs, and had hung out at the same malls in various suburbs' (ibid.: 143). From this common experience, they have elaborated a trans-Polynesian culture which is different from both their island-born parents and Pākehā (New Zealanders of European descent). Helen Morton Lee (2004: 145) also notes that a pan-ethnic identity is more likely to be claimed by those born overseas.

The term 'Pacific peoples' is now preferred to 'Pacific Islanders', and is commonly used by public authorities. This expresses a change in the criteria that define identity. Pacific peoples are not mainly defined by their land of origin, but by their belonging to a community and through a culture they are supposedly preserving and practising in New Zealand. And yet 'Pacific Islanders' is still frequently used by Polynesians themselves, who have to a certain extent appropriated the label.[5] The name of the Ministry of Pacific Islands Affairs has not been changed, even if its official purpose is 'to promote the development of Pacific peoples in New Zealand'. Winnie Laban explains:

> I think [Pacific Islanders is] very positive because, you know, we are people of this region and we always use the ocean [...] and I think that is the symbolism about bringing people together. [...] But there is a family connection that goes back to the ancient times of Polynesia, Melanesia, Micronesia, and I think that what links us together is the family model, in terms of the region.[6]

So these migrants enable New Zealand to emphasize its own Polynesian identity, its regional roots. From this perspective, Pacific peoples form a specific cultural category with a double status: a 'minority cultural group' but with acknowledged distinction due to political, historical, demographic and geographical factors (see MoJ/MPIA 2000). Today, New Zealand's official biculturalism has to cope with a *de facto* multicultural society. New Zealand was historically a British settler colony that emerged at the end of the nineteenth century from successive waves of migrants, and this Pākehā population rapidly exceeded the number of indigenous

Māori. During the 1970s and 1980s, the formalization of biculturalism through the reconsideration of the Treaty of Waitangi put the focus on an alliance between Māori and Pākehā, understanding this as the basis for New Zealand society.[7] But if new European and English-speaking migrants can easily fit into the Pākehā category, Polynesian migrants are excluded from the definition of Māori or *tangata whenua* (people of the land) as they have no specific rights to the land. Their experience of racist discrimination does not necessarily lead to trans-Polynesian solidarity based on common genealogical roots. On the contrary, Tracey McIntosh points out reciprocal negative representations: Pacific peoples criticize Māori for having lost their language and culture (through rural depopulation), and for the excessive politicization of cultural claims, while Māori tend to reproach Pacific peoples for their conversion to Christianity and capitalism (McIntosh 2001).

## Historical Polynesian Churches in New Zealand: Places of Memory and Changing Identity

### The Establishment of Polynesian Congregations in New Zealand

A distinctive feature of Pacific peoples is that they continue going to church in New Zealand – as the church is also a place for identity roots – while mainstream Pākehā churches have been declining since the 1960s.[8] The Christianization of the Polynesian islands began at the end of the eighteenth century with missionaries sent by the London Missionary Society (supported and followed by Polynesian teachers) and the Wesleyan Methodist Mission Society. But the Christian identity brought by European missions to Polynesia has today become an essential feature of the self-definition of a distinctive Polynesian cultural identity, fostering a sense of pride for having perpetuated both the missionaries' and the ancestors' heritages.

Among the mainstream New Zealand Protestant churches, the Presbyterian (then Congregational) Church and the Methodist Church are those which 'welcomed' Pacific peoples,[9] and therefore elaborated two distinct models. The first, advanced by the Congregational Church, consisted in assembling several Polynesian communities into a single congregation; in the second model, distinctive congregations were established for each community (Sāmoan, Tongan, Fijian). The first Polynesian congregation, established in 1946 within the Congregational Church of Newton in Auckland and called the Pacific Islanders Church (PIC), comprised Sāmoan, Cook Islander and Niuean congregations. This organizational model has been extended to other New Zealand cities to include Polynesian communities such as Wellington, Christchurch and Dunedin.

In 1968, when the Congregational and Presbyterian churches merged, they became Pacific Islanders Presbyterian churches. Each congregation conducts its own service in its own language, ideally with its own minister. At the beginning of the 1970s, a 'combined' service in English was added, first in the Newton PIC, as a concession to youth who hadn't mastered Polynesian languages. But most church activities are still run within each congregation. These churches, as Cluny and La'avasa Macpherson note, are conservative by nature, aiming to replicate the organization of the island 'mother' churches (Macpherson and Macpherson 2001: 28–29). But in New Zealand, the 'mother' church also commonly designates the first established congregation of Newton, now associated with a set of nostalgic memories from that 'good old time' when Polynesian communities were (truly or ideally) bound by solidarity. A 'map of memories' has progressively emerged that links the islands to those original places of Pacific peoples' gathering in New Zealand, which now serve as the landmarks of their establishment in the host society.

The PIC system is now in competition with Polynesian churches directly attached to island 'mother' churches. The Congregational Christian Church in Sāmoa (CCCS), set up in New Zealand during the 1960s, comprised fifty congregations in 1994.[10] The Cook Islands Christian Church (CICC), set up in New Zealand during the 1980s, comprised twenty congregations in New Zealand (and thirty in the Cook Islands) by 2005.

The Methodist minister Lynn Frith underlines the different perception of Polynesian identities involved in the two distinct church models:

> In the Methodist Church [...] we've got distinctly Sāmoans, distinctly Tongans and distinctly Fijians and we don't expect them all to function together, we don't assume that they can make one Church. [...] I think that's the difference: the general Pākehā perspective in the Presbyterian Church is 'all Pacific Islanders are the same'.[11]

The Methodist Church is also in competition with churches directly attached to the Methodist Church of Sāmoa and, above all, with churches attached to the Free Wesleyan Church of Tonga that have been established since the beginning of the 2000s.[12]

## Strengthening Cultural Identification

Among Polynesian migrants in New Zealand, congregations are considered 'new villages' (Macpherson 2004: 151), and the archetypal place for community gatherings. Ornaments, flowers, liturgical elements, hymns and clothes contribute to create a Polynesian atmosphere. The use of Polynesian languages and the presence of Polynesian ministers (whose first generation was trained at the island theological colleges) enable the communities to enjoy an atmosphere quite similar to that of their home island. These churches exemplify what Maurice Halbwachs (1994) has called the 'social frames of memory': a place where congregants elaborate a collective and homogeneous representation of the community of origin through the preservation of a common language and biblical interpretations. Closely tied to the communities,[13] Christian churches thus participate in the creation of new 'localities'. Appadurai (2005) has noted that groups rather than actual territorial limits create locality. Three specific features make it possible here: first, the strength of religious practice among Polynesian migrants; second, a strong urban concentration of these populations in New Zealand (79 per cent of Pacific peoples live in the Auckland and Wellington urban areas); and third, the cultural, linguistic and political commitment of these churches. They express this commitment through the organization of cultural or national events, the promotion of Polynesian languages and the role of community spokesmen held by Polynesian religious leaders in dealing with New Zealand's political authorities.

Regular or special activities organized by the Polynesian churches provide many opportunities to strengthen relationships between people with the same island origins. Inter-congregational meetings in particular, like those of women's groups or choir competitions, help different congregations of the same cultural group to maintain close ties. Special events like baptisms, birthdays (at twenty-one years), graduation ceremonies, weddings and funerals also offer opportunities for large gatherings. But these events can take a national and patriotic form: Sāmoan congregations celebrate the independence of Sāmoa on the first Sunday of June; Cook Islanders celebrate the arrival of the first Christian missionaries in the Cook Islands on 16 October; and Tongan congregations celebrate national official days like the Tongan king's birthday or the anniversary of his coronation.

The cultural commitment of these churches is illustrated by the use of Polynesian languages in the service, and the key role played by churches in the establishment of pre-schools in Polynesian languages. These pre-schools, providing total immersion in Polynesian languages or bilingual teaching, have been created by Pacific peoples since 1986, following the pattern of Māori pre-schools, and most are affiliated with a church (Hunkin-Tuiletufuga 2001). In 2003, 1,500 children attended a Sāmoan-speaking school, 850 attended a Cook Islander-speaking school and 750 a Tongan-speaking school (MoE 2004). These schools do not exclusively accept congregants' children, and thus contribute to the integration of the Polynesian churches into the local community.

Finally, while very few Pacific peoples currently hold political mandates, religious leaders do represent Polynesian communities before New Zealand's political authorities, and can serve as a mediation body. They strive to fulfil this purpose by establishing ecumenical island associations at the national and local levels. Following the initiative taken by his Sāmoan colleagues, the Cook Islander Presbyterian minister Toko Ine explains why he recently set up such an ecumenical association for Cook Islands ministers in the Wellington region:

> TOKO INE: That's the whole idea of this formulation of the Cook Islands body: the fact that each church has its people and now the ministers get together so the people come together, and then we can create a body, a Cook Islands religious advisory council. We are thinking on setting our strategy, our programme for our new group. We are eleven Cook Islands ministers in Wellington: Catholic, Seventh-Day Adventist, Assemblies of God, Apostolic, Presbyterian and CICC. So it's good to talk and to be united, and then the whole community will be united.
>
> Q: It could be a tool for lobbying, to talk with governmental departments?
>
> TOKO INE: Exactly. And I think all the departments will be aware now that, on things concerning Cook Islanders, they can come to us. And from the [Cook] Islands, we can look at it, because there are many groups from the [Cook] Islands who come to New Zealand, some groups are fundraising, some come for education, and we need to look at it and support them in all things.[14]

The recognition of the significant role played by these churches as actors in civil society reinforces the legitimacy of the ecumenical associations' leaders. Winnie Laban confirms:

> The prime minister has a meeting with all the church leaders twice a year, and that's an opportunity for the churches to tell us if there are happy or not, and I think it's good. The churches have an important role in the society, they are the civil society. It's very important and our job is to work closely with them, and we should consult them too. They make an enormous contribution to the well-being of our community and our families, and that makes a lot of sense for the state to work with them or to ask them their advice. Or if they are not happy about something, they can come to the government, because if they decide that they will not make their work anymore, who will carry this responsibility? It's a tension because some of the funding comes from the government too and sometimes it's not enough. […] They play an enormous role, a very important role, especially for the Pacific community, because the percentage of Christians is very high, Christians of many thoughts and differences.[15]

### Territorial Scattering and New Church Organizations in an Urban Setting

Despite their central role in the life of the communities of New Zealand's Pacific peoples, these Protestant churches are not merely a duplication of churches in the Pacific islands; moreover, the island churches themselves are experiencing change and transnationalization. At least four points distance them from one another.

Firstly, the parish organization in New Zealand reflects another relation to territory. Traditionally, the parish in the Polynesian islands is inseparably tied to a village. In the Cook Islands, for example, parishes and villages have the same boundaries, and each parish sub-division corresponds to a village's district, thus underlining the very strong territorialization of religious membership. Migration to New Zealand, on the other hand, tends to inspire gatherings on the basis of island or archipelago origins. But when congregations reach a sufficient size, then the possibility of replicating some aspects of village organization reappears, as in the Auckland Niuean congregation, which includes thirteen choirs representing the thirteen villages of Niue.[16]

The second point is the territorial scattering produced by the size of New Zealand's urban areas. In this context, the church can become the central place in which a scattered community converges, especially when an enduring attachment still links migrants to the church they first attended in New Zealand, despite successive changes of residence. This is the case with Sāmoan Methodists who still attend the church in Ponsonby, even if they no longer live near the city centre of Auckland due to changes in the property market:

> In the early 1970s, Pacific Islanders began immigrating to New Zealand in significant numbers, and many settled in neighbourhoods near the city centre. They naturally attended churches in the area, and Sāmoans in particular were attracted to St Johns Methodist Church in Ponsonby once it was designated a Sāmoan-language parish in 1984. This pattern began to change in the 1990s as Ponsonby became a trendy enclave and land prices skyrocketed. Sāmoan families found they could make significant profits by selling their properties and moving to the suburbs. [...] Revd Iakopo Fa'afuata is presbyter of the Auckland Sāmoan Parish in Ponsonby. When he took up the office, Iakopo believed the congregation would want to sell its church property and re-establish itself closer to the areas Sāmoans were moving [to]: 'We held [a] meeting to discuss it but the people were loyal to Ponsonby. Some cried at the thought of leaving'.[17]

Various organizations have tried to cope with this situation by concentrating all church activities on Sundays (or on another day, when the church is used by other groups), or by delegating certain activities to a local level, for example by meeting in congregants' homes. The first model is employed by the Rotuman Methodist congregation in Auckland, as Susau Stricking explains:

> Every Friday night and Friday evening from 7.00 PM to 9.30 PM we meet at the church. We have prayer meetings, cell groups, Bible studies and [the] youth programme [on] the same day because we scatter everywhere in Auckland: some families live in the south, some families live in the centre, in the west. So to make things short we all come on the Friday evening, do all our activities. So the youth do their own things, the women fellowships have their own meetings and their prayers, once a week. We come twice to the church, we come on the Sunday for our worship and then we come on Friday for our groups' activities and our prayer meetings.[18]

The second model has been set up by most Methodists of urban Tongan congregations. This decentralization of activities is adapted to the urban context and inspired by John Wesley's Bible classes and Wesleyan evangelization methods, which emphasize the need for missionaries to go and meet people where they live. Regarding Wesley classes, Tevita Finau says:

> Three families meet once a week or once a fortnight in the family house and do Bible studies and prayers. It was originated by John Wesley, but we have revived it in New Zealand, because in New Zealand we have to be more robust and more proactive. Because it's all right in Tonga [...] We have the dawn service, the morning service, Sunday school and the afternoon service, and also the evening service, in Tonga. But here, the space, we live far apart and there are distances between families. So rather than centralizing everything in the church, the Wesley classes look after themselves. And [...] in the Wesley classes, we group them in classes of families who live close together, so it means lighter responsibilities for the minister because it is home based and families look after themselves. And once every three months, Wesley classes meet together.[19]

With less success, the Cook Islander congregations of the PIC have also tried to group congregants living in the same areas, placing these local groups under the supervision of one or several deacons. This organization can contribute to integration at a sub-congregation level for those who no longer go to the church.[20] But this is sometimes hampered by the inability of aged deacons to visit the families under their charge.

Thirdly, the New Zealand context is marked by strong religious diversity and mobility. The Polynesian migrants are able to choose their church – including a Polynesian church – depending on various criteria (pastor's personality, location, theological orientation, attachment to a 'mother' church or a New Zealand denomination, and so on).

Finally, the deterritorialization of religious membership entails a redefinition of cultural identity focused on the issue of language. Different understandings of Polynesian identity coexist, and opposition can arise between elders (who consider mastery of language as a central part of identity) and New Zealand-born youth (who claim Polynesian identity even without language mastery) (Anae 1997). So rather than an unchanging landmark, churches tend to become a place of transition where New Zealand-born generations elaborate new identities by disentangling culture, family ties and religious choices.

## Churches in Transition: The Difficult Articulation of Familial, Linguistic and Cultural Logics

Churches have played a major role in facilitating the installation and integration of Pacific peoples in New Zealand, and in helping to maintain strong links with family remaining in the Pacific islands. Nevertheless, the decline of religious practice among New Zealand-born youth who have grown up in the Polynesian churches throws light on current tensions. And the institutionalization of cultural diversity within mainstream Protestant churches has some paradoxical consequences for Polynesian communities.

Familial changes and identity quests among New Zealand-born Polynesians have a significant impact on the churches. Services in Polynesian languages fitted the needs of first-generation migrants, but they are becoming a problem for the next generation due to the insufficient mastery of the language by New Zealand-born generations. Examining the example of Cook Islanders within the Presbyterian Church, Tokerau Joseph points out a dissociation between familial and church dynamics, while the church was traditionally organized as an extended family: 'As their focus shifted from church involvement to immediate family involvement, they found that demands or requirements of home life became more important than the demands and duties of church life' (Joseph 2005: 113–14). And yet, church initiatives aiming to contain the disaffection of 'youth' (a highly malleable social category) primarily seek the re-involvement of congregants' close family. Tokerau Joseph thus initiated new 'family services' within the Otara PIC, in South Auckland:

> We had a family service, not just for the young people but for the family: father, mother, grandfather, grandmother and children, let them work together in the service. It was very good, when we tried the family service, more people came to church because of their family, so that was good. […] [It was] like every three months or so, four services in a year, to bring families together. The purpose was to allow families to take part in the service, and encourage them to ask families to

come with them and to be together. Most of the families have no church, they stay home. So they were happy to do that.[21]

This transformation of families into a 'mission field' is occurring simultaneously with an increasingly political stance being taken by Polynesian religious leaders regarding the defence of 'family values', a trend that Winnie Laban regrets (she would prefer a mobilization of Pacific peoples around economic and social issues).[22]

Finally, institutional dynamics sometimes contradict the evolution of self-identification. While an increasing proportion of Pacific peoples tend to identify themselves with two (or more) ethnic groups,[23] the institutionalization of multiculturalism within the Presbyterian Church (for example) is implicitly based on the addition of ethnic groups seen as homogeneous. In 1998, this church decided to set up a Polynesian synod to ensure better representation of Polynesians within it. But in 2000, only 54 per cent of PIC congregations and 67 per cent of pastors of Polynesian origin had joined the synod. Reasons offered for this reluctance are numerous: the way in which the synod is run; the priority given to local solidarities (presbyteries) at the expense of cultural solidarities (synod); and the fear of being ascribed to a double minority position, in the Church and in the synod. This fear is notably strong among Cook Islanders, who often consider the synod as a 'Sāmoan thing' because of the dominant voice and number of Sāmoans within the group. The fact that a significant proportion of Polynesian pastors and congregants have declined the invitation to join the Polynesian synod shows the gap between the belief dimension and the identity dimension in religious practices: people do not always identify with the institutional bodies that supposedly represent them, especially when these bodies are based on cultural and linguistic characteristics. Within the PIC, the possibility of attending English-speaking services constitutes a first step in the dissociation between Polynesian languages and religious activities. This dissociation can finally produce personal itineraries of religious mobility shifting away from the frame of mainstream Polynesian Protestant congregations.

## Religious Change and Generational Shifts among New Zealand-born Pacific Peoples

Contemporary changes in Polynesian Protestantism occur primarily at the intersection of social and geographical mobility on the one hand, and intergenerational relationships on the other. For younger generations born in New Zealand, religious belonging is bound up with the complexities of local inclusion, cultural identification and transnational communities, as well as individual freedom, familial heritage and traditional patterns of authority. Most elders of Polynesian churches see youngsters' insufficient command of Polynesian languages as the most evident symptom of acculturation by mainstream New Zealand society. The new forms of expression promoted by church youth groups (often under evangelical influences), and their increasing reluctance to obey the traditional holders of authority in the church, reinforce this conviction. Whether youth still consider themselves 'true' Polynesians despite this disqualification, or instead look to other identities within New Zealand multiculturalism, they must go through an often painful process of self-definition.

In his study of Māori urban youngsters unable to match the *marae* model of Māori identity, Toon van Meijl argues that such conflict between several representations of the self can lead to a 'dialogical self[:] a dynamic multiplicity of *I*-positions in the landscape of the mind, intertwined as the mind is with the minds of other people' (Van Meijl 2006: 929). The religious itineraries of New Zealand-born young Polynesians show similar kinds of multiple identifications, as well as various attempts to disentangle their cultural self-identification from religious belonging: they can be 'true' Sāmoans without belonging to a 'purely' Sāmoan church, or embrace a 'Pacific people' identity by joining a regional evangelical network rather than a PIC Church, or claim to be genuine Christians not because of their Pacific heritage but because of a 'personal' experience of conversion, and so on.

Evangelical churches and missionary networks thus play a specific role in this process by providing a rhetorical frame focused on conversion understood as a 'new birth', which allows individuals to distance themselves – symbolically and/or concretely – from the compulsory membership that formerly defined their identity. Such churches also emphasize the need for individuals to 'move on' by presenting change as progress, and life as a matter of personal choices.

## From Social and Geographical Mobility to Religious Mobility

In New Zealand, as in the Polynesian islands, the youth groups of mainstream Christian churches have been a major field of evangelical influence over recent decades, often with the initial agreement of church leaders seeking effective ways to keep the younger generation within the church. Youth missionary organizations like Youth with a Mission and Youth for Christ have been at the forefront of this movement. Theological differences between mainstream and evangelical and charismatic Protestantism have not always been understood by youth as such, the difference seen rather as a way of escaping from the authority of elders through new freedoms of expression: the ability to speak more freely, or to dance or embrace contemporary styles of music.

The belief in a more personal salvation matches social and economic changes: in the religious field as in social life, it seems that one increasingly must find one's own way, as it becomes more difficult (and/or undesirable) to simply reproduce the situation of one's parents. And finally, increases in educational attainment spread the conviction that Christian life should also be a matter of progress, in biblical knowledge and religious experience – two opportunities that these movements seem to offer through their connection to a forum wider than the local church: global Protestant networks.

The definition of cultural identity itself is intertwined with these changes in religious identity induced by social, geographical and inter-generational mobility. In the Polynesian islands, the old Protestant churches today consider themselves guardians of cultural authenticity and tradition. But this tradition still includes the control, inherited from the early Western missions, of indigenous bodies and their 'impulses'. So the desire for more individual freedom of expression and the reluctance of younger generations to accept elders' authority can also encompass a rehabilitation of bodily expressions, like dance as an authentic expression of Christian faith.

In New Zealand, the possibility of 'choosing' a cultural identity as part of an evangelical 'new birth' can express a similar opposition to the compulsory cultural and religious heritage represented by Polynesian mainstream Protestant churches, as well as the elaboration of a distinctive identity within a multicultural and secular society. All these aspects are exemplified by the development of the Island Breeze movement since the beginning of the 1980s.

## Island Breeze: From Cultural 'New Birth' to Global Networks of Belonging

The Island Breeze movement was launched in 1979 by the American-Sāmoan Sosene Le'au, following contact with a New Zealand leader of Youth with a Mission. Le'au then attended a school of evangelism in Kona, Hawai'i (Le'au 1997). In 1979, he led his own school, training a group of twelve students, mostly Sāmoans and Hawaiians. These students, of mainstream Protestant family background, had converted to Pentecostal churches that did not welcome Polynesian cultural expressions. They were seeking a way to include their cultural heritage within the framework of predominantly Western charismatic Protestantism. During a time of worship, they began to move and dance in a Polynesian way. When they used these cultural expressions during an outreach campaign following training, at the South Pacific Games held in Fiji in 1979, they saw the significant impact this could have on young Pacific Christians. After the outreach campaign, the group went to Sāmoa and, with the support of friends involved in Polynesian show business, prepared a set of dances to be used in evangelism. In 1980, they took the name Island Breeze and flew to New Zealand for their first tour, making a significant impact on young Pacific Islanders and Māori.

Among New Zealand-born Pacific people, Island Breeze seemed to offer the possibility of reconciling Christian faith and Polynesian culture, with greater individual freedom. It was also a way to develop a new sense of belonging, halfway between a secularized English-speaking New Zealand society and the community churches that aimed to maintain religious traditions, Polynesian languages and the island system of authority. Due to the relative uncertainty about their identity caused by migration and multiculturalism, this individual freedom to be oneself, to find one's 'true' identity, has led to various circles of identification and belonging, beyond the national identity inherited from the older generation.

Pacific youth have expressed their ambivalent feelings towards cultural identities in the various ways they have used the notion of 'roots' to define a place where they want to belong. The conversion to evangelical Protestantism enables them to 'step out' of their culture, as Sosene Le'au puts it: 'Before you are a citizen of any country or culture, you must be a citizen of [God's] kingdom and His culture' (ibid.: 54). But Island Breeze also fosters a kind of cultural 'new birth', with the voluntary reappropriation of a cultural identity that is re-learnt, reformulated and, to a certain extent, chosen. As they felt their identity was inevitably bound to the land where they grew up, many of the first to join Island Breeze in New Zealand refused an 'uprooted' migrant identity and symbolically planted new roots in the local indigenous community:

> There are Polynesians [...] especially those who have grown up in a different culture, let's say for instance some Sāmoans especially in New Zealand, they grew up in New Zealand, born and raised in New Zealand, and they didn't like what they saw about their culture: a lot of trouble makers, you know, always bad news. So they felt ashamed, and so they don't want to be Sāmoans, they want to be Māori, New Zealander. And we have those in Island Breeze, some of our founding members were like that. For a long time they carried this thing that they didn't want to be Sāmoans.[24]

Thus the founder of the New Zealand branch of Island Breeze is a New Zealand-born Sāmoan who 'has always considered himself as a Māori'.[25] The further development of Island Breeze in the Pacific islands, and the new transnational connections that have emerged from tours and regional training sessions, have progressively shaped a different space of self-identification. Rather than identifying themselves with local references – Māori indigeneity or the New Zealand Pacific peoples' common experience – Polynesian youngsters involved in Island Breeze focused on their Pacific roots and extended their sense of belonging to a Pacific brotherhood that is both cultural and generational. In a kind of resurgence of what was known in the 1970s and 1980s as the Pacific Way, they articulated their own version of Pacific cultures away from the traditional authorities in charge of cultural memory. To learn and perform dances from all the Pacific islands symbolically helped members of the group to embrace this Pacific identity:

> We come on stage and we will be Māori, we get off stage and we have to change: now I have to put away my Māori way of doing things and now be a Hawaiian, come up and now be a Sāmoan. We dance all the dances, which is good, you know, one of our values is that we are called to embrace all the other peoples.[26]

A second and larger circle of belonging is the Indigenous Peoples networks. The UN International Decade of the World's Indigenous Peoples (1995 to 2004) has expanded the global network of indigenous claims. From similar experiences – land dispossession, exploitation, cultural repression – this solidarity has elaborated a sort of meta-identity or indigenous brotherhood, often defined in terms of a specific relationship with land and ancestors. Many evangelical movements, including Island Breeze, aim to tap into this global process, by formulating a Christian version of indigenous global identity, and fostering exchanges between so-called Christian indigenous peoples. This notably implies the 'redemption' of indigenous cultures, meaning both the rehabilitation of cultural expressions and the Christian reformulation of them, hollowing out a significant part of their initial content.

And thirdly, the larger circle of belonging is a global and multicultural world in which culture becomes a tool for evangelism, being considered a more authentic and therefore more effective way of presenting oneself to others. The use of touristic display codes helps to transform cultural differences into a medium of universal communication, providing easy figures such as the *haka* dance for Māori identity, *hula* for Hawaiians, and so on. Pacific peoples from New Zealand have been able to meet similar groups established in the Pacific but also in Missouri, Puerto Rico, the Philippines and Brazil, and to travel the world or join outreach meetings organized during international sporting events like the Olympic Games and various world championships.

These three circles of belonging exemplified by Island Breeze can be experienced within New Zealand society, through the articulation of self-identification and Pacific peoples' cultural communities, through relationships between New Zealand-born Polynesians and Māori of the same generation, and through the emergence of such new religious places as the Hosanna World Outreach Centre, which combines a local generational shift, a transnational Sāmoan identity and a global multiculturalism.

**Horizontal Multiculturalism: The Hosanna World Outreach Centre**

Hosanna World Outreach Centre is a charismatic Baptist church located in a northern suburb of Wellington. In 2007, it had about 1,000 members. It described itself as 'a radical, multi-cultural, new generation, cell church of multitudes from every nation, tribe, race, and language coming together to worship and to impact the community, the nation, and the world for God'.[27] It was established in Wellington during the 1990s by young Sāmoans, mostly New Zealand-born, and has recently set up several churches in Australia. The three stages in the development of this church underline most of the combined effects of the migration context and religious change on the self-definition of younger New Zealand-born Pacific peoples.

Coming from Sāmoan mainstream Protestant churches or historical Pentecostal churches (the Sāmoan Assemblies of God in New Zealand), the founders of the church strove to create a new place where the generational need for individual freedom could be fulfilled, away from traditional patterns of authority and community constraints. In doing so, they disconnected Sāmoan cultural identity, which they wanted to maintain, from the church and community institutions traditionally in charge of cultural memory: members can be Sāmoans and Christians on their own.

They also recreated a Sāmoan community with which New Zealand-born Sāmoans could easily identify. And part of this New Zealand-born identity includes a kind of multicultural duty, which has led them during the 2000s to welcome a significant community of black South African migrants. In the mid-2000s, the church established two Sunday services, one in Sāmoan and the other in English, and identified itself as both a Sāmoan and multicultural community. The emergence of this institution can be described as one of horizontal multiculturalism, not initiated by the Western dominant culture as a way to accommodate cultural diversity, but by a cultural minority itself in order to include other cultural minorities. This outcome of generational shifts occurring within Protestant groups of Pacific peoples in New Zealand significantly differs from the cultural identity articulated by a movement like Island Breeze, which tends to seek new circles of belonging beyond national origin. Here, Sāmoan identity is seen both as a piece of the New Zealand multicultural puzzle and as a transnational community that enables church leaders to develop a global evangelistic strategy.

At the New Zealand scale, they implicitly claim an active role in the making of society through their multicultural goodwill and, more explicitly, through strong activism in the defence of 'Christian values' as the core of a country's identity. Thus the Hosanna World Outreach Centre participated in demonstrations and petitions against liberal laws voted on by New Zealand's Parliament under Helen Clark's left-wing government (1999 to 2008). In 2007, they again joined conservative Christian networks to protest against a law labelled as 'anti-family' because it removed from the Crimes Act the statutory defence of 'reasonable force' to correct a child, meaning there will be no future justification for the use of such force.[28]

In its third stage of development, the church also embraces the current globalization and transnationalization of the Sāmoan community, following Sāmoan migration through the opening of new branches in Australia and the expression of a global ambition influenced by American televangelists and networks.

## Conclusion

Pacific peoples' experience in New Zealand shows that the influence of migration on religious sociability includes both conservative attempts to set up a religious place of cultural memory, and interactions with the host society leading to new church roles and organizational models. The tension between a self-identification based on shared religious memory inherited from the islands and the New Zealand multicultural context that imposes its own classification schemes greatly contributes to the reshaping of religious identities. Such tensions also reinforce a generational gap, producing religious mobility more effectively than did the geographical mobility of the first migrants.

Due to the increasing circulation of people, information and beliefs among Pacific island societies and migrants' host societies, today's reality has moved beyond the simple opposition between the assumed stability of identity in the islands and the disruption produced by migration or multiculturalism. The changes described in New Zealand are mostly embedded in transnational dynamics, and should be considered as prefiguring – and sometimes reflecting – similar trends in Polynesian societies. As Charles Forman has pointed out, religious pluralism in particular tends to become a significant phenomenon and a challenge to 'the well-established relation of Christianity to the communal sense of identity' (Forman 1990: 30). Thus the transmission of religious identity and cultural memory tends to depend increasingly on the ability of individuals to appropriate a coherent set of beliefs among competing representations of identity. Mobility and conversion are the more evident but not the only patterns of this process, which also entails a reshaping of traditional religious places. Thus, migrant communities like New Zealand's Pacific peoples may provide some clues to understanding how this individual elaboration of cultural and religious identifications can take place within the framework of the 'communal sense of identity' mentioned by Forman.

## Notes

1. Figures taken from '2001 Census Snapshot 6: Pacific People', Statistics New Zealand. Retrieved 6 October 2009, from: http://www.stats.govt.nz/Census/2001-census-data/2001-census-snapshot-downloadable-pdf-files.aspx.
2. On remittances, see Lee (2004: 136–38) and Spoonley (2001: 87–88). On the way in which new communication technologies such as the internet and e-mail can greatly contribute to the exchange of information, see Howard (1999).
3. Interview with Pastor Tourangi, a Cook Islander minister from Penrhyn, then in charge of the Manukau Presbyterian Pacific Island Church, 21 September 2005. For a more detailed analysis of migration and land among the Cook Islanders, see Pascht (this volume).
4. Interview with Aso Saleupolu, director of the Pasifika branch in Methodist Church of New Zealand, 20 September 2007.
5. For example, Fairbairn-Dunlop and Makisi write: '[we] have chosen to use the more colloquial PI (Pacific Islander); this is because PI was the term used when [we] were growing up' (Fairbairn-Dunlop and Makisi 2003: 17).
6. Interview with Winnie Laban, then Member of Parliament and Minister of Pacific Island Affairs, 10 December 2007.
7. The recognition of the Treaty of Waitangi was the first step towards the institutionalization of cultural diversity within the Methodist Church. The treaty was signed in February 1840 by a representative of the British Crown and Māori chiefs. It transferred sovereignty of the islands to the British Crown while maintaining Māori property rights to the land. It was first written in English, then translated into Māori with the help of the Anglican missionary Henry Williams. The significant differences between these two versions, especially the choice of the Māori word *rangatiratanga* (used in the Māori translation of the Bible for 'kingdom') to define the kind of authority that Māori tribes would maintain over the land, has generated deep misunderstandings and debates on the correct interpretation of the treaty (Schulte-Tenckhoff 2004).
8. In the 2001 census, 40 per cent of New Zealand's total population declared 'no religion' or did not answer the question on religious affiliation. Among Pacific peoples, this proportion varies from 9 per cent (Tokelauans) to 24 per cent (Niueans).

9. In 2006, 18 per cent of New Zealand's 266,000 'Pacific peoples' declared themselves Presbyterians, Congregationalists or Reformed, and 12 per cent as Methodists (these two religious groupings represented 10 per cent and 3 per cent, respectively, of the total New Zealand population).
10. For a historical study of the CCCS establishment in New Zealand, see Ioka (1998).
11. Interview with Lynn Frith, a minister in the Wesley Wellington congregation and former president of the Methodist Church of New Zealand, 27 November 2007.
12. At the beginning of the 2000s, the acceptance of gay and lesbian ordinations by the Methodist Church of New Zealand accelerated the process of recognition of these dissident New Zealand congregations by the Polynesian Island 'mother' churches.
13. The term 'community' is ambiguous: during interviews, this positively connoted notion designated in its wider sense the people involved in 'doing things together'. Two more specific senses also emerged: the community of origin (for example, people from the Cook Islands) and the local community (for example, the Auckland district of Mangere). There is no perfect equivalence between church and the community boundaries, but rather a relationship in which community encompasses church while the church reinforces the community.
14. Interview with Toko Ine, 14 November 2007.
15. Interview Winnie Laban.
16. *Spanz*, February 2003. This publication is a journal of the Presbyterian Church of New Zealand, and published in Wellington. For a more detailed analysis of the New Zealand Niuean community, see Thode-Arora (this volume).
17. 'Samoan Synod Woven from Many Strands', *Touchstone*, July 2004. This publication is a journal of the Methodist Church of New Zealand, and published in Christchurch.
18. Interview with Susau Stricking, a lay leader of the Rotuman congregation in Auckland, 6 October 2007.
19. Interview with Tevita Finau, a lay leader (steward) of the Tongan congregation at the Wesley Wellington Church, 13 December 2007.
20. See the description of St Luke's Pacific Island Presbyterian Church by Kenneth Harry (2003: 81).
21. Interview with Tokerau Joseph, 14 October 2005.
22. Leaders of Pacific peoples' churches notably took stances on the legalization of prostitution in June 2003 and on the civil union law (which established unions as open to both heterosexuals and homosexuals), voted on in December 2004.
23. According to the 2006 Census, 31 per cent of Sāmoans identify with two or more ethnic groups: this proportion reaches 47 per cent among Cook Islanders, 26 per cent among Tongans, and 51 per cent among Niueans. Figures retrieved

7 May 2008, from the Pacific Profiles series 2006, Statistic New Zealand: http://www.stats.govt.nz/Census/about-2006-census/pacific-profiles-2006.aspx.
24. Interview with June Mataia, an American-Sāmoan and former member of Island Breeze, 29 April 2005.
25. Interview with Ray Totorewa, director of Island Breeze New Zealand, Tauranga, 19 September 2005.
26. Interview with Ray Totorewa.
27. Statement retrieved 15 June 2008, from: www.hosanna.org.nz/.
28. 'Anti-smacking Bill Becomes Law', *New Zealand Herald*, 16 May 2007.

## References

Anae, M. 1997. 'Towards a NZ-born Samoan Identity: Some Reflections on "Labels"', *Pacific Health Dialog* 4(2): 128–37.

Appadurai, A. 2005. *Après le colonialisme: Les conséquences culturelles de la globalisation*. Paris: Payot et Rivages.

Fairbairn-Dunlop P., and G. Makisi (eds). 2003. *Making Our Place: Growing up P.I. in New Zealand*. Palmerston North: Dunmore Press.

Forman, C. 1990. 'Some Next Steps in the Study of Pacific island Christianity', in J. Barker (ed.), *Christianity in Oceania: Ethnographic Perspectives*. Lanham, MD: University Press of America, pp.25–31.

Halbwachs, M. 1994. *Les cadres sociaux de la mémoire*. Paris: Albin Michel.

Harry, K. 2003. 'Through Mangaian Eyes: Cook Islands Identity in Tokoroa New Zealand', in P. Fairbairn-Dunlop and G. Makisi (eds), *Making Our Place. Growing up P.I. in New Zealand*. Palmerston North: Dunmore Press, pp.75–88.

Hervieu-Léger, D. 1993. *La religion pour mémoire*. Paris: Cerf.

Howard, A. 1999. 'Pacific-based Virtual Communities: Rotuma on the World Wide Web', *Contemporary Pacific* 11(1): 160–75.

Hunkin-Tuiletufuga, G. 2001. 'Pasefika Languages and Pasefika Identities: Contemporary and Future Challenges', in C. Macpherson, P. Spoonley and M. Anae (eds), *Tangata O Te Moana Nui: The Evolving Identities of Pacific Peoples in Aotearoa/New Zealand*. Palmerston North: Dunmore Press, pp.196–211.

Ioka, D. 1998. 'Origin and Beginning of the Congregrational Christian Church of Samoa (CCCS) in Aotearoa New Zealand', Ph.D. diss. Dunedin: University of Otago.

Joseph, T. 2005. 'Cracked Coconuts: An Exploration of Why Young Cook Islanders Are Leaving Cook Islander Congregations of the Presbyterian Church of Aotearoa New Zealand', M.A. diss. Dunedin: University of Otago.

Le'au, S. 1997. *Called to Honor Him: How Men and Women Are Redeeming Cultures*. Tampa, FL: Culture Com Press.

Lee, H.M. 2004. 'All Tongans Are Connected: Tongan Transnationalism', in V. Lockwood (ed.), *Globalization and Cultural Change in the Pacific Islands*. Upper Saddle River, NJ: Pearson Prentice Hall, pp.133–49.

McIntosh, T. 2001. 'Hibiscus in the Flax Bush', in C. Macpherson, P. Spoonley and M. Anae (eds), *Tangata O Te Moana Nui: The Evolving Identities of Pacific Peoples in Aotearoa/New Zealand*. Palmerston North: Dunmore Press, pp.81–96.

Macpherson, C. 2004. 'From Pacific Islanders to Pacific People and Beyond', in P. Spoonley, C. Macpherson and D. Pearson (eds), *Tangata Tangata: The Changing Ethnic Contours of New Zealand*. Victoria: Thomson-Dunmore Press, pp.135–55.

Macpherson, C., and L. Macpherson 2001. 'Evangelical Religion among Pacific Island Migrants: New Faiths or Brief Diversions?' *Journal of Ritual Studies* 15: 27–37.

MoE. 2004. 'Pasifika Children in Early Childhood Education' in 'Pasifika Peoples in New Zealand Education: A Statistical Snapshot'. Wellington: Ministry of Education, section 2, pp.7–15.

MoJ/MPIA. 2000. 'Pacific Peoples', Constitution report. Wellington: Ministry of Justice and Ministry of Pacific Island Affairs.

Rallu, J.-L. 1997. *Population, migration et développement dans le Pacifique sud*. Paris: UNESCO.

Schulte-Tenckhoff, I. 2004. '*Te tino rangatiratanga*: substance ou apparence? Réflexions sur le dilemne constitutionnel de l'Etat néo-zélandais', *Politique et Sociétés* 23(1): 89–114.

Spoonley, P. 2001. 'Transnational Pacific Communities: Transforming the Politics of Place and Identity', in C. Macpherson, P. Spoonley and M. Anae (eds), *Tangata O Te Moana Nui: The Evolving Identities of Pacific Peoples in Aotearoa/New Zealand*. Palmerston North: Dunmore Press, pp.81–96.

Van Meijl, T. 2006. 'Multiple Identifications and the Dialogical Self: Urban Maori Youngsters and the Cultural Renaissance', *Journal of the Royal Anthropological Institute* 12(4): 917–33.

# 7

# Identity and Belonging in Cross-cultural Friendship

Māori and Pākehā Experiences

◆●◆

**Agnes Brandt**

In a world characterized by the increasing movement of goods, bodies, images and ideas, the ambiguities of cultural interchanges and borderline conditions generate multiple interconnections between persons, groups and places from which emerge a new variety of social relationships and modes of identification (cf. Clifford 1997; Featherstone 2001; Kirby 2009b).

In New Zealand, the colonial experience has had important implications for the place of both Māori and Pākehā New Zealanders – the descendants of the indigenous and the European settler population.[1] In conjunction with migration flows from the Pacific island area, Asia and other parts of the world, this has led to a situation characterized by rapidly changing culture composition. Against this background, present-day New Zealand identity-making processes are dominated by popular and political debates surrounding, on the one hand, indigenous rights and postcolonial settlements and, on the other, immigration issues.

Interestingly, in this contested field of power relations and identity politics, romanticizing post-Second World War images of a social fabric characterized by inter-group harmony, tolerance and egalitarianism (also referred to as the egalitarian myth) seem to persist in significant fractions of popular self-representation as well as in New Zealand's international reputation (cf. Consedine 1989). However, the long-term effects of colonization and existing social, political and economic inequalities contravene such an idealized scenario. The challenge of reconciling New Zealand's (post)colonial heritage with its growing cultural diversity is thus proving to be an extremely challenging task.

How do these complex processes bear on New Zealanders' everyday interpersonal relationships? What role do group loyalties and identifications play in this? Do friendships reproduce socio-cultural boundaries, or can they provide spaces for deconstructing them? Additionally, how is this related to the construction of identity and place-making processes? This chapter addresses these questions by investigating the dynamics of cross-cultural friendships as experienced by Māori and Pākehā New Zealanders. The focus is on the interrelation between friendship as an intimate bond and wider personal and public identity-making processes.[2]

This contribution draws on ethnographic material collected during fieldwork in the cities of Auckland and Wellington over thirteen months in 2007 and 2008. I would like to point out that my analysis is limited to the urban context.[3] My goal is to provide a contextualized account of individual present-day friendship experiences that accounts for those neglected social/political/historical roots of subjectivities raised by Kirby (2009a), among others. In what follows, I first delineate the specific historical political developments and their implications for identity and place-making processes, before turning to the discussion of some cross-cultural friendship practices and experiences by Māori and Pākehā actors. In the final section, some theoretical implications are explored.

As the analysis of the ethnographic data reveals, friendships surface as highly situational social constructs in which multiple, at times competing, conceptions of self and other are actively (re)constructed. Far from simply reproducing culture discourse, friendships emerge as processual phenomena that are experienced and lived in multiple ways, shaped and negotiated in a contested field of power relations. As I will argue, because of these characteristics, cross-cultural friendships in particular provide a worthwhile site for investigating processes of identity production and place-making in people's everyday lives and experiences.

In order to account for the complexities of this dynamic field of relations and identifications, a dialogical theoretical perspective will be utilized as a promising analytical avenue (see e.g. Holland et al. 1998; Holland and Lave 2001; Hermans 2002; Hermans and Dimaggio 2007). According to this view, the self is not only multiple, dialogical and polyphonous, rather than singular and static, but actors are seen as creatively fashioning imagined worlds in dialogue with the voices and actions of others. They do so in concrete places as they move about in their day-to-day lives. As I will be concerned to show, this approach is so compelling for the study of cross-cultural friendship and identity production because of its capacity to transcend the boundaries of self and other, inner and outer, while also accounting for human agency in personal interchanges.

## Cultural Diversity and Identity Politics in New Zealand

As in other postcolonial societies, such as Hawai'i, New Zealand's indigenous population is not only outnumbered by the non-indigenous Pākehā population, but Māori as a group are more affected by social and economic inequalities than Pākehā. This actuality not only stands in stark contrast to the already mentioned egalitarian myth, but it also poses a major challenge to biculturalism as an official policy.

Since the 1980s, a time when the political movements of the late 1960s and 1970s yielded their first long-term fruits, the New Zealand government has espoused a bicultural framework that acknowledges Māori cultural difference on the basis of their status as the indigenous peoples of New Zealand. This move was based on the acknowledgement of the Treaty of Waitangi (1840) as a central defining document in Māori and Pākehā relations (cf. King 2003: 515–20). Much has been written about the many versions and interpretations of the document signed between representatives of the British Crown and local Māori tribes (*iwi*).[4] It is in reference to the treaty that New Zealand is today imagined as a bicultural society, in which some form of comprehensive partnership is envisaged between the two treaty partners (cf. Schwimmer 1968; Sissons 1995). As a 'charter' for partnership and equality, the treaty constitutes an essential part of the decolonization project, for it provides the basis on which historical grievances can be addressed.

The bicultural framework has important implications for identity and place-making processes: From socio-political socio-historical perspectives, the construction of distinct Māori and Pākehā identities is inextricably linked to the (post)colonial experience, and has been shaped to a large extent by the contest 'for land, resources, status and power' (Walker 1989: 35).

In the case of Māori, the notion of a pan-tribal identity initially emerged as a result of the colonial experience. The contemporary notion of Māori indigeneity is based on their status as the 'custodians', or 'people of the land' (*tangata whenua*) (cf. Walker 1989: 35). A distinct relation to the land as both material and spiritual domain is claimed to be an important characteristic of Māori modes of identification. This is expressed in the double meaning of the term *whenua*, meaning both 'land' and 'placenta', the main function of which is the succouring of new life (cf. Mead 2003:

288–89). The connection to the land thus constitutes a central element of belonging as and being Māori.

However, for many present-day Māori living in the city, active links to their ancestral homelands have eroded over time. This can be problematic in terms of cultural identification and belonging, an issue that was often mentioned in my conversations with so-called urban Māori. One of them is Kahu.[5] In his own words:

> [M]ost Māori now live in urban centres away from their traditional lands and so their ... physical and their spiritual connection is lost .... [T]hrough the process of urbanization and assimilation, a lot of Māori identify with Pākehā .... [T]hey lose a lot of their identity. They lose a strong sense of who they are ... I guess for myself I go home as much as I can, and when I say 'go home' it means going up north ... or to the coast ... but predominantly I was brought up in the cities. So my knowledge and my connection to my past is not as strong as what I would like it to be, but I give it my best.

Like Kahu, many younger Māori in their twenties and early thirties actively seek to (re)connect to family relations and ancestral places as part of a wider project of identification and belonging. They learn their genealogies (*whakapapa*), retrace their parents' and grandparents' steps over time and go back to their rural homelands to meet their relations. While their experiences are often ambiguous to the point of being painful encounters for their sense of self, some succeed in renewing relations to ancestral places and family members outside the city as they move between different life-worlds and social connections. Others emphasize their connections to places and communities within the city, for example, to the local neighbourhood, to certain groups or to urban *marae* (ceremonial centres).[6] For them, their sense of place is tied up with the urban life-world they inhabit in their day-to-day lives (cf. Casey 1996: 34).

The significance of place in contemporary notions of Māori identity and belonging is also expressed in the revival of the custom of returning a child's placenta to the land. Nowadays, this can be the child's ancestral lands or a place of significance to the family in the city. The main function of this custom is to bind a child to the homeland and to secure its birthright to belong, expressed in the notion of *tūrangawaewae* (literally, 'a place for the feet to stand'). In the words of Kahu:

> In Māori culture we have a concept called *tūrangawaewae*. When a child is born, their *whenua*, or the placenta, is actually buried in the land, or the *whenua* [...] and that ... gives a spiritual connection of the child to their land, which is why land is so important to Māori. And it draws them to that place ... and the land tells the story of their history and of their peoples.

It is the spiritual dimension of this relationship that is often referred to by Māori when their own distinctiveness is contrasted with non-Māori notions of belonging. Linked to this discourse is the Māori political struggle for self-determination.

Also linked to this discourse is the notion of Pākehā identity. While the term 'pakeha' was already mentioned in the Treaty, a distinct notion of Pākehā identity came up in the 1980s, primarily as a reaction to the Māori nationalist movement, and as part of the processes that led to the official acknowledgement of biculturalism (Hoey 2004). Much of the discussion on being Pākehā deals with the acknowledgement of Māori indigenous status and the implications for Pākehā's as descendants of the settler population, who claim a distinct right to belong.

Against this background, Pākehā and Māori are not only construed in relation to one another, but they tend to be juxtaposed as different and exclusive, rather than inclusive. The specific historical processes and culture politics have led to the separation and 'turning inwards' of both cultures, a situation in which hybrid identifications are not easily embraced (Bell 2004). At the level of individual experience, this can be highly problematic, first and foremost because of the lack of flexibility and ambiguity in such politicized representations of 'culture' and 'identity'.

As Van Meijl (2006) has demonstrated for the case of young urban Māori, 'official' political representations of Māori identity often collide with personal experiences and may result in a crisis of self at the individual level. Similarly, Hoey (2004), among others, has argued that the socio-historical construction of Pākehā identity proves problematic for it is often linked to feelings of unease and dislocation. For some, the term 'Pākehā' carries with it such negative connotations that they feel threatened in their right to belong as New Zealanders (see also Spoonley 1986; King 1999). They feel dis-placed rather than em-placed (cf. Clifford 1997).

What is more, such singular and exclusive identifications as one or the other, Māori or Pākehā, do not adequately reflect a social reality – especially in culturally diverse urban environments – that sees a growing number of New Zealanders identifying with more than one group (cf. SNZ 2006). After all, since the arrival of the first Europeans, interaction between Māori and Pākehā has involved multiple relationships across cultural and ethnic boundaries including intermarriage. From these have come forth individuals who can – and do – identify in multiple and changing, rather than singular and static ways.

Personal representations of self are not only multiple and processual, but often contradictory and ambivalent (cf. Kolig et al. 2009: 10). In some respects, the decision to identify as neither Māori nor Pākehā reflects this confusion or mismatch between politicized identity discourse and personal experiences. As a result, a number of persons instead choose to identify as 'New Zealander(s)', or 'Kiwi(s)', a self-description of at least equally ambiguous connotation: While in some cases this can be counted as an attempt to move beyond existing boundaries, in others it may be the result of a lack of understanding and ignorance towards the position and needs of Māori (among other groups) in a Pākehā dominated society. From an indigenous perspective, such an equalizing label for all is regarded as highly problematic for it is seen as glossing over existing differences and inequalities, as well as threatening Māori status and rights as *tangata whenua* (Spoonley, Macpherson and Pearson 2004).

The issue is further complicated by recent migration patterns and the increase of 'other' groups in the country's urban centres, most notably Pacific island peoples and – more recently – immigrants from Asian countries. These 'new' immigrants carry their own images, identifications and modes of socializing with them en route to the place they are striving to make their home (cf. Clifford 1997), and for them becoming a 'Kiwi' or a 'New Zealander' – rather than a 'Pākehā' – is often an important part of their place-making processes. As ethnic and cultural diversity increases, New Zealand society's multicultural character has been debated extensively, especially in terms of its implications for the notion of biculturalism and Māori indigenous status.

As I will be concerned to show, these wider discourses surrounding culture politics and identity-making are highly sensitive, controversial and emotive topics, which reverberate in the way in which actors live and experience their close personal relations with others and in how they experience self and other in these relationships. As the ethnographic material discussed below shows, these wider processes are not only reproduced but also creatively reconstructed and re-imagined in cross-cultural friendships. Belonging plays an important role in this.

## Cross-cultural Friendship and Belonging in New Zealand

Like all social relationships, friendships are part of and influenced by the wider social processes in which they occur. As contemporary studies have demonstrated, friendships are diverse and multifaceted social phenomena that need to be analysed in their respective social, cultural, political and economic contexts (e.g. Adams and Allan 1998; Carrier 1990; Pahl 2000; Beer 2001). They are tied to notions of time as well as place in order to be formed, maintained and take the distinctive shape that makes their pursuit worthwhile for those engaging in them. Furthermore, friendships are relational and situational phenomena. As actors move about different localities in space and time, they not only carry different conceptions of sociality with them, but in engaging with others they simultaneously change and creatively refashion their relationships, themselves as well as those with whom they interact in the process. These processual characteristics of friendship echo the idea of 'landscape' put forward by Eric Hirsch, according to whom 'landscape' is the relationship between the two poles of experience in any cultural context, the 'foreground' (here and now actuality; us the way we are) and 'background' (horizon, potentiality; us the way we might be) of social life (Hirsch 1995: 3–5).

The main challenge for the anthropologist studying friendship in an increasingly interconnected world is – as in the case of all social phenomena – to allow for conceptions of sociality and relatedness that are fluid and flexible, rather than static and definite (see e.g. Appadurai 1990; Hannerz 1996). For the specific purpose of this chapter, a broad definition of friendship as an intimate bond beyond the context of family and kinship (albeit not exclusively) will be adopted. In most cases – but not necessarily so – this will involve some notion of voluntariness, reciprocity and stability.[7] I consider such a broad conception as useful, for it not only accounts for the processual characteristics of friendship – that is, as oscillating between foreground actuality and background potentiality – but it also allows for divergent and conflicting friendship conceptions and practices, which is of particular importance in cross-cultural contexts.

With this in mind, we can now turn back to the New Zealand setting. As we have already seen, in New Zealand the socio-historical experiences of colonization and migration are reflected in a somewhat ambivalent culture discourse surrounding indigenous rights and immigration issues, biculturalism and multiculturalism. What are the implications of these for Māori and Pākehā friendships?

When I started my fieldwork in Auckland in February 2007, it soon became clear that there were fewer cross-cultural friendships than popular and political rhetoric suggested. Even though many actors spoke of an increasingly 'multicultural' urban social fabric, where interactions with persons from a variety of ethnic and cultural backgrounds are possible, after further inquiry it was clear that in many cases this did not translate into interpersonal interactions at a more intimate level. Even in ethnically diverse neighbourhoods, such as the one in which I was staying during my first months in the field, it was difficult to find more intimate cross-cultural relations, especially where interaction between Māori and Pākehā was concerned. In fact, I found it much easier to trace out Māori–Pākehā relations once I moved to a Māori household situated in a less heterogeneous neighbourhood.

Taking into account findings which indicate that members of different ethnic groups in countries such as New Zealand and Australia mainly interact in the public sphere and only to a minor extent in terms of close personal relations, this mismatch between lived experience and politicized representation was to be expected to a certain degree. Nevertheless, it leaves the question as to how, under which circumstances and where, Māori and Pākehā engage in cross-cultural friendships with one another. This, as show below, is greatly influenced by the actors' life-worlds and identifications. What is more, ties of loyalty with certain groups and places play an important role in this.

As research has shown, in the formation of friendships, as in other relationships, the notion of homophily as a basic organizing principle plays a crucial role (cf. McPherson Smith-Lovin and Cook 2001).[8] Homophily is the tendency to associate or bond with similar others. Applied to friendship, this means that a friend is often experienced and imagined as similar to oneself, as alike. The construction of similarity in friendship is of particular interest in a social environment in which difference is employed strategically. Postcolonial Aotearoa New Zealand provides a good example of how difference may be either emphasized (such as in order to stress Māori identity as indigenous and different to Pākehā identity) or downplayed (such as emphasizing a shared 'Kiwi' identity). In friendship, too, actors may emphasize certain parts of themselves, and of their friends, for different reasons. Of particular interest for this contribution is the question on what basis similarity and – reversely – difference are constructed in cross-cultural friendships. As this depends to a large extent on the respective context and the individuals involved, there is no simple answer to it: shared history, common interests, activities and practices, shared values, beliefs or attitudes, but also social status, class, gender, age and ethnicity can serve as both dividing and uniting factors. Which combination of these factors is chosen, or can be chosen, usually depends on circumstances and power relations. Difference is, after all, an ongoing interactional accomplishment (West and Fenstermaker 1995).

As the examples below show, in the context of cross-cultural friendships between Māori and Pākehā, identifying with or belonging to a particular group or place often gives two (or more) persons a basis to relate to one another, in its simplest form something to talk about upon first encountering one another, something to 'build on'. This is connected to feelings of familiarity, comfort, and security. As actors move about their day-to-day lives between different social spaces, they engage in multiple relations in which different, at times competing, notions of self and other are negotiated. And while opportunity structures and inequalities play an important role, the empirical data suggest that a shared sense of belonging can facilitate friendships that reach beyond cultural and ethnic boundaries.

## Some Pākehā Friendship Experiences

My findings indicate that, consistent with the principle of homophily, Pākehā tend to socialize with others of similar socio-demographic background. By and large this means that Pākehā, at least in the urban setting, tend to be friends with other Pākehā – a pattern that we also find in the choice of sexual partner (cf. Schäfer 2007). For many, there is neither the need nor a particular interest, nor the opportunity, to engage in close cross-cultural friendships. Reversely, Pākehā who engage in cross-cultural friendships usually share certain socio-demographic characteristics and social spaces with their non-Pākehā friends. In many cases these persons are part of a social environment that facilitates cross-cultural relationships, and which provides places in which cross-cultural encounters are assisted. Some of these Pākehā are involved in cross-cultural intimate-couple relationships or another cross-cultural family constellation. Others have grown up or live in a social environment, pursue a lifestyle, a career or simply have interests in areas in which cross-cultural relationships are encouraged or a given as part of everyday life. Social opportunity structures thus influence cross-cultural friendship formation. Affiliation to social collectivities and places often plays an important part in this context.

Take the case of Jonathan, a Pākehā man in his mid thirties; or, as he describes himself to me at our first meeting, a 'white married male, born and bred in New Zealand'. It is Jonathan's involvement in different softball and soccer teams that has enabled him to develop a range of cross-cultural friendships. He describes softball in this context as a Māori-dominated sport, soccer as Pākehā dominated – a description that was also supported by others in my study regardless of cultural or ethnic affiliations. Also supported by others' experiences is Jonathan's observation that throughout his life this split between the two sports, and groups, has led to relatively separate social groups and circles of friends. In Jonathan's words:

> Softball in New Zealand is a very Māori-dominated sport. So at school in the summertime, I would hang out with all the Māori boys playing softball and just hang out. Then, during the winter, because I played soccer, I hung out with all the white boys because they were the soccer players. In winter, Māori boys played rugby, and softball in the summer. The white boys played cricket in the summer and soccer in the winter. So, I used to swing between both sides ... I developed heaps of friends in both directions. I look at my life now, and just being able to fit into both cultures ... I just find it so easy to fit in either way.

As he explained to me during one of our conversations, Jonathan ultimately experiences this 'swinging between both sides' in a positive way as it has enabled him to 'fit into both cultures', as he says, and to feel comfortable in either environment. His account illustrates well how different groups and places are experienced as relatively closed, or bounded, socio-cultural spheres – a central finding of my research. At the same time, their boundedness may be transcended by individuals such as Jonathan, who feel part of both and who move back and forth with ease. The sport in this case provides a shared social space that allows for cross-cultural friendship through personal interaction. Since each sport is tied up to specific times and places, Jonathan is required to actively step out of one sphere and into the other at different times in order to maintain his social relations.

An equally important factor is effort. In our conversations, Jonathan repeatedly underscored his active involvement in establishing friendships. By his own account, he makes an effort because he finds friendships with a variety of persons rewarding. He talks about the extension of knowledge and engagement in new practices and activities, such as singing and dancing with his Pacific island friends – activities he feels he could not or would not do with most Pākehā friends. The benefits of stepping out and across one sphere to the other are important factors in his quest for self-learning and growth.

Even from the short account cited above, it is clear that Jonathan sharply distinguishes rhetorically between his own cultural identity and his non-Pākehā friends' identities. Personally, Jonathan identifies as a 'New Zealander'. He finds 'Pākehā' an inappropriate label for himself because, as he points out, it can be used to depict any non-Māori person, including non-New Zealanders. Here, the aforementioned unease with the historically imbued category 'Pākehā' and its incongruity with personal representations of self are evident.

By calling himself a New Zealander, Jonathan represents himself as belonging to New Zealand, a place experienced and imagined by him. Despite perceived cultural difference, he constructs his friends as also belonging to this image of New Zealand. For him, a shared interest in sport and shared belonging to what he calls 'New Zealand sporting culture' are important factors in the process of constituting self, other and the relationship between them. His account underscores the importance of engaging in shared activities in common social spaces in order for more intimate friendship ties across group boundaries to develop. Sport for Jonathan is a unifying force between individuals and groups. He even goes so far as to say that sport is the focal point of New Zealand culture. He perceives his friends as Māori, as Pacific Islander, Brazilian, Korean as well as New Zealander or Kiwi. Being Kiwi marks them as belonging to New Zealand – like Jonathan.

What this example shows is how multiple identifications and belongings as well as shared social space influence and assist the formation of cross-cultural friendships. As Jonathan moves back and forth he crosses boundaries, but he also reconstructs them by recognizing the boundedness of the groups and places he engages in. As he does so, he constructs himself as a Kiwi, a New Zealander, a soccer-placer, rugby player and so forth. The perceived cultural differences between self and other are bridged or overruled by shared interests and a strong sense of shared belonging that is articulated at different levels and in specific places (cf. Rose 1995; Lovell 1998): the sports team, the New Zealand sporting community and a macro-image of New Zealand culture. Jonathan's reference to New Zealand as an imagined place and community reflects the wider culture discourse and identity politics. His insistence on difference within a joint 'Kiwi' culture in some ways resembles the idea of an essentially egalitarian society in which everyone can engage on equal terms, regardless of where they are from. While this enables him to cross over with ease, difference in experience (for instance, on the basis of socio-economic position) is largely rendered invisible.

A shared sense of belonging to a group and/or a place as a facilitator of cross-cultural friendship is a recurrent theme in my data. Apart from sports, other frequently mentioned collectivities and social spaces in this context were churches, educational institutions, voluntary associations and organizations, as well as music and arts communities, the workplace and sometimes the neighbourhood. The actors in these settings relate to one another on the basis of shared experiences, roles and interests. Familiarity, comfort and belonging are frequently mentioned qualities that facilitate the formation and maintenance of friendships.

However, this logic also works the other way around: If friendships are – at least to a certain degree – dependent on a shared sense of belonging and comfort, then, reversely, different notions of belonging and feelings of unease or discomfort may create divergence rather than convergence. The fragility of commonality as a basis for friendship is particularly salient in situations where one party is more comfortable and 'at home' than another. Furthermore, the extra effort involved in stepping out and across boundaries is not always enough for friendships to be established. In some cases, the boundedness of social spaces emerges as too strong for a person to succeed in actually establishing more intimate connections – even if they actively make an effort to do so.

Take the case of Linda, who exemplifies well the point that an outgoing personality and good social skills, combined with effort and shared space, do not necessarily suffice in order to establish friendships across boundaries: A Pākehā woman in her fifties, Linda has been learning the Māori language for several years. Like many other Pākehā who make an effort to learn it, Linda attends Māori language classes and engages with Māori people in order to gain greater insights into Māori culture and, by implication, also into New Zealand culture. While personal growth is an important motivator for her, she also sees in it an important contribution to meaningful and positive relations between Māori and Pākehā at a wider societal level. She invests time and effort in this undertaking, and she would like to establish some personal relations with Māori beyond a general level of friendliness, but finds this difficult to accomplish. Linda's social network reflects a predominantly Pākehā middle-class background. Her friendship universe is diverse, in that her friends come from different phases in her life, but the principle of homophily applies in regard to gender, age, socio-economic background and cultural affiliations as well as lifestyle, values, shared interests and experiences. In contrast, in her Māori language classes, Linda is older than most of her classmates, the majority of which are Māori and come from different socio-cultural and economic backgrounds. Even though she is liked and well integrated, she feels a bit 'on the outer', something that she puts down to her different life-world.

I have known Linda for more than ten years, since I first started learning the Māori language myself. Over the years, Linda and I often talked about the problem of getting access to and establishing more intimate relations with Māori people. As she told me during one of our interviews: 'I don't have Māori friends, [...] [M]y life has got a certain number of orbits, and I move in those, and it's like I don't have any Chinese friends either, you know, or, you're quite limited'. This feeling of being limited she also attributes to her urban environment, which makes it difficult for her to come into contact with non-Pākehā on a day-to-day basis. Participating in Māori language classes is also an attempt to cross over this boundary. At this she feels only partially successful:

> LINDA: I still feel, I still want to be in the club, and I'm not in the club [...] And I'm not in the club because I'm not born into it and I don't, you know, all that stuff about *whakapapa* [genealogy] [...] I mean, even if you learn the language you're still not Māori, you know, you're learning the language but you're not Māori and so there's always that, you have a much greater sense of comfort in situations where there are Māori people or on the *marae* [ceremonial centre], because you know so much more and you're open to it, but you're still not quite there.
>
> Q: Will you ever be?
>
> LINDA: I think you can, I think you could be, but it would be – I think it's dependent on forming relationships with Māori people, actually.

In this case, the shared space of the classroom and the learning community do not quite suffice for the formation of intimate cross-cultural friendships.

In some ways, Linda says, learning about the other language and culture even makes her feel more isolated and different. In a cultural context where genealogical reckoning (*whakapapa*) is an important way of relating to one's land and people in both material and spiritual terms, Linda, because of her inability to draw on these connections, sometimes feels disconnected and dislocated as a Pākehā in New Zealand. Being Pākehā is experienced in this context as being 'other'. Non-belonging emerges as much as a defining factor as belonging (cf. Rose 1995).

Again, the boundedness of the 'two worlds', Māori and Pākehā, come to the fore. Friendship as an intimate bonding is imagined by Linda as potentially providing her with a deeper level of interaction, and as a way of bridging the perceived divide between her own and the other culture. Cross-cultural friendship is thus ideally constructed as a space in between, in which the actors are seen as capable of transcending cultural boundaries. By doing so – that is, by transcending the boundaries in friendship – Linda also expects to feel more emplaced as Pākehā. However, even though she is prepared to move out of her comfort zone, Linda finds it difficult to find shared social spaces with Māori that would enable such friendships. Furthermore, she is aware that they would most probably remain outside or peripheral to her main 'life-orbits'. The limits of the problematic notion of multiculturalism come to the fore here as the so-called multicultural city she lives in fails to provide for her spaces of encounter with Māori people.

## Some Māori Friendship Experiences

For many Māori, the problematic takes a different shape. Whereas Pākehā often have to make a conscious effort to engage in friendships with Māori, the latter, because of their minority status and fewer numbers, frequently interact in a Pākehā dominated environment on a regular basis. Not surprisingly, Māori tend to engage in a greater number of cross-cultural friendships.[9] It is important to note that the urban environment itself, and society in general, are usually experienced as Pākehā places: places that follow the logic and norms ascribed to a Pākehā 'way' and culture.

Unlike many Pākehā, Māori actors not only conceptualize themselves frequently as bicultural, but they also frame and experience their social worlds along bicultural lines: they talk about their Māori side and their Pākehā side, their Māori friends and their Pākehā friends, the Māori world and the Pākehā world. As these actors move between their multiple worlds, biculturalism becomes part of their daily experience. At the same time, however, they describe how in their individual life-worlds and experiences the two 'sides' do not just collide; they also cross and merge. The result is a rather ambiguous and at times confusing field of contested identifications.

And whereas for some this is a source of personal friction and instability, for others it provides surplus opportunities. In any case, Māori – more so than Pākehā – identify along multiple pathways, which very often follow the bicultural logic laid out by the wider identity politics outlined above. And since multiple identities are nurtured in multiple relationships, these actors juggle their 'competing needs, roles and self-awarenesses' (Kolig et al. 2009: 10) in different friendships in creative ways.

A central finding of my research is that many Māori tend to maintain largely separate Māori and Pākehā friendship groups. These groups are frequently maintained in different socio-cultural spaces, which follow different norms and codes, and in which different identities or 'sides' are enacted or lived. The friendships in these spaces also tend to follow different cultural rules and norms, depending on whether they are associated with Māori or with mainstream Pākehā worlds. Hence, as the actors move between different groups and places, they live different 'cultural' parts of themselves with different people. Their Pākehā friends are often oblivious to all of this. Importantly, these Māori friendships with Pākehā often stay within the realms of mainstream society, and only few Pākehā friends engage in Māori spaces on a regular basis. Friendships with other Māori on the other hand may take place in either or both worlds.

Not surprisingly then, many Pākehā experience feelings of discomfort when encountering this 'other' world and 'other' side of their Māori friends – something that both Māori and Pākehā actors frequently pointed out to me in the course of my fieldwork. For instance, Hemi, a Māori student in his early twenties, told me about his university friends' surprise when he brought them to the department's Māori room:

> I had [...] invited a couple of my Pākehā friends to come into the Māori room [...] I found that they tended to be very uncomfortable being around so many dark-skinned people, who spoke differently to how they did outside that room. We joked in a very different way, we found different things about different people funny [...] [A]fter taking my friend out I said, 'Oh, were you okay? I could tell that you were a little bit uncomfortable', and she told me that she [...] just wasn't used to that.

Here, the separation of the two socio-cultural worlds becomes particularly obvious as existing social relations are reversed. Hemi's friends felt uncomfortable because of the unfamiliar situation and the different social norms in the Māori room, and also because they experienced a new side of their friend, a side that they were not used to and with which they had to familiarize themselves.

Whereas Māori are often used to moving between a range of Māori and Pākehā environments, many Pākehā are not. This can lead to quite distinct experiences and life-worlds. Not surprisingly, a number of Māori describe their shared experiences as Māori as the main distinguishing factor between their friendships with Māori as opposed to their friendships with Pākehā, friendships that they also associate with different norms, behaviour and places. However, while this was a very clear pattern in the data, in most cases this difference is regarded as secondary in ordinary friendship interactions by those who engage in them.

Take the example of Tino, a Māori man in his mid twenties: Tino's cultural identification does not play a primary role in his friendships. Rather than identifying as 'Māori', he prefers to identify along tribal lines, as this refers to places and people that he knows and feels connected to. His account exemplifies well the significance of localized forms of identifications and belonging (cf. Lovell 1998). It also demonstrates the interweaving of culture, class and gender. Tino's friends are mainly Pākehā. They are young, male musicians and writers, like him, and describe themselves as belonging to a distinct community. Value homophily and belonging are the main formative friendship factors. It is only when his Pākehā friends are engaging with the Māori world that cultural difference comes to the fore. In Tino's words:

> I mean ... they're only seeing, like, the tip of the iceberg [...] This is where even though I have mostly Pākehā friends there's a whole side of me that I can't really communicate with them, [...] just what it is to be Māori and to grow up Māori. Those are things that [...] get shared with other Māori people.

Tino's strategy for dealing with difference on such occasions is to accept it, although he would also like to show his friends his own perspective on 'being Māori'. However, on the whole he finds this difference rather irrelevant for his friendships, which are based on other qualities and commonalities, mainly writing, music and something like a 'young urban lifestyle'.

Tino's case demonstrates well the deep entanglement of gender, socio-economic and socio-cultural milieu in the formation of friendships. Even though these factors are hardly ever consciously reflected by the actors in their friendship choices, they play a decisive role for the initial establishment and successful maintenance of close cross-cultural friendships across all age groups. All three tend to be downplayed as friendship-constituting factors. Of the three, gender homophily seems to be the most readily acknowledged by individual actors. In contrast, class and culture are frequently conflated under the rather vague notion of a 'shared background' – a recurrent theme in the data. There is an especially marked tendency for conflating 'class' and 'culture' in friendship rhetoric. This corresponds with the blurring of socio-economic and cultural boundaries, and a reality that sees Māori more socio-economically disadvantaged than Pākehā. In any case, Māori actors tend to acknowledge difference more willingly. According to Hine, a Māori woman in her early thirties:

> Friendship is built on economics as well. So, because I'm a colonized, middle-class, educated Māori, I'm so not middle class – yet, I'm still platinum in the ghetto. I can't run around with Māoris who, you know, went to the boarding school and […] were wealthy […] If there were more Pākehā in the working class that I'm from, which is truck drivers and cleaners, but they're not, […] I would have more Pākehā friends if they were within the class that I was in, and as I grow up and as I come into my own, […] then I suppose I will have more Pākehā friends.

Hine clearly expects more cross-cultural friendship opportunities as she 'moves up' in society. Whether this indicates greater prospects for cross-cultural friendships in the middle levels of society is difficult to estimate. In any case, quantity does not necessarily indicate intercultural content. While cross-cultural friendships certainly exist at all societal levels, class only constitutes one friendship-constituting factor among many. In any case, even though Māori and Pākehā engage in cross-cultural friendships with one another, their experiences of these relationships differ strikingly at times. This is because of the boundedness of the 'two worlds' as brought forth by identity politics and colonial heritage, worlds that are not always visible in friendship interactions, but which can nevertheless become salient in certain situations. It is in these situations that the difference between one and the other comes to the fore.

## Cross-cultural Friendship in Context: Some Implications for Identity and Belonging

The foregoing analysis points to the need for a contextualized study of cross-cultural friendship that takes into account wider social processes. The dynamics of identity and belonging emerge as important factors in cross-cultural friendship practices. In what follows, some of the main findings will be summarized and placed in theoretical context.

As the examples above demonstrate, friendships work in relation to a variety of intersecting and changing factors. A prominent characteristic is their relatively informal and situational nature. In cross-cultural friendships, this implies that cultural difference and potential resulting tensions and conflicts can – though not in all cases, but remarkably often – be ignored or bridged by the individuals involved by means of focusing on other commonalities and similarities such as shared interests and lifestyle. The actors themselves choose what differences and similarities count in their relationship with one another. Whereas in some cases the perceived cultural difference between self and other can effectively impede the formation of particularly intimate friendships, in other instances new spaces can open up, spaces 'in-between', in which actors may equivocally articulate self and other, and potentially transcend both (cf. Bhabha 1994, 1996). In such instances, cross-cultural friendships can open up spaces in which social boundaries may be challenged and even transformed.

As the ethnographic material further reveals, wider public and political discourses surrounding identity and culture are reflected in Māori and Pākehā actors' conceptions of self and other in their close cross-cultural friendships. In all of the cited examples, the construction of cultural difference is influenced by the politically framed policy of biculturalism, and by and large proceeds along available modes of identification as laid out by culture discourse.

The data thus tellingly demonstrate the fluidity and fragmented nature of multiple identifications referred to by Hall (1996), when he writes of identities as temporary points of attachment to subject positions constructed by discursive practices and moulded within the play of power and exclusion. In the case of New Zealand, this is accompanied by the construction of socio-cultural spaces that are experienced as largely separate and ambivalent. The idea of 'two worlds', one Māori and one Pākehā, influences the ways in which both Māori and Pākehā actors engage in friendships, but also their sense of self in these friendships. Māori in particular seem to construct their identities along bicultural, or multiple, life-worlds, which are experienced in emotional ways and which may or may not come to the fore in their cross-cultural friendship interactions depending on the respective situation and the individuals involved.

While a sense of dislocation as Māori or as Pākehā and the experience of different life-worlds and histories, may effectively inhibit close cross-cultural friendships, a shared sense of belonging to a group or a place may serve as a facilitator. As we have seen, ties of loyalty can be articulated at a range of intersecting levels (cf. Rose 1995; Lovell 1998), from being a member of a particular sports team or an association to a shared sense of belonging to New Zealand as an imagined place and community. Transcultural lifestyles, interest in the 'other', and some degree of effort to engage with the 'other', assist in the formation of friendships. As shared interests, lifestyles and values come to the fore, other potentially dividing factors become less pronounced.

In most instances of interaction, the cultural dimension appears to be regarded as largely irrelevant, or at least secondary, for the friendship at stake in terms of interaction or affection. However, when the 'two worlds' collide in practice, cultural difference is not only recognized, it may become problematic as it challenges conceptions of self and other. This is expressed in Jonathan's learning of how to 'swing in between', in Linda's frustration at being unconnected, also in the case of Hemi's friends who feel out of place in the Māori room, and finally, in the example of Tino, who suddenly feels a bit uncomfortable when his Pākehā friends start engaging with the Māori world. Belonging and non-belonging to imagined places and groups are equally important factors here (cf. Rose 1995).

Depending on respective friendship constellations and contexts, these processes play out differently with varying consequences for self and other, and their interrelationship. In cross-cultural friendships, as in other cross-cultural situations, the recognition of self through difference is particularly prominent or observable (cf. Woodward 1997). Self and other emerge as the products of their interaction, as relational. Both Jonathan and Linda experience self-growth through their engagement with non-Pākehā people, but where Jonathan constructs his sense of self in the wider realm of New Zealand sports culture, Linda finds it more challenging to root herself as a Pākehā in New Zealand. And where Jonathan more or less reproduces the myth of a society in which everyone can equally participate on friendly terms, Linda reflects more readily on socio-economic boundaries and opportunity structures. For her, the idea of an egalitarian society, in which people are not only equal but also engage equally in cross-cultural intimate relations, is indeed a myth. For Hemi, Tino and Hine, the picture is a different one. As Māori, they are used to moving in between different worlds that are not only bounded socio-culturally but also economically. Their multiple bicultural identities are a given, identities that they live and reproduce in their relationships with other Māori and non-Māori, and which are situated in specific socio-cultural places.

The findings are thus in accord with more recent theoretical developments favouring dynamic conceptualizations of culture and identity as processual, multivocal and polyphonous phenomena (e.g. Appadurai 1990; Gupta and Ferguson 1992; Bhabha 1994, 1996; Friedman 1994; Robertson 1995; Hall and Du Gay 1996; Wright 1998; Featherstone 2001; Kolig et al. 2009). However, as laid out above, the socio-historical specifics of New Zealand have led to a situation of postcoloniality in which close cross-cultural ties are not as easily established at a personal level as some theorists suggest. Rather, the findings support Gupta and Ferguson's (1992) argument for a historically grounded analysis of the dynamic production of difference in interconnected spaces and power relations (see also Kirby 2009b). What is required is a theoretical framework that captures the dynamics of discourse, friendship and identity, both at the individual and the group level.

Situated in cognitive anthropology and social psychology, I believe a praxis-oriented dialogical perspective may hold the answer to this difficult task. Such a framework seeks to transcend the boundaries of self and other, inner and outer, self and society. It aims at a thorough understanding of the interconnectedness between self and society. Most importantly perhaps for the analysis of cross-cultural friendships in New Zealand, this theoretical framework seeks to account for the impact of power relations and human interchange on the construction of identity and belonging without discarding the important factor of human agency (cf. Holland et al. 1998). The purveyors of this approach follow a Bakhtinian conceptualization of identity as processual, dialogic and polyphonous, which is reflected in the notion of a 'dialogical self'. The self in this view is not singular and static; it is a 'society of the mind', multiply constructed within dialogues across difference (Holland et al. 1998; Holland and Lave 2001; Hermans 2002; Hermans and Dimaggio 2007; also see Van Meijl 2006). This means that the notion of a self not only encompasses internal I-positions (I as a student, I as a daughter and so on), but also external ones (my friend, my colleague, the group to which I belong and so forth) among which dialogical relationships can be established. This multiplicity of I-positions thus allows for fractured, ambiguous and contradictory self-understandings.

Going back to the ethnographic data discussed above, this means that seemingly unconnected and contradictory notions of self and belonging can be integrated within this analytical framework. This is essential if we are trying to understand under which circumstances, for what reason and in what ways individual New Zealand actors establish common grounds, or homophily, across differences (cultural, economic, social, gender and so forth) in their close personal interactions and relationships with others.

Actors like Jonathan, Linda, Hemi, Tino and Hine identify in multiple and sometimes conflicting ways. According to context and needs, they emphasize in their interactions with friends certain aspects about themselves, and about those they are engaging with. They escalate commonalities and they try to ignore differences depending on 'what is needed' in order for a particular relationship to work. By doing so they not only maintain a particular relationship, but they actively fashion a sense of self and belonging within and outside these relationships. Their interactions are not only contextualized in time and place, but also improvised (cf. Kirby 2009a).

The actors inhabit what Holland et al. (1998) have termed 'figured worlds'. Figured worlds are socially and culturally constructed realms of interpretation and action that take shape within and grant shape to the co-production of activities, discourses, performances and artefacts (ibid.: 51–52). They are imagined worlds peopled by characters 'who carry out its [meaning: the worlds'] tasks and who also have styles of interacting within, distinguishable perspectives on, and orientations toward it' (ibid.: 51). Actors reproduce cultural knowledge and identity, but they also innovate, improvise and reconfigure their social and cultural lives. In the process they deconstruct and re-imagine both themselves, others and their relationships by mutually engaging with one another. The crucial point is that a person's relationships and notions of self and belonging are not just influenced by wider social and cultural processes. Rather, as the above examples show, close personal relationships such as friendships are creatively imagined and fashioned by actors in dialogue with a multiplicity of sometimes colliding and fractured voices and actions of others.

In certain ways, the data reflect the ideal of a multicultural New Zealand society in which actors can belong as well as retain some sense of difference. Theoretically at least, polyvocality, difference and cultural diversity are accommodated by such an ideal notion. However, as we have seen, at the level of social praxis, actors frequently experience the limits of the multicultural or bicultural ideal. Firstly, official representations only rarely match individual life experiences and identifications. Individual actors manoeuvre much more flexibly within different, often conflicting, notions of self and belonging than the comparatively static culture discourse suggests. Secondly, some actors are more multicultural than others, depending on their respective socio-cultural and economic backgrounds and individual interests. As we have seen, whereas many Māori actors frequently move between different 'worlds', their Pākehā friends are often ignorant of the bicultural lives their friends are engaged in. Finally, it is safe to assume that whereas the ideal of a multicultural New Zealand society suggests a multitude of cross-cultural interactions and relationships, this does not hold for the level of social practice. The ethnographic data reveal here relatively limited cross-cultural friendship interactions. Where they occur, they are frequently experienced as ambiguous and as less intimate than intra-cultural interactions. On the other hand, the data reveal the desire of individual actors to establish more close cross-cultural friendships. What they also show is that the actors themselves retain the ideal notion of a bicultural or multicultural society in which friendships are established among actors of diverse socio-economic and cultural backgrounds.

## Conclusion

As we have seen, cross-cultural friendships as experienced by individual Māori and Pākehā actors in urban New Zealand are inextricably linked to wider processes of identity-making and culture politics. Belonging and non-belonging to certain groups and places have important political and emotional implications for the ways in which Māori and Pākehā establish relationships with one another, and how they construct themselves and others.

Unfortunately, the multicultural city often fails to provide spaces of encounter (at least for Pākehā such as Linda) for close cross-cultural friendships to develop. On the other hand, the ideals of biculturalism and multiculturalism (however problematic they may be) also hold out the possibility for diverse and multiple identifications to coexist. The multicultural ideal of friendly social interaction across difference is not only upheld by actors, but is actively pursued in their cross-cultural friendships. Friendships, because of their relatively informal and voluntary characteristics (as opposed, for instance, to family relations), allow for a relatively high degree of flexibility in the construction of difference and similarity. Because of this flexibility, cross-cultural friendships in particular may provide important spaces 'in between' in which actors can re-imagine themselves and others through their mutual interactions with one another.

Friendships thus provide an interesting and under-researched site for the study of cross-cultural relations in New Zealand and elsewhere. With regards to the New Zealand data in particular, a dialogical perspective on identity and belonging in friendship, in conjunction with a socio-historically grounded analysis of power relations and identity discourse, seems a promising avenue for further analysis and theoretical exploration.

## Notes

1. The term 'Māori' refers to the indigenous peoples of New Zealand. While 'Pākehā has no unitary definition, in common usage it refers to 'a person of predominantly European descent' (Williams 2000: 252), and is sometimes associated with (white) skin colour. As Spoonley (1988) has elaborated, Pākehā identity has been shaped by their experience as members of the dominant group in society. In this article, pakeha refers to New Zealanders of European descent who identify as Pākehā and/or New Zealand-European. This may include persons identifying as 'New Zealanders' but acknowledging a cultural heritage linked to the settler population.
2. For a more detailed analysis of my argument, see also Brandt (2013).
3. The data were collected as part of a project on cross-cultural friendship in New Zealand. While data have been collected in Auckland's more rural surroundings, the focus was on the urban context, in particular in Auckland, New Zealand's largest city. During my time in the field, I stayed in different households, comprised of persons identifying as Māori, Pākehā, New Zealanders, European, and any combination of these.
4. Walker counts four English versions of the text and a Māori translation: 'The English version from which the translation was made has yet to be found' (Walker 1990: 90–91).

5. For reasons of data protection and anonymity, all personal names and identifying information in this chapter have been altered.
6. The term *marae* refers to the open area in front of a meeting house (*wharenui*), where formal greetings and discussions take place. In common usage, this includes the whole complex of buildings around the *marae*. It should be noted that nowadays only a minority of Māori visit a *marae* regularly: see e.g. Salmond (1975).
7. This is not to deny the existence of a variety of friendship conceptions. For instance, Māori notions of relatedness, especially the notions of *whānau* (extended family) and *whanaungatanga* (relationship, kinship), often coexist with more individualized conceptions. A detailed analysis of these is beyond the scope of this discussion.
8. This is not to deny the existence of other friendship constituting factors, for instance strategic considerations. Most of the studies alluded to here were conducted in the USA and follow a sociological or psychological approach. For an overview, see McPherson, Smith-Lovin and Cook (2001).
9. As I have already mentioned, this also applies to intimate-couple relationships (cf. Schäfer 2007).

## References

Adams, R.G., and G. Allan. 1998. 'Contextualizing Friendship', in R.G. Adams and G. Allan (eds), *Placing Friendship in Context*. Cambridge: Cambridge University Press, pp.1–17.

Appadurai, A. 1990. 'Disjuncture and Difference in the Global Cultural Economy', *Theory Culture and Society* 7(2): 295–310.

Beer, B. 2001. 'Anthropology of Friendship', in N.J. Smelser and P.B. Baltes (eds), *International Encyclopedia of the Social and Behavioral Sciences*. Kidlington: Elsevier, pp.5805–8.

Bell, A. 2004. 'Half-castes and "White Natives": The Politics of Maori-Pakeha Hybrid Identities', in C. Bell and S. Matthewman (eds), *Cultural Studies in Aotearoa New Zealand: Identity, Space and Place*. Oxford: Oxford University Press, pp.121–38.

Bhabha, H. 1994. *The Location of Culture*. London: Routledge.

―――― 1996. 'Culture's In-between', in S. Hall and P. Du Gay (eds), *Questions of Cultural Identity*. London: Sage, pp.53–60.

Brandt, A. 2013. *Among Friends? On the Dynamics of Maori–Pakeha Relationships in Aotearoa New Zealand*. Göttingen: Vandenhoeck & Ruprecht.

Carrier, J.G. 1990. 'People Who Can Be Friends: Selves and Social Relationships', in S. Bell and S. Coleman (eds), *The Anthropology of Friendship*. Oxford: Berg, pp.21–38.

Casey, E.S. 1996. 'How to Get from Space to Place in a Fairly Short Stretch of Time: Phenomenological Prolegomena', S. Feld and K.H. Basso (eds), *Senses of Place*. Santa Fe, NM: School of American Research Press, pp.13–52.

Clifford, J. 1997. *Routes: Travel and Translation in the Late Twentieth Century*. Cambridge, MA: Harvard University Press.

Consedine, B. 1989. 'Inequality and the Egalitarian Myth', in D. Novitz and B. Willmott (eds), *Culture and Identity in New Zealand*. Wellington: GP Books, pp.172–86.

Featherstone, M. 2001. 'Postnational Flows, Identity Formation and Cultural Space', in E. Ben-Rafael and Y. Sternberg (eds), *Identity, Culture and Globalization*. Leiden: Brill, pp.483–526.

Friedman, J. 1994. *Cultural Identity and Global Process*. London: Sage.

Gupta, A., and J. Ferguson. 1992. 'Beyond "Culture": Space, Identity and the Politics of Difference', *Cultural Anthropology* 7(1): 6–23.

Hall, S. 1996. 'Introduction: Who Needs "Identity"?' in S. Hall and P. Du Gay (eds), *Questions of Cultural Identity*. London: Sage, pp.3–17.

Hall, S., and P. Du Gay (eds). 1996. *Questions of Cultural Identity*. London: Sage.

Hannerz, U. 1996. *Transnational Connections: Culture, People, Places*. London: Routledge.

Hermans, H.J.M. 2002. 'The Dialogical Self as a Society of Mind', *Theory and Psychology* 12(2): 147–60.

Hermans, H.J.M., and G. Dimaggio. 2007. 'Self, Identity, and Globalization in Times of Uncertainty: A Dialogical Analysis', *Review of General Psychology* 11(1): 31–61.

Hirsch, E. 1995. 'Landscape: Between Place and Space', in E. Hirsch and M. O'Hanlon (eds), *The Anthropology of Landscape: Perspectives on Place and Space*. Oxford: Clarendon Press, pp.1–30.

Hoey, D. 2004. 'There Will Always Be a Taupo: Some Reflections on Pakeha Culture', in C.B.S. Matthewman (ed.), *Cultural Studies in Aotearoa New Zealand: Identity, Space and Place*. Oxford: Oxford University Press, pp.188–202.

Holland, D., and J. Lave. 2001. *History in Person: Enduring Struggles, Contentious Practice, Intimate Identities*. Santa Fe, NM: School for American Research Press.

Holland, D., D. Skinner, W. Lachicotte and C. Cain. 1998. *Identity and Agency in Cultural Worlds*. Cambridge, MA: Harvard University Press.

King, M. 1999. *Being Pakeha Now: Reflections and Recollections of a White Native*. Auckland: Penguin.

——— 2003. *The Penguin History of New Zealand*. Auckland: Penguin.

Kirby, P.W. 2009. 'Lost in "Space": An Anthropological Approach to Movement', in P.W. Kirby (ed.), *Boundless Worlds: An Anthropological Approach to Movement*. New York: Berghahn, pp.1–27.

Kirby, P.W. (ed.). 2009. *Boundless Worlds: An Anthropological Approach to Movement*. New York: Berghahn.

Kolig, E., et al. 2009. 'Introduction: Crossroad Civilisations and Bricolage Identities', in E. Kolig et al. (eds), *Identity in Crossroad Civilisations: Ethnicity, Nationalism and Globalism in Asia*. Amsterdam: Amsterdam University Press, pp.9–20.

Lovell, N. 1998. 'Introduction: Belonging in Need of Emplacement?' in N. Lovell (ed.), *Locality and Belonging*. London: Routledge, pp.1–22.

McPherson, M., L. Smith-Lovin and J.M. Cook. 2001. 'Birds of a Feather: Homophily in Social Networks', *Annual Reviews of Sociology* 27: 415–44.

Mead, H.M. 2003. *Tikanga Maori: Living by Maori Values*. Wellington: Huia.

Pahl, R. 2000. *On Friendship*. Oxford: Polity Press.

Robertson, R. 1995. 'Glocalization: Time-Space and Homogeneity-Heterogeneity', in M. Featherstone, S. Lash and R. Robertson (eds), *Global Modernities*. London: Sage, pp.25–44.

Rose, G. 1995. 'Place and Identity: A Sense of Place', in D. Massey and P. Jess (eds), *A Place in the World? Places, Cultures and Globalization*. Oxford: Open University Press, pp.87–132.

Salmond, A. 1975. *Hui: A Study of Maori Ceremonial Gatherings*. Auckland: Reed.

Schäfer, G. 2007. 'The Social Construction of Cross-cultural Couple Relationships in New Zealand', *Sites: A Journal of Social Anthropology and Cultural Studies* 4(2): 85–111.

Schwimmer, E. 1968. 'The Aspirations of the Contemporary Maori', in E. Schwimmer (ed.), *The Maori People in the Nineteen-sixties: A Symposium*. Auckland: Blackwood and Janet Paul, pp.9–64.

Sissons, J. 1995. 'Tall Trees Need Deep Roots: Biculturalism, Bureaucracy and Tribal Democracy in Aotearoa New Zealand', *Cultural Studies* 9: 61–73.

SNZ. 2006. 'Census of Population and Dwellings'. Wellington: Statistics New Zealand. Retrieved 7 April 2007 from: www.stats.govt.nz/Census/2006CensusHomePage.aspx.

Spoonley, P. 1986. 'Introduction: Being Pakeha – In Search of Ethnicity', *Sites: A Journal of Social Anthropology and Cultural Studies* 13(1): 1–5.

―――― 1988. *Racism and Ethnicity*. Auckland: Oxford University Press.

Spoonley, P., C. Macpherson and D. Pearson (eds). 2004. *Tangata Tangata: The Changing Ethnic Contours of New Zealand*. Southbank: Thomson Dunmore Press.

Van Meijl, T. 2006. 'Multiple Identifications and the Dialogical Self: Urban Maori Youngsters and the Cultural Renaissance', *Journal of the Royal Anthropological Institute* 12(4): 917–33.

Walker, R. 1989. 'Maori Identity', in D. Novitz and B. Willmott (eds), *Culture and Identity in New Zealand*. Wellington: GP Books, pp.35–52.

―――― 1990. *Ka whawhai tonu matou: Struggle without End*. Auckland: Penguin.

West, C., and S. Fenstermaker. 1995. 'Doing Difference', *Gender and Society* 9(1): 8–37.
Williams, H.W. 2000 [1971]. *Dictionary of the Maori Language*. Wellington: Legislation Direct.
Woodward, K. 1997. 'Concepts of Identity and Difference', in K. Woodward (ed.), *Identity and Difference*. London: Sage, pp.7–62.
Wright, S. 1998. 'The Politicization of "Culture"', *Anthropology Today* 14(1): 7–15.

# Epilogue

# Uncertain Futures of Belonging

Consequences of Climate Change and
Sea-level Rise in Oceania

──────── ◆●◆ ────────

## Wolfgang Kempf and Elfriede Hermann

Theoretical perspectives of movement, place-making and multiple identifications provide an analytical frame for capturing and representing core aspects of the realities which Pacific Islanders now face at home and abroad. The previous chapters in this volume offer insights into this world of contacts, networks and articulations. Place, culture and identity are seen as open, changeable, intrinsically heterogeneous domains of experience. Belonging describes a complex process of dialogue, involving diverse dimensions and directions. At the methodological level, the principal challenge is to combine the analysis of historically evolved practices of Pacific Islanders, including their politics and place-making, with a contemporary, more relational perspective on Oceania. Just how important it is to consider the extent to which Oceania is integrated into global flows and forces can be gauged from the existential challenges the Pacific island states and their peoples face nowadays.

Chief among these existential challenges is doubtless the anticipated impact of anthropogenic climate change and sea-level rise. This prospect of fundamental change throughout the region has prompted us to view in a new light the relevance of movement, place-making and multiple identifications as an analytical configuration. We argue that the manner in which place, culture and identity are specifically constituted by mobility, connectivity and articulation matters for an adequate understanding of the agency of Pacific Islanders in respect of climate change and sea-level rise. At the same time, we assume that the future impact of climate change and sea-level rise will not leave unchanged the processes and practices whereby multiple belongings are constituted.

The idea of anthropogenic climate change rests on two interlinked insights. On the one hand, human-induced emissions have over the last century raised concentrations of greenhouse gases (chiefly carbon dioxide) in the atmosphere. Over the same timescale, the earth's mean temperature has risen worldwide. According to current models and projections by climate scientists, any further increase in greenhouse gas concentrations can, depending on the scenario, lead to global mean temperatures rising by anywhere between 1.1 and 6.4 degrees centigrade by the year 2100 (see Archer and Rahmstorf 2010: 150). One consequence of global warming will be a rise in sea levels, the chief causes of which are the thermal expansion of water induced by warming and the increased volume of water from the melting of ice sheets. The average rate of sea-level rise over the last twenty years has been put at about 3 mm a year; by the year 2100, scientists expect the level of the planet's oceans to have risen by at least one metre (Rahmstorf 2010: 44).

The first point to make is that a prolonged rise in sea levels at this scale poses a grave risk to ecological and social structures, especially those situated in coastal regions. Given that seaboards in all parts of the world are among the most thickly populated areas on the planet, experts assume that a higher sea level means, certainly over the longer run, that there will be a need for comprehensive protective measures as well as resettlement schemes (see e.g. Hetherington and Reid 2010: 274–75). Current estimates of how many people will likely be affected by such measures are, however, more in the nature of speculation than genuine science (see Kempf 2012b: 227). Small islands and island states are seen as especially vulnerable to sea-level rise (Mimura et. al. 2007: 689), and the region of Oceania is no exception.[1] Here, a combination of rising waves and a general increase in extreme weather events (such as hurricanes, floods, droughts) will increasingly result in the submergence of coastal plains, a higher incidence of erosion and damage to land, infrastructure, settlements and installations, chiefly along seaboards – and not least, an adverse effect on existing drinking-water resources.

Yet the consequences of rising sea levels are only part of a broad spectrum of changes that global climate change is likely to unfold in the islands of the Pacific. Increased sea-surface temperatures, increased acidification of the ocean and the bleaching and reduction of coral formations will, in all probability, negatively impact on the size and distribution of local fish stocks and other maritime resources. All the above changes would be especially detrimental to such economically important arenas as the subsistence economy, agricultural production, fishing and tourism. There will inevitably be implications for income structures, the dependability of food supplies, the quality of life and certainly the lifestyles of the peoples of the Pacific. Furthermore, climate change will have a direct bearing on the health of the region's population, since infectious disease will increase (water-borne and vector-borne alike).

But these generalizing statements are no more than preliminary assays. Not taken into account is the multiplicity of geographic, socio-ecological, economic, political and cultural structures in Oceania, which largely contribute to the fact that the impact of climate change and sea-level rise on the islands, populations and regional states will have varying results (Barnett 2005: 206–7). To be sure, geographic diversity is a frequently cited factor. On the scale of vulnerability, clearly the larger, high-rising volcanic islands are among the more robust zones, whereas the smaller, low-lying reef islands and atolls are among the most sensitive. This disproportionate vulnerability on the part of atoll states – such as the Marshall Islands, Tuvalu and Kiribati – has played no small part in attracting (public and) scientific interest, especially over issues of national integrity and security (see Barnett and Adger 2003; McAdam 2010), representation (see Connell 2003; Farbotko 2005, 2010), cultural and social transformation (Rudiak-Gould 2013), and climate-related migration (see Mortreux and Barnett 2009; Farbotko and Lazrus 2012).

One key aspect of relevance to our analysis is the heterogeneous terrain of national sovereignty, political alliances and global networks, which, especially in the case of small island states, impacts hugely not only on the economy, as well as on development generally, but on the praxis and demography of migration. Basically, we encounter three varieties of political status in the Pacific island region (see Lockwood 2004: 13; Barnett and Campbell 2010: 5): fully independent island states; autonomous island states freely associating with metropolitan states like the USA and New Zealand; and direct dependencies of France, New Zealand and the USA. Barnett (2002: 25; 2005: 206–7) argues that such specific configurations of political autonomy and international ties influence whatever ability individual Pacific island states have to react to future challenges from climate change.

Lazrus (2012) has suggested conceptually combining differential perspectives on contacts and entanglements, power effects and vulnerabilities, knowledge systems and options for action. The strength of this integrated model lies, she claims, in its ability to link two complementary aspects.

Lazrus draws on Hauʻofa's relational perspective of a 'sea of islands' (Hauʻofa 1994) to view the global networking of island populations as representing an opportunity for the latter to display resilience and adaptive agency. This first aspect she combines with a second, the concept of social vulnerability developed in anthropological disaster theory, in order to grasp analytically the structural limitations of agency (Lazrus 2012: 289). Her concern is to trace contours of a 'totality of relationships that provide opportunities and constraints in the face of climate change – namely, the political and economic scaffolding erected through processes of colonialism and engagement with market globalization' (ibid.: 289).

Our analytical perspective has the advantage of letting us identify processes and practices within this wider field of entanglements and dominant vectors of power, processes and practices that in Lazrus's account, it must be said, remain largely implicit. The mobility of the inhabitants of island states, whether at the national or the international level, or both, gives rise to modes of place-making and identification that find expression in multiple belongings. Moreover, it is this terrain of multiple belongings (in all its historical and cultural specificity) that we must be alive to when rating factors of vulnerability, resilience and adaptive ability, since it creates the conditions under which Pacific Islanders develop their agency in the face of the consequences of climate change and sea-level rise. But it is equally necessary to note the ways in which the ongoing constitution of multiple belonging – along with relevant forms of mobility, place-making and identification – are recontextualized and modified by the effects of climate change and sea-level rise. Here we will primarily be dealing with realms of discourse and imagination – for, in respect of the primary perils facing Pacific states and their peoples from climate change, we are only talking as yet of future scenarios. One key aspect of those discourses and imaginations is future belonging. Thus, in contemporary discourses, the postulated effects of climate change and sea-level rise might well strengthen existing uncertainties of belonging or contribute to giving rise to new ones.

## Movement

Anthropological studies of the impact of climate change and sea-level rise must take into account the dominant modes of movement found among Pacific Islanders. Only by doing so can they attain an adequate understanding of contemporary constructions of place, culture and identity as variables of human agency. One important node of study is international migration, and the transnational links to which this gives rise. In her survey of Pacific transnationalism, Lee (2009a: 2; 2009b: 15) points out how important reciprocity, kinship relations and cultural identity are for constituting mutual ties between countries of origin and residence. Lee also considers it essential, in her analysis, to factor in the mutability of transnational links. She points to processes of weakening ties and diminishing contacts to countries of origin, especially in the second and third migrant generations; the development of an indirect (that is, mediated by third parties) engagement with former homelands, a process she terms indirect transnationalism; and an intensification of lateral contacts between diaspora communities, which she terms intra-diasporic transnationalism (see Lee 2009b: 17, 28).

Knowledge of the nature and causal efficacy of these shifting configurations of transnational links and enmeshments is essential for anthropological investigations into the consequences of climate change and sea-level rise in Oceania and the management of these (cf. ibid.: 30). Thus, for instance, the material support extended by members of the various diasporas to their countries of origin in the wake of extreme weather events is to be deemed a key indicator that transnational solidarity and transfer structures have contributed, and will probably continue to contribute, to the resilience and adaptability of island communities throughout the Pacific (Barnett 2002: 26; Barnett and Campbell 2010: 50). One further aspect – significant in our view – concerns the circulation of information, knowledge and narratives of climate change and sea-level rise within transnational networks, whether through electronic media or through personal encounters. Take, for example, the chapters by Pascht and Thode-Arora (both this volume) on the network of relationships, entitlements and obligations – mediated via various modes of belonging (to land, family, village, church and so on) – that have been constructed in New Zealand by Cook Islander and Niuean migrants with their respective islands of origin. This network describes just such a terrain of potential communication pathways and discursive vectors. Transnational links maintained by Christian churches in the Pacific and beyond have likewise put in place viable networking structures, within which perceptions, assessments, official positions and action programmes concerning climate change, sea-level rise and relocation are increasingly being circulated (see Kempf 2012a; Wasuka 2013).

The studies by Garond on Palm Island in Australia and by Rollason on Panapompom in Papua New Guinea remind us that not only are international migration and transnational enmeshments but also movements within nation-states relevant variables for anthropological studies of climate change and sea-level rise. Here the political, economic and social conditions in such very different countries as Australia and Papua New Guinea supply operative frameworks for the adaptive capacities and resilience of two island communities whose present composition is the product of forced resettlement (Palm Island) and migrant labour during the colonial era (Panapompom). Evident in both instances is just how important historical conditions and constraints can be for any understanding of present self-perceptions, movements and modes of belonging among marginalized island populations. That this postcolonial terrain of recent repositionings and multiple belongings is often, from the indigenous perspective, permeated with ambivalence, stagnation and uncertainty seems worthy of consideration as a modality for coping with the consequences of climate change and sea-level rise. Indeed, all the more so when we recall that uncertainties of belonging also play a role in the area of international migration and transnational links (Pascht; Thode-Arora; Fer and Malogne-Fer, this volume).

Relocations, especially when great distances are involved, give rise to landscapes of uncertain belonging, and this needs to be factored into any analysis of indigenous agency in the face of climate change. The case of the Banabans sheds light on one such landscape. This community comes originally from Banaba, an island in the central Pacific whose ecology was ruined by multinational phosphate mining. In 1945, the entire community was resettled on Fiji's Rabi Island, from whence, in subsequent decades, Banabans have articulated multiple belongings underpinned by a feeling of uncertainty. This emotion is referred to in the vernacular as *raraoma*, which includes notions of insecurity, uncertainty and worry. The first point to make is that *raraoma* has long dominated how Banabans relate to their island of origin, since they were extremely worried as to whether the rights based on belonging to the latter would remain in force after Banaba was incorporated into the state of Kiribati. The second is that the rise of ethno-nationalism in multicultural Fiji has caused Banabans to fear that full recognition of belonging to the present postcolonial state of Fiji might be withheld, along with the rights and entitlements deriving from such membership (Hermann 2004: 211–12; Hermann and Kempf 2005: 319–20).

Let us turn now to how the consequences of climate change and sea-level rise impact on the field of movement in the Pacific region. Dürr's study of travel and how place and identity are constructed in the contact zones of intercultural encounters can serve as a point of departure for looking at what would seem a promising area of study, one that has received little attention to date: the terrain of movements formed by travelling Pacific Islanders who are propelled by the discourse of global warming. We are referring to the growing number of government and church representatives, academics, technical experts, members of NGOs, activists, film-makers and artists, all of them hailing from the Pacific island region. They give their own accounts of the special vulnerabilities and existential perils facing islands and island states in the wake of global climate change, doing so at political meetings, international congresses, church assemblies, workshops, discussion rounds, tours, exchange programmes and the like. Moreover, such contributions are tantamount to a process of negotiation. In thus striving to use international forums and contact zones to advertise projected risks and coming upheavals, always with a view to securing the attention, empathy and support of the international community, these Pacific Islanders have taken to stressing the integrity, uniqueness and indispensability of place, identity and nation, which must at all costs be preserved from destruction and loss.[2]

The projected consequences of climate change and sea-level rise will lead to significant changes in environmental and living conditions throughout the Pacific region. Worth noting is that the expected ecological transformations will increasingly undermine the ability of local populations to provide for themselves to any acceptable extent. Especially in those regions that have to face existential degradation of their overall situation in combination with a growing population, we may expect that many will feel driven to emigrate. It is the prospect of such developments that permits social scientists to make the assumption that migration movements involving Pacific Islanders will increase at both national and international levels (Boncour and Burson 2009: 15–16; Barnett and Campbell 2010: 172; Hugo 2010: 34; Barnett and O'Neill 2012: 9).

Against the background of earlier debates on the growing numbers of 'environmental' and/or 'climate refugees' worldwide, in which massive criticism was raised against apocalyptically worded crisis scenarios, exaggerated estimates, alarmist media accounts and imprecise conceptualizations, not to say uncertain causalities between environmental change and displacement, experts now strive for a more differentiated perspective on the Pacific island region. Thus Farbotko and Lazrus (2012: 388) note that any future climate-induced migration by Pacific Islanders does not necessarily have to take the form of flight. Other experts counter sweeping generalizations to the effect that climate-induced migration is primarily a (security) problem by arguing that we should not overlook the positive contribution migration can make to adaptation, and so to reducing vulnerability (Boncour and Burson 2009: 15–16, 19; Barnett and Campbell 2010: 171; Barnett and Webber 2010: 38, 44–45).

Basically, it is the case that increased movement within the context of existing migration systems is far more likely than the advent of entirely new flows (Barnett and Webber 2010: 42, 51; Hugo 2010: 24–25, 34). This terrain of future options that authors derive from present movement patterns also affords insight into the nature of the constraints. In terms of the Pacific island region, this means that political alliances with metropolitan states – the association of Niue and the Cook Islands with New Zealand is a case in point – will continue to hold the door open for migration, a door that will remain shut for people from the independent island states that are without comparable political enmeshments. As a consequence, those in the latter category run the risk of destitution, should their ability to provide for themselves be further undermined by climate change and sea-level rise (see Barnett and Campbell 2010: 172). Relocation of whole communities, whether as a preventive measure or as a last resort, will likely entail considerable risk. International relocations have a reputation of often increasing the vulnerability of affected communities (Barnett and Webber 2010: 53; Barnett and O'Neill 2012: 9). Internal relocations, on the other hand, are limited not infrequently in many Pacific island states as a result of historically evolved structures of indigenous land ownership (Campbell 2010; Barnett and O'Neill 2012: 9). The Christian churches of the Pacific position themselves as political actors and mediators at both national and international levels concerning issues of climate-induced migration – however, their growing influence is still too rarely factored into such scenarios (see Kempf 2012a; cf. Pareti 2013).

Expanding the volume of voluntary migrant labour is currently favoured as a practical way to bolster the adaptive capacity of Pacific Islanders (Barnett and Webber 2010: 42, 44; Barnett and O'Neill 2012: 9). While the voluntary aspect is primarily intended to underwrite the socio-cultural specifics of decision-making processes and to secure indigenous participation in the latter, migrant labour as such would contribute to (re)organizing socio-economic networks and solidarity structures, so that these could be depended on across broad tracts of space-time (Barnett and Campbell 2010: 171; Barnett and Webber 2010: 42; Lazrus 2012: 293–94). But if there is to be a more flexible *modus operandi*, especially in terms of migrant labour on an international scale, there will first need to be a lowering of existing hurdles erected by the metropolitan states of the Pacific region; in this process, bilateral agreements are more likely to prove implementable than global agreements, at least initially (Boncour and Burson 2009: 19).

Concrete steps directed towards making it easier for their people to find work abroad are being taken by, for example, the government of Kiribati. In a further attempt to counter the risks of climate change and sea-level rise for the atoll state, a few years ago President Anote Tong and his government began to back up the Kiribati Adaptation Program (KAP) with a political initiative they call 'Migration with Dignity'.[3] The measures are designed to support emigration at its present levels, while also ensuring that the younger generations especially have the professional qualifications needed to be accepted in the new host countries.[4] Representatives of Kiribati's government argue that it makes more sense to put in place a managed process of labour emigration now, rather than to wait fifty or sixty years for disaster to strike, with people then moving uncontrollably on a grand scale.

The discourses circulating in Kiribati about the problem of climate change and sea-level rise, especially in combination with local adaptive measures decreed by the government, are having a significant impact on the younger generation's attitudes to place, belonging and mobility. Here is one response to a survey we carried out in 2009 with a cohort of pupils on Tarawa, Kiribati's principal atoll:

> I think some people have been saying that in fifty years our beloved country will have disappeared as a result of sea-level rise. But what I do know is this: our beloved country cannot disappear under the waves because our beloved country is in the middle of the world ... But just in case, we should prepare ourselves by:
>
> *Going overseas.
>
> *Saving up money.[5]

These remarks would seem to turn on a fundamental paradox. On the one hand, the possibility is denied – it is simply too great an imaginative leap – that Kiribati might in the foreseeable future disappear below the waves, meaning the whole country will simply cease to be. On the other hand, the pupil recognizes that such a development can no longer be discounted entirely. Hence it seems to him reasonable, just in case it ever happens, to have a contingency plan worked out: quitting the country to build up a new existence elsewhere. His repeated characterization of a threatened Kiribati as his 'beloved country' gives us a taste of the emotional discourses to which people in this atoll state now have recourse to in view of the projected impacts of climate change and sea-level rise (Hermann 2011, 2012). This formulation is symptomatic of the younger generation of I-Kiribati, whose emotional bond with their country of birth is increasingly marked by the uncertainty of future belonging.

Attachment to one's land – something which Pacific Islanders generally value highly – is in many places acquiring a new dimension, as a result of the discourses of climate change, sea-level rise, migration and/or relocation. Future scenarios portraying forced migration and relocation as ineluctable consequences of climate change are helping to amplify indigenous conceptualizations of an integral connection between place, person, culture and way of life. In the states and islands of the Pacific most at risk, this trend is traceable to the fact that significant majorities there are unwilling to turn their backs on their land forever (see e.g. Gemenne and Shen 2009; McNamara and Gibson 2009; Mortreux and Barnett 2009; Lazrus 2012; Barnett and O'Neill 2012). Nor is it the case, let us add, that all migrants are ready to abandon their country of origin or their family land, either as places of socio-cultural reference or as places they might one day wish to return to. Against this background, demands are readily understandable that more will need to be done by scientists and politicians in terms of putting in place, at least over the medium term, mitigating and adaptive measures of a kind that will preserve highly exposed islands as homelands and reference points – chiefly of course for the local population, but also for the many distant diasporic groups (see Barnett and Campbell 2010: 173–74; Barnett and O'Neill 2012: 10).

## Place-making

Articulations of attachment to land are integral to the praxis and politics of place-making. Adopting an analytical perspective that attempts systematically to incorporate movement into the process of place-making, our primary aim is to conceptualize the emergence of place and identity as mutable, relational and multiple configurations within an analytical field of far-flung enmeshments and power relationships. The heterogeneous and multivocal structuration of such places – constituted as they are by movement – offers, we believe, a useful point of entry for anthropological studies wishing to shed light on the consequences of climate change and sea-level rise in Oceania. This is a perspective that lets us critically evaluate existing conceptualizations of place in the social-science literature on climate change and sea-level rise. We believe this field is still largely given over to a decidedly conventional view of what places are.

Anthropological studies of anthropogenic climate change not infrequently foreground the natural anchoring and reciprocal integration of place, culture and identity (see Crate 2008, 2011; Crate and Nuttall 2009). Cultural difference here is primarily a function of natural space and its ecological zones. Each handed-down configuration of place, culture and identity embedded therein is 'part of the ethnodiversity that, like biodiversity, is essential to the robust health and continued human, plant, and animal habitation of the planet' (Crate 2008: 585; cf. Crate 2011: 184). Here, the specific connectivity of indigenous groups with, and/or their dependency on, intact ecological systems is central to the concept of place-based or island-based communities (see Crate 2008: 573; Lazrus 2012: 290). Lived human–environment relationships in such communities are depicted as the linchpin of a cultural essence thought to reside in traditional ecological forms of knowledge, everyday practices, symbolic structures and ideological orientations, all of which are now being jeopardized by the inroads of global climate change (see Crate 2008, 2011; Crate and Nuttall 2009).

Lazrus (2012: 290) partly takes her lead from this analytical perspective, but has little to say on just how the essentializing conceptions of place-based or island-based communities are ultimately to be reconciled with Hau'ofa's idea of a 'sea of islands' involving multiple contacts, combinations and extensions.

The natural and cultural uniqueness of places is also postulated by Adger et al., who argue 'that localized material and symbolic values have hitherto remained undervalued in the standard political and welfare economic calculus of climate change policy and science' (Adger et al. 2011: 2). These authors enlist the idea of place to pinpoint the identity-conferring quality that environment and culture have, especially for indigenous communities. The insight they wish us to share is that any altering, endangering or degrading of the environment due to climate change and sea-level rise will impact not only on the material but also on the immaterial plane of meaning. In their eyes, such changes will have an effect on how people ascribe value to and identify with places. The challenge facing science and policy-making alike, the authors assert, is how to bind the socio-cultural relevance of place and identity more strongly into risk management and decision-making processes linked to climate change and its ramifications for local communities. To illustrate their argument, Adger et al. (ibid.: 6–13) cite Pacific atolls and the Arctic as instances of regions at risk from climate change. In more or less remote parts of these exposed regions, they see natural uniqueness as combining with cultural difference in local communities to yield an authentic constellation of environment, culture, place and identity which, in their view, needs to be factored into any political assessment of the risks of climate change and any counter-measures adopted.

Social-science narratives of this kind turn on the opposition between tradition and modernity; they construct naturally anchored, culturally homogeneous places and autochthonous communities whose uniqueness is now coming under threat from destructive forces. This essentializing perspective is founded on two key exclusions. For one thing, historical transformations in those places they have in mind are left out. Atolls in Kiribati, to give one example, are described as 'remote and underdeveloped' places, where traditional, ecological modes of knowledge and praxis characterize how local populations interact with the environment (ibid.: 8) – this despite the fact that Christianity and work-related migration to the phosphate mines on Nauru and Banaba (Williams and Macdonald 1985; Shlomowitz and Munro 1992), as well as in connection with international sea-faring (Borovnik 2005, 2009), have long formed part of the constituent features of all these islands. For another thing, places and identities seemingly less traditional and authentic are entirely excluded on the analytical plane. The essays in this collection supply exemplary reference points for places that are ignored. Thus in the conceptual terrain of a bounded and sequestered homogeneity of environment, place, culture and identity we find no room being left for, say, absentee landowners (Pascht, this volume). It is a terrain in which the uniqueness of such colonially constituted places as reservations (Garond, this volume) and plantation islands (Rollason, this volume) is almost never taken into consideration – nor, for that matter, is their historically evolved heterogeneity, their hybrid nature, their constant changeability.

Omitted too have been the making (real and imagined) of places by Pacific people in the context of travelling and international migration (see the chapters by Dürr, Pascht, Thode-Arora, Fer and Malogne-Fer, this volume). In any event, positionings outside one's country of origin hardly play any role at all in the debate over the consequences of climate change and sea-level rise. When it comes to anthropogenic climate change and its aftermath, the interest of many current studies is firmly focused on those Pacific islands, or island states, deemed to be vulnerable. Countries like New Zealand are, at best, accorded the status of potential havens for islanders fleeing endangered regions in the Pacific. Although such a calculus does make plenty of sense from a geographic, political and humanitarian perspective, we can only urge the importance of attending to the plurality of ways in which place, culture and identity are constituted in the diaspora, since these too form a specific platform for the reception of discourses bearing on climate change and sea-level rise. Lazrus (2012: 296), who has similarly recommended paying more attention to the Pacific diaspora in this connection, is thinking especially of the relationships diasporic communities forge with their countries of residence. As we see it, any perspective focusing on the Pacific diaspora in the future must additionally address the issue of transnational links. The aim must be to incorporate into our analytical framework the impact climate change discourses from the diaspora have on the construction of places and landscapes in the islands of origin, and vice versa, as well as giving an account of the resultant transformations in the perception of the diaspora and islands of origin.

For an indication of how official discourses on climate change and sea-level rise – in combination with an ongoing process of planning and implementing adaptive measures – impact on the perception and constituting of places, we need but turn to the atoll state of Kiribati. In this choice we are building on our discussion of Kiribati in the previous section. In Kiribati the government is endeavouring to create in the population an awareness of climate change. This is usually done via official declarations, parliamentary debates, conferences, consultations, days of action, workshops, competitions and the like. The main media channels used are national radio, newspapers and local video productions. An example of this policy being put into practice is the 'National High Level Public Hearing on Climate Change', which was held on 19 April 2013 on the main atoll of Tarawa, close to government headquarters. In their concern to reach as broad a section of the population as possible, the organizers chose as their venue Bairiki Square, which has a long history of staging public events.[6] The speeches by the president, church representatives, members of the parliamentary opposition and spokespersons for various social interest groups were not only heard by a large crowd but were also carried live by radio. People were then given the opportunity to direct questions at the speakers, either orally (in the case of those attending the event) or (in the case of absentees) via telephone and Facebook.[7]

This political process, the purpose of which is to acquaint the people of Kiribati with the climate change problematic and what it may mean for them, factors in a second goal no less dear to the government. This is to implement measures directed at climate-change adaptation and disaster risk reduction. The Kiribati Adaptation Program (KAP) plays a decisive role in this connection. Core concerns of the KAP are the safeguarding and improvement of available drinking-water supplies, the protection of coastal regions and the fortification of key areas of infrastructure. New sea walls (to stabilize the infrastructure) and the planting of mangroves (to counter coastal erosion) are visible signs of the government's policy of adaptation.[8] In the general context of a prevalent discourse of climate change and sea-level rise, Kiribati's people are increasingly seeing their familiar places and landscapes in a different light. That the constitution of place and identity can – additionally – incorporate aspects of movement is shown, for example, by the responses one pupil gave in a survey we carried out in 2010 on Tarawa:

Q: Have you heard about climate change, and if so, where did you hear about it?

A: Yes, I've heard about it. I first heard about it when I was in Rarotonga (the Cook Islands).[9] The people from the environment ministry always go into the schools and tell them about climate change. This was where I first heard about it.

Q: Do you think that Kiribati may be affected by climate change?

A: Yes, of course Kiribati will be affected by climate change. We can individually experience the shores on our beach washing away little by little, causing government people to build sea walls to protect our beach sand from being carried away by the sea. Kiribati is one of the vulnerable islands in the Pacific that will be greatly affected by climate change.[10]

This quotation is significant in three respects. First, it hints at the fact that younger generations of I-Kiribati are now confronting climate-change discourse in a variety of walks of life and educational contexts. Second, it indicates that movement – in this case between the Cook Islands and Kiribati – enables people to see Kiribati's atolls in relation to other Pacific islands at risk. Third, the internalized discourse of climate change and sea-level rise conditions how younger generations interpret alterations to places and landscapes and, building thereon, how they intend to realize and routinize the constitution of place and identity in the future.

The broad-based reception of official discourses on climate change (and migration), in combination with the publicly visible reconfiguring of many places through the implementation of adaptive measures, has caused several I-Kiribati to ponder the indissoluble bonds tying them to their lands. For climate-change discourses, spatial alterations and migration policies all create a regime of truth, which, among other things, makes future displacement seem plausible. In the previous section, we noted that the prospect of forced migration and relocation is only helping to underscore the local discourse of the enmeshments of place, culture and identity. As for the reaction of the older generation, respondents usually wanted to stay put and end their days on their own land, rather than take their chances abroad. Their priority is therefore mainly to ensure continuity in place-making. Other I-Kiribati, this time chiefly from the middle and younger generations, are focused more on the discontinuity that would accompany a collective relocation and the irreversible loss of land and country. To illustrate the radical breach that the long-term effects of climate change and sea-level rise would surely entail, especially for land ownership and the issue of belonging, some I-Kiribati refer to the dead relatives who lie buried there – resting in the same earth they have worked during their lifetimes. One I-Kiribati woman – she had lived for some time in New Zealand before returning to Tarawa to work as a freelance consultant to the government and a number of aid agencies, formulated the matter as follows:

> The most important part, the angle that I always [insist on], is our sense of belonging to our own country. If we remember the past, our ancestors fought to have their land, and ownership is a proof of blood being spilt for that land! Plus the victory. It is a sign of victory for them to get that land. Okay. So now we have that. If we run into big trouble and have no more country left, all of that will be wiped out. But it's not only that. All of our loved ones who have passed away and been buried will now be floating somewhere. But anybody with a loved one would like to have them laid to rest and, you know, resting in peace. But that will then be a kind of floating rest. It's not something that we look forward to.[11]

The generations who have gone before are seen as custodians of the land, ensuring its continuity. They have literally given substance to the soil and, in doing so, legitimized the right of those coming after to hold the land. Not for nothing does the vernacular term *te aba* stand for both 'land' and 'people'. The graves of relatives – digging them, maintaining them, the mnemonic function they fulfil – are signs (today mostly Christian) of a social and spatial connectedness with the land, and are therefore rightly seen as integral to I-Kiribati's place-making. The prospect of their dead relatives floating away on the rising waters signifies more than just the loss of land. It is a metaphor for dissociation, the dissolution of all kinds of historical, social and cultural anchoring. It is a vision of ultimate placelessness, in which the certainty of belonging has melted away into thin air or – to stay with the metaphor – been washed away. Representations of this kind alert us to how cultural conceptualizations of place-making and belonging are being mobilized by I-Kiribati as a counter-discourse, in an effort to appeal to the morality, sense of responsibility and willingness to help of the international community.

Climate-change discourses, migration policy and adaptive measures also influence how place and identity are constituted by Banabans living in Kiribati. The background lies in the fact that a small number of members of the Banaban community, itself relocated over sixty years ago to Fiji's Rabi Island, have migrated in the first decade or so of the new millennium to Kiribati, settling mostly on the main atoll of Tarawa. The political instability in Fiji in particular, as well as the peripheral geographic, socio-political and economic position the community finds itself in back on Rabi Island (cf. Teaiwa 1997: 131), prompted Banaban families to look for educational facilities, scholarships and job opportunities in urban Kiribati. Some of those Banabans who migrated also had the advantage of having land holdings on Tarawa, given their close kinship ties with I-Kiribati. Here, then, they settled, building houses, digging wells, laying out gardens, digging graves, fetching their relatives from Fiji, and raising children (who would then marry into I-Kiribati families).

If climate change and sea-level rise hardly registered with Kiribati-Banabans initially, over the years they have become increasingly aware of Tarawa as a vulnerable place (and the vulnerability of their own places there). This progression is shown by the way a group of Banabans, who were constructing a sea wall and a belt of mangroves, originally saw in this just a measure for saving their own land holdings from erosion. But as discourses of climate change and its aftermath finally hit home, they began to see in the sea wall and mangroves an adaptive measure against sea-level rise. From the growing realization of a dim future facing precisely such atoll states as Kiribati, it was only a short step to grasping that their own future on Tarawa, including their belonging to land and society there, was anything but certain. It was in this nexus that the Banabans' multiple identifications paved the way for them to ponder new options.

## Cultural Identifications

Recent work on migration and transnational links in the Pacific (including the present volume) have alerted us to the complexity of multiple identifications, on which discourses of climate change and its aftermath are now increasingly having an impact. By considering the case of those Banabans who have, over the last decade and a half, emigrated to Tarawa from Rabi Island, we will now briefly turn to such plural identifications and their articulation in the context of climate change. As is true of all the Banaban community, these émigrés identify with their island of origin (Banaba), including the unique way of life that once existed there in pre-colonial and colonial times, but also – and no less so – with Rabi Island and the culture that has developed there over time, blending elements taken from the cultural repertoire of autochthonous Fijians, Indo-Fijians and other ethnic groups. Like their fellow Banabans on Rabi, they have internalized many aspects of so-called Western culture – Banabans, after all, have been integrating these into their lifestyle ever since phosphate mining commenced on Banaba (without let-up later on Rabi). Whereas Rabi-Banabans identify in some contexts with specific cultural characteristics associated with specific Kiribati islands, basing these on family ties and thus derived claims to ownership of plots of land there, Kiribati-Banabans do so on a daily basis. Thus, many Banabans who have migrated to Tarawa from Rabi Island feel they now belong to their new country of residence, culturally as well as nationally. Like I-Kiribati themselves, they view their plots of land on Kiribati's atolls not simply in an economic light, but rather as objects of intense attachment.

When climate change in all its forms meets with configurations of cultural identifications, such complexity cannot remain unaltered. Of particular note, in the case of Banaban migrants to Tarawa, is that they, by dint of belonging to their new country of residence, feel affected by the countless discourses circulating there on the consequences of climate change. Whereas only a few years ago Banabans of the older and middle generations had seen Kiribati as offering opportunities for their children and grandchildren, they are no longer so sure about this. Many now worry about the future there. Confronted with news of global warming and projected sea-level rise, Banabans reflect on their multiple identifications with land, people and cultural practices – both within Kiribati itself and on Rabi Island. If as a first consequence of their migration to Kiribati they were driven to highlight their new I-Kiribati identity in the making, what we find now is that the increased prevalence of climate-change discourses is causing them to stress their Banaban identifications. Both Banaba (a raised limestone island) and Rabi (an island of volcanic origin) rise considerably higher than Kiribati's atolls; thus, as people recognize, they offer rather more in the way of protection against flooding. Banaba, because it is difficult to supply, is hardly suited at present to take in any migrants, but not so Rabi; as a result, that island is looming ever larger in the calculations of Kiribati-Banabans. Not coincidentally, they remind themselves that they are still Fijian nationals. If the political situation in Fiji once gave the Banaban community reason to feel insecure, Rabi Island now seems like a comparatively safe haven in view of the scientific reports of what climate change will do to Kiribati's atolls. With Rabi, they have fewer worries, as a Banaban father of five made clear:

> Sometimes I worry about the sea level. Because I don't know when my time will come. And what will happen with my kids then? What will they do? So I think: we'd better think about how to protect them. And yet, we are not so worried after all, we have a homeland, you know, and we have mountains there. [...] We do have a homeland. That's why we don't worry or really care about the sea level rising here. Because we have our own island: Rabi.[12]

By designating Rabi as a homeland, the interlocutor was affirming his Banaban identification. He went on to state that he had talked over with his wife the possibility of resettlement in New Zealand or Australia, along with other I-Kiribati, should Kiribati's government ever embrace this solution. For, he added significantly, 'we are part of the I-Kiribati, too'. Statements of this kind draw attention to the discourse of multiple identifications circulating among Banabans. In the context of climate change, we found that most Kiribati-Banabans see their plural belonging as resources definitely to be drawn on for solutions in difficult times.

True, Banaban migrants to Kiribati are but a special instance among all those others where identifications have been expressed and partially altered in the context of climate change. There is still a paucity of studies exploring how the knowledge of climate change affects identifications among Pacific Islanders. Yet studies of Tuvaluans and I-Kiribati have already tabled some provisional findings, namely that identifications play a pivotal role in the context of discourses on climate change and planning for the future. For Tuvalu, a discourse has been documented where islanders articulate a sense of close belonging to their threatened place – and also the culture associated with that country. Mortreux and Barnett (2009), as well as Gemenne and Shen (2009), have described this discourse in highly graphic terms, showing the extent to which stay-at-home Tuvaluans justify their decision not to emigrate by citing it. But at least some of those Tuvaluans who have emigrated to New Zealand – whether for economic reasons, or on account of family ties, or through a general sense that staying put meant risking their future – no longer identify exclusively with Tuvalu, but weigh the option, now perfectly thinkable, of citizenship in their new country of residence (Gemenne and Shen 2009: 15–16).

A dominant discourse of identification with the country of origin, co-existing with initial, cautious voices imagining what it would be like to belong to another nation, can be noted too in Kiribati. In an environment characterized by climate-change discourses, many I-Kiribati have taken to expressing their sense of identification with land and country in loving terms, acknowledging the bond they feel with their home islands and the culture found there, and in no way hiding the worries they feel for the land and its people (Hermann 2012). To be sure, it is not as if love (*tangira*) for the land and its people has not been thematized in the past. However, existing discursive formations have taken on new meanings as a result of present worries and insecurity (*raraoma*), to the point where today's I-Kiribati emphasize their determination not to abandon their threatened homeland and unique culture.

But does this mean we must conclude that the islanders have single ties, exclusively fixed on Kiribati, as if their identifications were not already constituted by movement? To suggest this would be to do scant justice to the complex social (and often economic) networks and identifications in which the I-Kiribati participate. Not all I-Kiribati were born in Kiribati, nor is it the case that all I-Kiribati have always lived on the same Kiribati atoll where they are currently residing. Other places of origin, as well as the social ties they have built with the communities living there, mean that they feel themselves as at least partly belonging to these – dependent, to be sure, on context. Thus one elderly lady – as an I-Kiribati she strongly identified with a certain atoll in her country – mentioned, when voicing her thoughts on the risks to Kiribati's atolls of increased flooding, that she had herself been born on Banaba, where her father once worked in the phosphate mines, adding significantly: 'We should go to Banaba'. To this more elevated island, she already had a close biographical link. Recalling that it would be decades before any upheavals due to climate change could seriously threaten her country, this is what she had told her husband: 'We won't be around when Kiribati will be under the sea. But what about the people who will be alive then? I hope they'll find a better place to live in. Maybe that's why some people have started to evacuate to New Zealand'.[13] Shortly afterwards she explained that her son too wanted to emigrate to New Zealand, where his brother-in-law was living already. For members of the younger generation, such future plans no longer seem in any way unusual. Speaking with young I-Kiribati, there is invariably a broad majority who stress that they want to go on living on their islands and that they will do their best to preserve them. However, as a result of the information campaigns waged by the government, many are now contemplating an uncertain future for their country. That is indeed why some are starting to address worst-case scenarios and, consequently, thinking of migration. In the event of extreme existential risk, one I-Kiribati young woman admitted, she could imagine relocating to another country – adding: 'if the government will send us people to places where they can find jobs and become citizens at that particular country, e.g., New Zealand and Australia'.[14]

Even if such reactions are as yet relatively rare, they do suggest that the I-Kiribati, struggling to take on board discourses of climate change and the uncertain future awaiting their country are now rethinking their identifications. They are pondering the ties, based on past movements, which they have built (or might conceivably build) with other places and other communities, the better to activate these ties for purposes of plural belonging, should this become necessary.

## Conclusion: Climate Change and Uncertain Futures of Belonging

Discourses of climate change and sea-level rise encounter a terrain of high diversity in Oceania, a terrain long permeated by multiple movements as well as by the connections, processes of place-making and cultural identifications these have occasioned. This is the space in which Pacific Islanders relate discourses on the consequences of climate change to their belonging to one or several places, countries and social communities. It is in this discursive context that we find projections being made for an uncertain future, and this is no less true for stay-at-home Pacific Islanders than for those who have migrated and are now residing abroad.

Pacific Islanders living in their country of origin have to worry for its and their future, depending on how grave the projected inroads of climate change are in their specific case. In particular, the inhabitants of atoll states like Tuvalu, Kiribati and the Marshall Islands, which are among the most vulnerable regions in the Pacific, need to address the challenge of working out what belonging to their country means. It is to be noted that their interaction with climate-change discourses cuts two ways. On the one hand, many islanders contribute to strengthening the local discourse of belonging to land and country, including an (imagined) community with which they associate this. We should avoid seeing this as a natural reaction by these islanders. What we have instead is a cultural reaction to powerful discourses of climate change, a reaction also attesting to a determination to do whatever it takes to protect their homeland. On the other hand, a discourse on the possibilities for migration is plainly underway, a discourse which the younger and middle generations in particular now invoke as they begin to imagine what it might mean to one day belong, additionally, to a different society in a new host country.

Migrants who are already established abroad but think back to the atolls or coastal settlements of their old homelands will, in all likelihood, be caused by climate-change discourses to reckon with imponderabilities, so that their sense of belonging to these places will hardly be free of worry. For people whose existence in the diaspora is precarious enough already, presumably this will further ratchet up their uncertainty of belonging. Not so, however, for those migrants whose new place of residence is threatened by sea-level rise or other consequences of climate change, while their old homelands are not so threatened to a comparable degree. The Banaban case has shown that migrants falling into this latter category, irrespective of any worries they may feel about the future plight of their new country of residence, are already entertaining the possibility of returning to where they came from. And there are some among them who consider moving on to yet another country of residence, should the need arise and the opportunity present itself. Migrants falling into this third category, therefore, consider the multiple identifications at their disposal, knowing they may one day have to choose other identifications than those currently prioritized, and so mobilize specific belongings to another place – inhabited by other communities – for purposes of building a future life there.

Contemplating how Pacific Islanders deal with the uncertainties posed by discourses of climate change, not to mention the consequences thereof, it is clearly the case that they, for all their worries about the future, are also actively searching for ways to rein in the imponderabilities. This holds equally for those remaining in their countries of origin and for those living abroad in the diaspora. In their search for options, islanders position themselves as belonging to one or more places and to plural networks. And when multiple belongings are discerned, then a number of options are recognized, ranging from staying put in an endangered place and adapting to the consequences of climate change to migrating elsewhere in the Pacific. Which options are ultimately chosen depends not only on the economic means they can muster, but also on such factors as international support, national policies, bilateral and multilateral agreements and policies pursued by the countries of destination. Nor should we overlook the fact that Pacific Islanders are demonstrating a capacity to act. Faced with powerful discourses of climate change, they exercise agency by mobilizing the fact of their belonging to a particular land and its people – or, and increasingly so, to many communities, which may or may not transcend national borders and embrace a number of countries.

## Notes

1. The following account of what climate change and sea-level rise will mean for the Pacific islands is heavily indebted to Mimura et al. (2007) and SPREP (2008).
2. The film by Nei Tabera Ni Kai (2010) on a governmental delegation from the atoll state of Kiribati, screened at the Copenhagen Climate Conference in 2009 and the 'The Water Is Rising', a project aimed at inviting dance groups from Tuvalu, Tokelau and Kiribati (all countries at risk from climate change and sea-level rise) to tour the USA (see www.waterisrising.com/), may both be said to exemplify this thematic. See also Hermann and Kempf (n.d.).
3. On KAP's priorities, see: www.climate.gov.ki/category/action/adaptation/kiribati-adaptation-program/. On 'Migration with Dignity', see: www.climate.gov.ki/category/action/relocation/, last accessed 12 April 2013.
4. This information derives from interviews with the president of the Republic of Kiribati, Anote Tong (14 September 2009); the deputy secretary of the Ministry of Foreign Affairs and Immigration (7 September 2009); and a representative of the Ministry of Labour (22 September 2010).
5. Response of a male pupil, aged 18. The pupil had, in fact, inserted a third asterisk, so plainly he had more in mind than these first two points. For whatever reason, he broke off at this point, leaving us to speculate about what further steps he was envisaging.
6. This event was organized by members of the Parliament Select Committee on Climate Change (PSCCC). See on this matter: www.climate.gov.ki/resources/parliament-select-committee-on-climate-change/ and http://www.climate.gov.ki/wp-content/uploads/2013/03/National-High-Level-Public-Hearing-on-Climate-Change-Official-Programme.pdf, last accessed 13 August 2013.
7. See: www.climate.gov.ki/2013/04/19/wet-weather-fails-to-dampen-public-hearing-spirits/, last accessed 13 August 2013.
8. See: www.climate.gov.ki/category/action/adaptation/kiribati-adaptation-program/kiribati-adaptation-program-phase-iii/, last accessed 12 April 2013; and www.climate.gov.ki/2013/07/25/mangrove-education-and-planting-on-its-way-to-four-more-islands-3-islands-complete/, last accessed 13 August 2013.
9. The Cook Islands have a tiny diaspora community of I-Kiribati, so it is not unusual for some children to get at least part of their schooling there.
10. Response by a male pupil, aged 17, September 2010.
11. Nei L., 12 September 2009.
12. Ten M.K., 5 September 2009.
13. Nei A., 22 September 2012.
14. Female pupil, aged 17, September 2010.

# References

Adger, N.W., J. Barnett, F.S. Chapin and H. Ellemor. 2011. 'This Must Be the Place: Underrepresentation of Identity and Meaning in Climate Change Decision-making', *Global Environmental Politics* 11(2): 1–25.

Archer, D., and S. Rahmstorf. 2010. *The Climate Crisis: An Introductory Guide to Climate Change*. Cambridge: Cambridge University Press.

Barnett, J. 2002. 'Rethinking Development in Response to Climate Change in Oceania', *Pacific Ecologist* 1: 25–28.

——— 2005. 'Titanic States? Impacts and Responses to Climate Change in the Pacific Islands', *Journal of International Affairs* 59: 203–19.

Barnett, J., and N. Adger. 2003. 'Climate Dangers and Atoll Countries', *Climatic Change* 61(3): 321–37.

Barnett, J., and J. Campbell. 2010. *Climate Change and Small Island States: Power, Knowledge and the South Pacific*. London: Earthscan.

Barnett, J., and S.J. O'Neill. 2012. 'Islands, Resettlement and Adaptation', *Natural Climate Change* 2: 8–10.

Barnett, J., and M. Webber. 2010. 'Migration as Adaptation: Opportunities and Limits', in J. McAdam (ed.), *Climate Change and Displacement: Multidisciplinary Perspectives*. Oxford: Hart, pp.37–55.

Boncour, P., and B. Burson. 2009. 'Climate Change and Migration in the South Pacific Region: Policy Perspectives', *Policy Quarterly* 5(4): 13–20.

Borovnik, M. 2005. 'Seafarers "Maritime Culture" and the "I-Kiribati Way of Life": The Formation of Flexible Identities?' *Singapore Journal of Tropical Geography* 26(2): 132–50.

——— 2009. 'Transnationalism of Merchant Seafarers and their Communities in Kiribati and Tuvalu', in H. Lee and S.T. Francis (eds), *Migration and Transnationalism: Pacific Perspectives*. Canberra: Australian National University Press, pp.143–50.

Campbell, J. 2010. 'Climate-Induced Community Relocation in the Pacific: The Meaning and Importance of Land', in J. McAdam (ed.), *Climate Change and Displacement: Multidisciplinary Perspectives*. Oxford: Hart, pp.57–79.

Connell, J. 2003. 'Losing Ground? Tuvalu, the Greenhouse Effect and the Garbage Can', *Asia Pacific Viewpoint* 44(2): 89–107.

Crate, S.A. 2008. 'Gone the Bull of Winter? Grappling with the Cultural Implications of and Anthropology's Role in Global Climate Change', *Current Anthropology* 49(4): 569–96.

——— 2011. 'Climate and Culture: Anthropology in the Era of Contemporary Climate Change', *Annual Review of Anthropology* 40: 175–94.

Crate, S.A., and M. Nuttall. 2009. 'Introduction: Anthropology and Climate Change', in S.A. Crate and M. Nuttall (eds), *Anthropology and Climate Change: From Encounters to Actions*. Walnut Creek, CA: Left Coast Press, pp.9–36.

Farbotko, C. 2005. 'Tuvalu and Climate Change: Constructions of Environmental Displacement in the Sydney Morning Herald', *Geografiska Annaler B* 87(4): 279–93.

―――― 2010. 'Wishful Sinking: Disappearing Islands, Climate Refugees and Cosmopolitan Experimentation', *Asia Pacific Viewpoint* 51(1): 47–60.

Farbotko, C., and H. Lazrus. 2012. 'The First Climate Refugees? Contesting Global Narratives of Climate Change in Tuvalu', *Global Environmental Change* 22: 382–90.

Gemenne, F., and S. Shen. 2009. 'Tuvalu and New Zealand: Case Study Report for the EACH-FOR Project'. Bonn: Institute for Environment and Human Security, United Nations University. Retrieved 5 July 2011 from: http://www.ehs.unu.edu/file/get/7739.

Hau'ofa, E. 1994. 'Our Sea of Islands', *Contemporary Pacific* 6(1): 148–61.

Hermann, E. 2004. 'Emotions, Agency and the Dis/placed Self of the Banabans in Fiji', in T. van Meijl and J. Miedema (eds), *Shifting Images of Identity in the Pacific*. Leiden: KITLV Press, pp.191–217.

―――― 2011. 'Emotions and Belonging vis-à-vis News of Climate Change', unpublished paper delivered at the symposium 'Climate Change in Pacific Island Communities', annual meeting of the Association for Social Anthropology in Oceania, Honolulu.

―――― 2012. 'Social Capital in the Face of Climate Change: Voices of Emotional Belonging from Kiribati', unpublished paper delivered at a conference held at the University of the South Pacific, Suva, July.

Hermann, E., and W. Kempf. 2005. 'Introduction to Relations in Multicultural Fiji: The Dynamics of Articulations, Transformations and Positionings', *Oceania* (special issue) 75(4): 309–24.

―――― n.d. '"Prophecy from the Past": Climate Change Discourse, Song Culture and Emotions in Kiribati', in P. Rudiak-Gould and T. Crook (eds), *Appropriating Climate Change: Pacific Reception of a Scientific Prophecy*. Warsaw: De Gruyter Open.

Hetherington, R., and R.G.B. Reid. 2010. *The Climate Connection: Climate Change and Modern Human Evolution*. Cambridge: Cambridge University Press.

Hugo, G. 2010. 'Climate Change-induced Mobility and the Existing Migration Regime in Asia and the Pacific', in J. McAdam (ed.), *Climate Change and Displacement: Multidisciplinary Perspectives*. Oxford: Hart, pp.9–35.

Kempf, W. 2012a. 'Climate Change, Migration, and Christianity in Oceania', in K. Hastrup and K.F. Olwig (eds), *Climate Change and Human Mobility: Global Challenges to the Social Sciences*. Cambridge: Cambridge University Press, pp.235–57.

―――― 2012b. 'Climate, History, and Culture: The Power of Change', *Reviews in Anthropology* 41(4): 217–38.

Lazrus, H. 2012. 'Sea Change: Island Communities and Climate Change', *Annual Review of Anthropology* 41: 285–301.

Lee, H. 2009a. 'Introduction', in H. Lee and S.T. Francis (eds), *Migration and Transnationalism: Pacific Perspectives*. Canberra: Australian National University Press, pp.1–6.

—— 2009b. 'Pacific Migration and Transnationalism: Historical Perspectives', in H. Lee and S.T. Francis (eds), *Migration and Transnationalism: Pacific Perspectives*. Canberra: Australian National University Press, pp.7–41.

Lockwood, V. 2004. 'The Global Imperative and Pacific Island Societies', in V.S. Lockwood (ed.), *Globalization and Culture Change in the Pacific Islands*. Upper Saddle River, NJ: Pearson Prentice Hall, pp.1–39.

McAdam, J. 2010. '"Disappearing States": Statelessness and the Boundaries of International Law', in J. McAdam (ed.), *Climate Change and Displacement: Multidisciplinary Perspectives*. Oxford: Hart, pp.105–29.

McNamara, K.E., and C. Gibson. 2009. '"We Do Not Want to Leave Our Land": Pacific Ambassadors at the United Nations Resist the Category of "Climate Refugees"', *Geoforum* 40(3): 475–83.

Mimura, N., L. Nurse, R.F. McLean, J. Agard, L. Briguglio, P. Lefale, R. Payet and G. Sem. 2007. 'Small Islands', in M.L. Parry, O.F. Canziani, J.P. Palutikof, P.J. van der Linden and C.E. Hanson (eds), *Climate Change 2007: Impacts, Adaptation and Vulnerability – Contribution of Working Group II to the Fourth Assessment Report of the Intergovernmental Panel on Climate Change*. Cambridge: Cambridge University Press, pp.687–716.

Mortreux, C., and J. Barnett. 2009. 'Climate Change, Migration and Adaptation in Funafuti, Tuvalu', *Global Environmental Change* 19: 105–12.

Rahmstorf, S. 2010. 'A New View on Sea Level Rise', *Nature Reports: Climate Change* 6(4): 44–45.

Nei Tabera Ni Kai (dir.). 2010. *COP 15 – Side Event*. Film produced by L. Uaan and J. Anderson. Tarawa: NTNK Video Production.

Pareti, S. 2013. 'Climate Refugees? More Coastal Villages May Have to Relocate Due to Eroding Shorelines and Coastal Flooding', Islands Business. Retrieved 30 May 2013 from: www.islandsbusiness.com/2013/5/fiji-business/climate-refugees/.

Rudiak-Gould, P. 2013. *Climate Change and Tradition in a Small Island State: The Rising Tide*. New York: Routledge.

Shlomowitz, R., and D. Munro. 1992. 'The Ocean Island (Banaba) and Nauru Labour Trade, 1900–1940', *Journal de la Société des Océanistes* 94: 103–17.

SPREP. 2008. 'Factsheet: Pacific Climate Change'. Apia: Secretariat of the Pacific Regional Environment Programme. Retrieved 4 February 2013 from: www.sprep.org/climate_change/pycc/documents/pacificclimate.pdf.

Teaiwa, T.K. 1997. 'Rabi and Kioa: Peripheral Minority Communities in Fiji', in B.V. Lal and T.R. Vakatora (eds), *Fiji in Transition: Research Papers of the Fiji*

*Constitution Review Commission*, Vol. 1. Suva: University of the South Pacific, pp.130–52.

Wasuka, E. 2013. 'Climate Change, Relocation High on PCC's Agenda: Churches to Be More Involved in Community', Islands Business. Retrieved 30 May 2013 from: www.islandsbusiness.com/2013/4/politics/climate-change-relocation-high-on-pccs-agenda/.

Williams, M., and B. Macdonald. 1985. *The Phosphateers: A History of the British Phosphate Commissioners and the Christmas Island Phosphate Commission*. Carlton: Melbourne University Press.

# Notes on Contributors

◆●◆

**Agnes Brandt** holds a Ph.D. in anthropology from Albert Ludwig University in Freiburg, where she was a member of the interdisciplinary DFG-research group Friends, Patrons, Followers. After holding posts as research assistant in Bochum and as lecturer at Ludwig Maximilian University in Munich, she currently works as a parliamentary assistant at the European Parliament in Brussels. She has conducted fieldwork in New Zealand in 2001/2002, 2007 and 2008. Her research interests include the study of interpersonal relationships and identity-making processes and transculturation.

**Eveline Dürr** is Professor at the Institute for Social and Cultural Anthropology, Ludwig- Maximilians-University, Munich. Previously, she held a position as associate professor in the School of Social Sciences, Auckland University of Technology, New Zealand. She received her Ph.D. and *venia legendi* (Habilitation) from the Albert-Ludwigs-University in Freiburg. She has conducted fieldwork in Mexico, the USA, New Zealand and Germany on topics ranging from patterns of transcultural encounters to migration and the formation of cultural identities. Her research projects and publications reflect her interests in urban anthropology, spatiality, tourism, environmental issues and globalization, and take into consideration the historical trajectories that have formed present conditions.

**Yannick Fer** and **Gwendoline Malogne-Fer** are sociologists at the research group Societies, Religions, Secularisms (GSRL) at the École Pratique des Hautes Études, and the Centre National de la Recherche Scientifique, Paris, and specialists in Polynesian Protestantism. They began doing fieldwork in 1995 in French Polynesia, then extended their area of interest to the Polynesian communities in New Zealand and the Cook Islands (Rarotonga). Gwendoline Malogne-Fer is more specifically interested in women's roles within Protestant churches, the Polynesian islands and migration contexts. Yannick Fer's research focuses on evangelical churches and missionary networks. In 2012, he coordinated the special issue of the

Archives de sciences sociales des religions on *Christianismes en Océanie / Changing Christianity in Oceania*. They are editors of *Anthropologie du christianisme en Océanie* (L'Harmattan, 2009).

**Lise Garond** is currently lecturing at the Victor Segalen University, Bordeaux, as well as an associate researcher at the Laboratoire d'Anthropologie Sociale, Paris. She has conducted research with the Aboriginal people of Palm Island (North-East Queensland, Australia) since 2006. Her research interests include the making of (post)colonial history and memory, the relationships between Aboriginal and non-Aboriginal people, and the state.

**Elfriede Hermann** is Professor at the Institute of Cultural and Social Anthropology at the University of Göttingen, and holds degrees from the University of Tübingen (M.A. and Ph.D.) and from the University of Göttingen (Habilitation). She has conducted research with the Ngaing of Papua New Guinea, the Banabans of Rabi Island (Fiji) and Banaba Island (Kiribati), and the inhabitants of Kiribati. From 2005 to 2011 she was a research fellow with the Honolulu Academy of Arts, Hawai'i. The foci of her research and publications are identifications, belonging, emotions, historicity, ethnicity, migration, cultural transformations, transculturation and cultural perceptions of climate change.

**Wolfgang Kempf** holds a Ph.D. from the University of Tübingen and has taught cultural anthropology at the Universities of Tübingen, Heidelberg and Göttingen, where he is currently a researcher at the Institute of Cultural and Social Anthropology. He has conducted fieldwork among the Ngaing of Madang Province, Papua New Guinea, the Banabans of Fiji, and in Kiribati. His research interests focus on climate change, migration, diaspora, space, colonialism, power and resistance, biography and religious transformation. He is currently doing research on perceptions of climate change in Kiribati and Fiji.

**Toon van Meijl** is Professor of Anthropology at Radboud University, Nijmegen, and director of the interdisciplinary Centre for Pacific and Asian Studies at Nijmegen. He studied social anthropology and philosophy at the University of Nijmegen and at the Australian National University, Canberra, from which he obtained his Ph.D. in 1991. Since 1982 he has conducted fieldwork among the Tainui Māori in New Zealand. He has published widely on issues of cultural identity and the self, and on socio-political questions emerging from debates about the property rights of indigenous peoples.

**Arno Pascht** lectures at the Institute of Social and Cultural Anthropology of the University of Cologne, and studied social anthropology, psychology and political science in Munich, and at the University of Bayreuth. His research has focused on changing land tenure and on the system of chiefs in the Cook Islands. His research interests include ethnicity, land tenure, legal pluralism, leadership, migration, transnational processes, cultural transformations and climate change.

**Will Rollason** is a lecturer in anthropology at Brunel University, London. He conducted ethnographic research on Panapompom Island, Papua New Guinea, between 2004 and 2006. His interests in Papua New Guinea include race, development and the postcolony, mimesis, parody and abjection. His publications deal with various aspects of contemporary Papua New Guinean experience, including football, fashion, action films, wage labour and economic exclusion.

**Hilke Thode-Arora** is currently a research associate with the Munich State Museum of Ethnology in affiliation with Victoria University, Wellington, and has previously held an honorary affiliation with the University of Auckland. She has conducted fieldwork with the Niuean community in Auckland and on Niue, and her research interests include interethnic relations and ethnic identities, and material culture and its social and historical implications. Her current project focuses on Sāmoan oral traditions about specific artefacts in museum collections, and about Sāmoan travellers to Germany around 1900.

# Index

Aboriginal people (Australia), 2, 5, 9, 15–17, 49–68, 193–94
adaptation, 192–93, 195–98, 200–3, 208
agency, 30, 166, 190, 192, 194, 208
adaptive, 192
alterity
    construction, 16, 26
    and self, 26
Aotearoa. *See* New Zealand
Auckland, 5, 10, 12, 17, 94–113, 129–30, 142, 146, 150–53, 165, 170
Australia, 5, 16, 18, 49–68, 74–75, 77, 83–85, 103, 117–18, 128, 158–59, 193

Bakhtin, Mikhail, 13–14, 182
Banaba, 194, 199, 204–6
Banabans, 19n4, 194, 203–5, 208
belonging, 169–78
    ambiguities of, 15, 51, 56–58, 60–61, 65, 168, 176, 183
    to communities, 14–15, 109, 127, 130, 132–33, 145, 158, 167, 171, 173–74, 178, 180, 207–8
    cultural, 9, 143, 145–48, 152–53, 156–60, 205
    exclusions of, 2, 15, 60, 104–5
    global circles of, 18, 157
    future, 192, 197, 202, 207–8
    and identity, 5, 13, 17, 19, 56, 59–60, 127, 156, 167, 171, 173
    multiplicity of, 1–2, 5, 14–16, 27, 49–50, 57–59, 176, 190, 192, 194, 205, 208
    to places, 10, 14–15, 18, 126, 130, 167, 171, 173–74, 180, 197, 203–5, 207–8
    and self, 5, 167, 173, 182–83
    sense of, 19, 65, 127, 142, 156–57, 167, 171, 174, 179–80, 202, 208
biculturalism, 5, 18, 30, 145–46, 166, 168–70, 176–77, 180–81, 183–84
boundaries
    ethnic, 54, 68n19, 95, 150, 168–69, 171, 176, 178–80
    socio-cultural, 5, 11, 19, 28, 165, 168–69, 173–74, 177–78
    socio-economic, 169, 178, 181
    socio-geographic, 52, 150, 161n12
    transcending boundaries, 13, 26, 29, 166, 169, 174–76, 178, 180, 182
    (un)making, 26, 28, 54

churches in the Pacific, 5, 10, 14, 18, 99–100, 105–9, 142–60, 193, 196. *See also* missionaries; Pacific Islanders Church
class, 28–29, 31, 35, 39, 171, 178–79
    affiliation, 39
    conflicts, 45n7
    middle-class, 25, 29, 31, 33–35, 39, 175, 179
climate change, 4, 189–209
community, 1, 7, 11, 17, 40, 54, 64, 68n20, 76, 78–82, 86, 119, 144–45, 161n12, 174, 207

colonialism
  colonial administration, 18, 51, 54–55, 75–79, 82–85, 119–20
  colonial categories, 56, 192
  consequences of, 9
connectivity, 1, 3, 190, 198
Cook Islanders, 2, 5, 9, 17–18, 117–38, 143, 145–53, 161n22
culture, 11–12, 16, 18, 26–40, 42–43, 67n18, 96–97, 152, 156–58
  Aboriginal, 56, 67n18
  authentic, 67n14
  changing, 13
  Christian, 156
  construction of, 11, 16, 28
  contact, 13, 16, 26–28
  culture areas, 2
  culture discourse, 11, 165, 170, 174, 180, 183
  culture politics, 168–69, 183
  cultures, 2–3, 6, 11–13, 25–29, 33–34, 37, 42, 157
  cultures in motion, 2, 43
  exchange, 36
  as experience, 25, 28
  and identity, 2–3, 6, 10, 12–13, 167–68, 173–74, 177–78
  indigenous, 31, 40, 157
  loss of, 40, 56, 65, 104, 108, 146
  Māori, 30–32, 35–37, 43, 96, 146, 168, 172–73
  Mexican, 37
  Niuean, 97
  Pākehā, 168, 172–73
  performing, 32, 37
  pre-European, 29, 37
  Torres Strait Islander, 62, 67n18
  traditional, 50, 56
  trans-Polynesian, 145
  Western, 158, 204

development, 17, 64, 75, 77, 82–87, 88n6, 191
dialogical perspective, 13, 19, 165, 181, 184
dialogical process, 10, 14–16
dialogical self, 154, 182
diaspora, 1–2, 4–5, 9, 57, 67n15, 99, 104, 106–7, 111nn10–11, 113n24, 144, 193, 200, 208, 209n9

displacement, 2–3, 5–7, 9, 15, 50–61, 65, 99, 130, 195, 202

ecology, 8, 190–91, 194–95, 198–99
economy, 5, 9, 17, 19, 29, 71–74, 77–78, 83–88, 99, 103–4, 108, 118, 128, 133–34, 145, 191–93, 196, 203, 206, 208
emotion
  discourses of, 194, 197
encounters, 7, 13, 16, 25–29, 33–36, 38, 44n2, 45n11, 99, 167, 171, 176, 193
  cross-cultural, 10, 16, 27–28, 40, 43–44, 172
  cultural, 5, 10, 13, 16, 25–44, 172, 177, 184, 194
  transpacific, 25
enlargement, 3, 117
environment, 73, 195, 198–200
ethnic marking, 17, 108
exchange, 10, 16, 28, 36, 42, 74, 79, 82, 86 125, 128, 131, 134–35, 144, 157
exploitation, 3, 52, 157

Fiji, 112n19, 156, 194, 203–5
friendship, 164–88
  and comfort, 171, 173–77, 181
  cross-cultural, 10, 13, 19, 164, 166, 169, 172–74, 176, 179–80, 183–84
  definition, 170
  and difference, 171, 173–84
  and homophily, 171–72, 175, 178
  and similarity, 171–72, 176, 179, 184
future, 62, 72, 128, 192, 195, 200
  uncertain, 88, 134, 197, 202–8

global warming, 190, 194, 204
globalization, 3, 6–7, 27, 36, 74, 118, 159, 192

Hau'ofa, Epeli, 3–4, 88n7, 117, 129, 192, 199
health, 66n8, 68n20, 191, 198
histories of origin, 50, 58–59, 65–66
home, 25, 27, 32, 41, 169, 174

Index 219

homeland, 1, 7, 13, 15, 33, 53, 118–19, 128–32, 134–35, 138n26, 167, 193, 198, 205–8

identifications, 118, 126, 127, 129, 133–35, 137n23, 167, 171, 180–82
  competing, 13, 63, 76, 168, 176, 182
  modes of identification, 164–65, 180
  multiple, 1–2, 9, 12–14, 28, 50, 63–65, 72–73, 118, 126, 154, 155–58, 166–68, 173, 177, 183, 189, 204–5, 207–8
identity
  as changing, 12–13, 126, 145, 152–53, 155, 165, 181, 182, 189
  cultural, 12–13, 146, 152, 155, 156, 158, 192
  and culture, 167–68, 173–74, 177–78
  and difference, 11–12, 29–31, 171, 174, 177–79, 181, 183
  ethnic, 98–99, 102, 109, 111n10, 127, 145
  identity-making, 164–66, 169, 183
  identity politics, 164, 166–69, 174, 177, 179
  as multiply constructed, 12, 15, 18, 42, 118, 126, 129, 154, 155–58, 165, 176–77, 181–82, 192, 194, 198
  pan-tribal, 166
  and sameness, 11–12, 31, 171, 179, 183
  and self, 1, 5, 11–12, 29, 31–33, 40, 154, 156, 165–66, 168, 173–74, 180–83
I-Kiribati, 197, 202–7, 209n9
indigeneity, 30–31, 35, 65
  and Aboriginal 'tribal' identifications, 50, 56–57
  in Australian Aboriginal land claims, 50, 57, 59–61, 67
  and identity, 26
  Māori, 18, 157, 166
  recognition of, 18, 50
  reified notions of, 56–57, 65

kinship, 17–18, 54, 81–82, 86, 97–98, 107, 124–25, 127, 135, 143–44, 192
  kinship ties, 9, 128, 130, 203
Kiribati, 2, 4, 191, 194, 196–97, 199–207, 209n2

land, 166, 176
  attachment to, 9, 17, 56–57, 67n17, 82, 105, 130, 133–34, 157, 176, 197–98
  damage to, 190
  and kinship, 82, 98, 105–6, 124, 203
  land conflicts, 9, 126–27, 132, 135, 136n3
  land rights, 9, 17–18, 60, 98, 104–5, 109, 118–22, 125, 129, 131–35, 138n31
  land tenure, 17, 104, 118–21
landowners, 8, 15, 203, 136n5
  absentee, 5, 14, 17, 104–5, 109, 118–23, 129– 34, 200
  landownership, 15, 79, 105, 119–21, 125
landscape, 8–10, 14, 17, 51, 73, 82–84, 98, 123, 124, 170, 200–2
  transnational, 14

Māori (Cook Islands). See Cook Islanders
Māori (New Zealand), 2, 4–5, 13, 15–16, 18–19, 25–45, 95–97, 101, 103, 108, 146, 148, 154, 156–58, 160n6, 164–85
  and friendship, 176–79
  identity, 166–68, 171
  urban, 167–68, 176
marginalization, 3, 5, 9, 50, 64, 68n20, 99, 194
Marshall Islands, 4, 191, 207
memory, 18, 51, 75, 79, 82, 89n19, 98, 124, 135, 142–43, 146, 148, 157–59
Mexico, 4, 10, 13, 16, 25, 28–45
migration
  climate-related, 191, 195
  forced, 4–5, 49–51, 53, 58–59, 197, 202
  imagination of, 4, 207–8
  internal, 4–5, 9, 143

international, 4–5, 9, 11, 14, 118, 129, 143–50, 164, 169–70, 192–94, 200, 204
labour, 97, 112n21, 128, 193, 196, 199
missionaries, 76, 80, 112n21, 137n19, 146, 148, 151, 154–58, 160n6
mobility, 1–6, 9, 26–28, 34, 83, 103, 106, 128, 151, 153–55, 159, 190, 192, 197
multiculturalism, 11, 18, 145, 153–54, 156–59, 169–70, 176, 183–84, 194
multilocality and -vocality, 8–11
Munn, Nancy, 73–75, 80, 86, 88n7

networks, 2, 8, 65, 72, 75, 128, 154, 175, 193, 196, 206, 208
global, 155–57, 191–92
social, 33, 175
transnational, 4, 97, 128, 144, 155–57, 193
New Zealand, 2, 4–5, 9–10, 12–19, 25, 94–113, 117–19, 122, 127–29, 131–35, 142–62, 164–85, 191, 193, 195, 200, 202, 205–7
Niue, 10, 12, 15, 94–116, 143, 150, 195
Niueans, 2, 5, 10, 12–13, 17, 94–16, 117, 138n23, 146, 150, 160n7, 161n22, 193

Pacific Islanders Church (PIC), 99–100, 105–9, 146–47, 151–54
Pākehā, 5, 10, 15, 30–31, 36, 40, 95–96, 98, 102–4, 108, 111n8, 145–47, 164–81, 183–84
and friendship, 19, 172–76
identity, 168–69, 184nn1–2
Palm Island, 5, 9, 15–16, 49–68, 193–94
Palm Island Aboriginal reserve
and Aboriginal 'tribal' camps, 52–56
and displacement, 49–51, 58–59, 65
and place-making, 51–56
and segregated settlement patterns, 52, 56
Panapompom, 5, 9, 15, 17, 71–90, 193–94

Papua New Guinea, 2, 5–6, 17, 71–90, 193
Pasifika Festival, 96, 101, 103–4, 106, 108
performance, 26–27, 32–33, 35, 37–38, 64, 85, 106, 135, 182
cultural, 36, 55, 96, 104, 126
Māori, 13, 35–36
representation, 42
traditional, 31
place
constitution of, 3, 7, 14, 51–52, 88, 200–2
as dynamic configuration, 6
dynamics of, 5–6, 26, 38
and identity, 1, 3, 5–6, 8, 10, 12, 15, 17, 26, 34, 41, 43, 51–54, 56, 61, 75, 94–113, 126, 146–48, 150, 156, 159, 165–66, 177, 189–90, 192, 194–95, 198–203
multi-dimensionality of, 6, 8–9, 37, 41, 43
multiplicity of, 8–9, 12, 198
as product of historical praxis, 6, 8, 34, 51–56, 60–61, 62
replacement, 30
sense of displacement, 168, 176
place-making, 1–2, 5–7, 9–10, 14, 16–17, 26, 38, 50–51, 55, 56, 61–62, 65, 98, 108–9, 165–66, 169, 189, 192, 198–204, 207
Polyfest, 96, 107
Polynesian migrants, 10, 99–106, 127–28, 142–48, 151–52, 193
poverty, 3

Rabi Island, 194, 203–5
Rarotonga, 9, 14–15, 118–31, 133–34, 201
relationships (social), 1, 3–4, 8–10, 13–14, 16–17, 26–27, 29, 43–44, 45n11, 65, 72, 74, 80, 88, 108, 126, 128, 135, 148, 153, 158, 164–65, 168, 170, 172, 175, 177, 179, 181–83, 185n7, 185n9, 193
relocation, 5, 15, 51, 111n14, 193–94, 196–97, 202–3
remittances, 4, 18, 128, 134, 137n18, 144, 160n2

representation, 2, 11, 26–28, 30–31, 41–43, 95–96, 148, 153, 183, 191, 203
  Aboriginal, 64
  cultural, 13, 16, 26, 37, 168
  of identity, 5, 11, 31, 159, 168
  Māori, 31, 45n7, 111n8, 146
  Mexico, 29, 37, 168
  non-Aboriginal, 64
  Pākehā, 111n8
  performative, 35, 42
  of place, 10, 74, 99, 103
  politicized, 171, 168
  of the self, 154, 168, 173
  self-representation, 32
resettlement, 8, 190, 193–94, 205
resilience, 192–93

Sāmoans, 138n23, 146–47, 153–56, 158–59, 161n22
sea-level rise, 4, 189–209
sea of islands, 3–4, 192, 199
self
  and community, 1, 17
space, 3–4, 17, 31–33, 51, 53, 55–56, 61, 73, 85, 98–99, 105, 108–10, 111n13, 151, 157, 165, 169, 171–77, 180, 184, 207, 215
  and the idea of 'worlds', 167, 171, 174, 176–80, 182–83
  natural space, 198
  public space, 41, 95, 102, 109
  space-making, 17

space-time, 17, 73, 75, 80, 82, 86, 98, 111, 169, 196
spaces in between, 176, 180–81, 184

transnationalism, 2–4, 10–11, 14, 18, 19n2, 111n10, 117, 143–44, 153, 158–59, 192–93, 200, 204
travel, 1–2, 9, 13, 15–16, 26–27, 37, 45, 57, 105, 117, 128, 138n24, 157, 194, 200
  experience, 26–27, 33–34, 38, 45
  and identification, 27, 43
  impact of, 26, 28, 43
  as a privilege, 34
Tuvalu, 4, 143, 191, 205–7, 209n2

uncertainty, 58–59, 87–88, 128, 134, 156, 194, 207
underdevelopment, 9, 17, 72, 74, 75–86, 199

vulnerability, 190–92, 195–96, 200–1, 203, 207

work, 17, 73–76, 78–88, 89n19
worlds, 27
  figured worlds, 182–83
  imagined worlds, 165
  life-worlds, 28, 34, 167, 171, 174, 176, 178, 180

youth, 4, 147, 151–52, 154–56